# Cults
# and
# The Family

The *Marriage & Family Review* series:

# Cults
# and
# The Family

Florence Kaslow and Marvin B. Sussman
Editors

Marriage & Family Review
Volume 4, Numbers 3/4

The Haworth Press
New York

The Haworth Press, Inc., 28 East 22 Street, New York, NY 10010

**Library of Congress Cataloging in Publication Data**
Main entry under title:

Cults and the family.

(Marriage & family review : v. 4, no. 3/4)
Includes bibliographical references.
1. Cults—United States—Psychological aspects—
Addresses, essays, lectures. 2. Sects—United States—
Psychological aspects—Addresses, essays, lectures.
3. Family—United States—Addresses, essays, lectures.
I. Kaslow, Florence Whiteman. II. Sussman, Marvin B.
III. Series.
BL2530.U6C84      291.1'783587      81-20264
ISBN 0-917724-55-0                  AACR2
ISBN 0-917724-81-X (pbk.)

65104

# Cults and The Family

Marriage & Family Review
Volume 4, Numbers 3/4

# FOREWORD

We are delighted to present this collection of original papers on the subject of ''Cults and the Family.'' This particular process of creation took over two years. The editors sought a wide range of perspectives, feelings, and experiences regarding the relationship of cult membership to the family and its reciprocal. As a consequence, the particular articles range in disciplinary approaches, use of empirical data, expression of experiences and feelings, and therapeutic interventions to help families whose members were or are currently members of different cults. Various authors present sharply divergent data and conclusions. Historical, sociological and psychological perspectives examine developmental processes, how beginnings become recognized and then institutionalized in structures through dogma and ideologies and behavioral practices. Ethical and moral issues are presented and discussed.

Views from the psychiatric catbird seat are portrayed and efforts are made to look at the similarities and differences between therapeutic communities and the new wave of cults. Options in helping distressed families whose offspring are satisfied or dissatisfied members of cults and also those who have had their young adult children go through the experience of deprogramming are also examined.

We view this collection of original articles as a most comprehensive, eclectic, and insightful one regarding the dynamics and interrelationships between families and various existing cults on the contemporary American scene. We recognize that some of the statements made by the authors will be questioned and challenged in various ways and in various arenas. We as editors and publisher disclaim any responsibility for the particular viewpoints presented by the various authors. These articles represent solely the reports of the individual contributors. Neither the publisher nor the editors have conducted independent research to confirm or disprove any of their statements or reports. We have requested that the authors document their particular statements and have given them the freedoms guaranteed under the U.S. Constitution to state freely their analyses as they see them from their particular perspectives. They alone are responsible for the authenticity of the material.

*1*

It is our earnest hope that you will find this a provocative, informative, and highly readable anthology.

*Editors for this issue*
*and The Haworth Press, Inc.*

# THE CULT PHENOMENON: HISTORICAL, SOCIOLOGICAL, AND FAMILIAL FACTORS CONTRIBUTING TO THEIR DEVELOPMENT AND APPEAL

Lita Linzer Schwartz, AB, EdM, PhD
Florence W. Kaslow, AB, MA, PhD

## Introduction

An examination of the contemporary cult phenomenon requires investigators to utilize data from several of the social and behavioral sciences as well as analytic skills. One cannot, for example, look at the prevalence of cults today without considering the marked and rapid changes of the post-World War II decades which have contributed to the emergence of youth counter-culture movements. Technological developments, international conflicts, and economic changes have created mass uncertainty and anxiety. The political and sociological movements of the 1960s and 1970s have had pervasive effects on our attitudes, values, and behaviors. Changing, and often contradictory, psychological theories have been popularized and sometimes exaggerated to the point of causing parental confusion in the area of child-rearing. All of these events have exacerbated the search for identity of adolescents and young adults, making them at least potentially vulnerable to groups that promise acceptance, security, and freedom from unwanted responsibility and decision-making.

History is also involved in relating the development of each cult. Anthropology and sociology help to explain similarities and differences not only among the cults, but also between the cults and other restrictive religious groups. Particular attention is paid here to the Unification

Lita L. Schwartz is professor of Educational Psychology at the Pennsylvania State University, Ogontz Campus. Florence Kaslow is a family therapist and editor of the *Journal of Marital and Family Therapy*.

Church, Hare Krishna movement, Church of Scientology, Divine Light Mission, and Children of God. These are the most prominent of the estimated 2500-3000 cults in the United States. The cults exist world-wide, but our focus is on them in this country.

The characteristics of youths vulnerable to the approaches of cult recruiters are generally unremarkable for the age-group and its life-style. They tend to be upper-middle-class students who are lonely, depressed, uncertain, outer-directed, and searching—searching for *the* answer to their own and society's problems. They seek acceptance, for a "cause," for commitment. The interaction of this constellation and exquisite timing by cult recruiters produces vulnerability.

Once recruited, the young adult meets instant acceptance through "love-bombing;" is subjected to repetitive lectures, chants, and rituals that have an hypnotic effect; is kept in an encapsulating environment that allows for no contradictions or outside information; and is manipulated by highly effective conditioning techniques and psychological pressures. Questions and negative comments are met with resistance designed to make the individual feel guilty for such behavior. Those who succumb to the indoctrination process experience marked changes in personality as they assume a new identity within the cult (Conway and Siegelman, 1978).

Meanwhile, the parents of those recruited are frequently bewildered at the sudden disappearance of the youth, stunned by the personality changes, and grief-stricken at being abandoned and rejected in favor of the new "family." They need and seek help from clergy, therapists, and parents who have already suffered this experience. When and if they succeed in recovering their child from the cult, they and the youth continue to need therapy to reduce the problems that contributed to his/her vulnerability, to confront the emotions aroused by the involvement in the cult and subsequent departure from it, and to gain strength to face the future in more constructive ways. Several alternative modes of therapy are discussed as different families require different approaches to deal with this critical situation.

Of great concern to families, and to family therapists specifically and much of society generally, is the rise of modern cults, most of them purportedly religiously-oriented. In this review of literature relevant to the issue of the cults, a brief historical background is provided to place the phenomenon in perspective. Following this, the origins and main principles of major cults will be examined. Causes of vulnerability to the cults, recruiting and conversion techniques, and deprogramming approaches will then be discussed. The effects of cult membership on the recruit's family, and therapeutic techniques which appear to have efficacy when used in treating the family and the ex-cult member, completes the paper.

## Historical Background

Looking at life in the United States since the end of World War II, one notes numerous and varied changes affecting family and individual life styles occurring at a rate more rapid than earlier in our history. Military and international political events such as the nuclear threat, the "Cold War," the Korean War, and the Cuban crises in the first half of this period combined to keep much of the population in a state of anxiety, with a resulting fatalistic attitude of "Let's live for today; there may be no tomorrow."

As industry returned to consumer production and expanded rapidly to utilize new technologies in meeting demands of the civilian economy, employees moved about the country to new jobs and new communities. Suburbs were developed almost overnight where families of similar income level, but lacking most other characteristics in common, established new, if temporary, roots. Government grew in size and functions, leading to increased bureaucratization. These events, plus the advent of computerization in almost all walks of life, have contributed to feelings of anonymity and depersonalization in a burgeoning and increasingly complex society.

The civil rights and Third World movements can also be viewed as forerunners and concomitants of the extremist wing of the "Third Force" movement in psychology. This has led to an exaggeration of self-actualization as a goal, "Do your own thing." The most anarchistic proponents of this philosophy aver that only the self is important and the "other" and society should not interfere with one's impulse gratification. These movements, as well as the growth of instant communication via television, also led to an increase in the amount of violence. Crimes against property mounted as more people saw attractive consumer goods displayed and sought instant possession. Crimes against people, highlighted by the assassinations of John and Robert Kennedy and Martin Luther King, Jr., became more commonplace. The "body counts" of the Viet Nam war and incidents like My Lai were shown nightly on television news programs. Distinctions between public and private behavior faded, and "let it all hang out" was a slogan in common use.

Within the family, the roots provided by stable neighborhoods and the proximity of extended family members often disappeared, reducing sources of reinforcement for family values. Parents, particularly fathers, became preoccupied with their orientation toward demonstrable material success. Changes in child-rearing patterns in the direction of greater permissiveness, as urged by mental health professionals and progressive educators, led to parental confusion and, ultimately, impotence in the parental role. Liberated by their parents' abdication of power, and encouraged by advocates of individuality, adolescents soon discovered that the price of this freedom was increased responsibility for making decisions and forging their own life style, often prematurely. At the same time, they were witnesses to the spectacle of national political figures, as well as their own parents, lying their way through assorted crises, and being slapped on the wrist for their transgressions. The "Big Lie" these figures preached differed often only in content from those of earlier totalitarian dictators. It climaxed in the national debacle of Watergate (1974).

In the world of psychology, B. F. Skinner's (1938) operant conditioning theories and techniques assumed prominence in some educational programs and clinical practices, and seemed to promote a mechanistic view of people as easily manipulable. The potential for programming people like robots horrified those who were aware that such practices were commonplace in nations having authoritarian governments, as American POWs had discovered in Korea.

Given the normal stresses of evolving an identity in late adolescence or as young adults (Erikson, 1968), our middle-class, educated youth could have adapted as earlier generations had. Sororities and fraternities, which formerly had offered a family-like network of "sisters" or "brothers" and a house-mother as well as an attractive residence representing a "home away from home," had diminished in popularity when they were branded in the 1950s as elitist and undemocratic. Post-war dormitories tended to be huge, cold, and impersonal cinderblock edifices where undergraduates could easily feel unimportant and lonely on a mammoth, uncaring campus far from home. Instead, they met the turbulence of the post-war decades, the clashes between their idealism and surrounding realities, and the problems of the changing economy by forming a counter-culture.

During the sixties and early seventies, the counter-culture was a violent echo of those nineteenth century socialist groups that had withdrawn into isolated, supposedly utopian, communities in response to overwhelming social changes and an inability to cope with the breakdown of social restraints (Kanter, 1972). Angry at affluence ignoring poverty, an unpopular war in Viet Nam, and parents who could no more face frustration than they could, middle-class youth "took off," "popped pills," protested in song and sometimes in violence, and "dropped out" of society.

When, in the seventies, the Viet Nam war was over and many of the "causes" with which they could identify had disappeared, many of the counter-culture rebels were still floundering, ill-equipped to function in the larger society or to cope with its demands. They sought to replace the chaos and turbulence of the sixties with the soothing philosophy and repetitive chants or mantras of Eastern religions—calm, serene, fatalistic, the antipathy of the Judeo-Christian ethics of responsibility and achievement orientation. The appeal of today's cults lies as much in their apparent offer of tranquility as in their being a haven from a still-frightening world that imposes unwanted responsibilities, complexities, and choices to be made (Rice, 1976).

## Development of the Cults

Spokespersons for those groups generally designated as cults perceive themselves as little different from the early Christians who broke with Judaism almost 2000 years ago. Whether milennial in doctrine or preaching that a new Messiah has arrived or is imminent, the cults do diverge in significant ways from more traditional religious groups, even those that are clearly minority sects. The question has been asked, for example, "How does the Unification Church differ from the Amish or the Mormons?" Therefore, before discussing briefly the development of each of several major cults (among the 2500-3000 extant in this country), let us compare dominant characteristics of the current crop of cults and other religious groups.

Although all eight groups compared in Table I require substantial or complete "submission to authority" and some financial contribution to the group, only four practice restriction of communications, physiological (diet, sleep) deprivation, and generate feelings of fear and hatred toward non-members that border on paranoid delusions (Edwards, 1979; Stoner and Parke, 1977). These same four also each have charismatic leadership, undemocratically selected.

By contrast, the communal life style of the Amish (Denlinger, 1975; Hostetler, 1963) and the Lubavitcher Chassidim (Mintz, 1977; Rubin, 1972; Shaffir, 1978) is based on the mutual support of discrete *families* to preserve the beliefs, behaviors, and identity of the group. Active proselytization is practiced by the Catholic Church, Mormons, Jehovah's Witnesses, and numerous evangelical sects, but is carried out principally through persuasion and education. Potential converts *are fully aware* of the identity of the group which seeks to convert them and the nature of expected

Table I: Comparison of Characteristics among Religious Groups and Cults

| | Lubavitcher Chassidim | Amish | Roman Catholic | Mormons | Unification Church | Church of Scientology | Alamo Feder. | Children of God |
|---|---|---|---|---|---|---|---|---|
| Charismatic leader | | | | | X | X | X | X |
| Submission to authority | X | X | X | X | X | X | X | X |
| Communal life-style | | | | | X | X[1] | X | X |
| Rigid ideology | X | X | X | X | X | X | X | X |
| Restricted communications | | | | | X | X[1] | X | X |
| Isolation from family | | (2) | | | X | X[1] | X | X |
| Active recruiting | | | X | X | X | X | X | X |
| Physiologic deprivation | | | | | X | X | X | X |
| Hate/fear of outsiders | | | | | X | X | X | X |
| Assets turned over to group | Tithing | Tithing | Tithing Contribution | Tithing | X | X[1] | X | X |

[1] These hold true for members living within the group's community, but not for all members.

[2] The Amish practice "shunning," or separation from the community (including the family), when an individual violates the principles of their Church. This is an extreme measure, and is not a condition of membership.

commitments is explained. The "heavenly deception" inherent in cult recruitment is not practiced in these groups.

Cults tend to arise in periods of socially pathological conditions (Gillin, 1946, p. 545). They are seen as being responsive to feelings of economic, social, organismic, ethical, and/or psychic deprivation (Glock, 1964, 26-29; Kuttner and Shaw, 1977, 480-481) or disorganization. The cults discussed here tend to be responding primarily to ethical and psychical feelings of deprivation and confusion. In so doing, they misuse faith— what Cox calls "the seduction of the spirit" (1973, p. 118). According to him,

> the seducer twists authentic inner impulses into instruments of domi-
> nation. Vulnerable persons and powerless peoples are maneuvered
> into seeing themselves through images thrust upon them by the dis-
> torting mirror of the managers. People's needs and hopes are cleverly
> parlayed into debilitating dependencies. (p. 118)

The Unification Church of Rev. Sun Myung Moon is the best-known and probably the largest of the cults operating in the United States today. Moon is a Korean whose theology is allegedly entwined with his nation's politics. That theology, as propounded by Moon in his *Divine Principle,* has as its goal the ultimate unification of all the world's religions, hence the name Unification Church. Like other milennial movements, it foresees the advent of a new messiah en route to the restoration of mankind to God's divine grace. It is implied that Moon himself is the Lord of the Second Advent. He and his wife are perceived by church members as their "true parents" (Sontag, 1977; Yamamoto, 1977).

In the United States, Moon's first disciples established a center in the San Francisco Bay area early in the 1960s. *Doomsday Cult* (Lofland, 1966) is a study of that group in its early days. The revised 1977 edition provides details of the changes in recruiting techniques and group practices that resulted in the phenomenal growth and enrichment of the Unification Church in the following decade. The "Moonies," like most of the cults to be discussed here, aim their recruiting efforts to the middle- and upper-middle class, white college student who appears to be adrift.

Despite Brent's allegation that "Indian guru cults won't work here," (1979), the Hare Krishna movement, officially called the International Society for Krishna Consciousness or ISKCON, has attracted several thousand young people to a strictly spiritual, ascetic, and vegetarian way of life. The origins of this religion lie in Vishnuism, the dominant division of

Hinduism. Lord Krishna himself was a charismatic holy man in the 16th century.

The modern leader, A. C. Bhaktivedanta, Swami Prabhupada, founded the Krishna society in New York in 1965 (Daner, 1976). This American group follows its own variation of Hindu beliefs, and considers itself to be above and outside of the public law. Devotees of the cult, unlike their clean-cut and neatly dressed "Moonie" brethren, have been easily recognizable by their shaven heads, saffron robes, and continuous mantra chanting. However, recent developments have caused some members to don "straight" clothing and even wigs when "witnessing" (speaking of their beliefs to others) or soliciting, so that their strange appearance does not alienate potential recruits or contributors.

Also drawn from the Indian guru tradition is the Divine Light Mission, led by the youthful Guru Maharaj Ji. Characterized by its leaders as a philosophy rather than a religion, many of the practices are drawn from Hinduism. These include celibacy, a vegetarian diet, and abstention from tobacco, alcohol, and drugs (Downton, 1979). The Guru does not claim to be God, but claims that through teaching his followers ("Premies") meditation and discipline, he can put them in touch with the God who has been with them all along (Stoner and Parke, 1977; Enroth, 1977). His advertisements promise "peace" to those who give him love. Like Rev. Moon, Guru Maharaj Ji lives in luxurious circumstances, in sharp contrast to the ascetic surroundings and meagre fare provided for many of his disciples.

David Berg's Children of God movement also claims to be a religion and, in some ways, resembles missionary Christianity. Berg often refers to himself as "Moses," and is perceived by his followers to be in direct communication with God. The Children of God are hierarchically organized in colonies and communes, originally (although no longer) based on Berg's interpretation of the kibbutz model. Although much of the Children of God's time is spent in Bible study and prayer, the group is not sexually as ascetic as those previously discussed. Begun as a "Teens for Christ" group in 1968, and renamed the "Family of Love" in 1978, the Children of God was and is strongly evangelistic (Ward, 1978). Like the "Moonies" and others, members of the group solicit donations or sell small items to raise money for a wide variety of non-existent humanitarian causes, part of the "heavenly deception" practiced by the cults on outsiders (Davis and Richardson, 1976; Ward, 1978). That is, they claim to be collecting funds for an orphanage, church, or group aiding the poor, none of which exist. Following the Lefkowitz hearings in New York State in which the Children of God had been investigated, Berg and the majority of his followers left the United States for more hospitable surroundings in Europe (Wallis, 1976).

Scientology was not founded as a religion at all. Rather, L. Ron Hubbard, its founder, first published his ideas on a new "psychotherapy" in *Astounding Science Fiction* in May 1950. The techniques were called "Dianetics" (Evans, 1973, 32–33). From this beginning, the organization developed expensive therapy sessions, a unique jargon, use of the psychogalvanometer (called "E-meter"), and, about 1955, became a definite, if eccentric, religion. As early as 1968, the English Parliament denounced Scientology as a cult that alienated family members from each other and that was a menace to the health of its followers (Evans, 1973). Similar conclusions were reached by an investigatory commission in Australia. More recently, the Church of Scientology has been investigated by the United States Department of Justice (Philadelphia *Inquirer,* 16 August 1978). In October 1979, nine members of the Church pleaded guilty to having infiltrated the Department (*New York Times,* 26 October 1979).

To illustrate the strong internal discipline of the group and the hold that Hubbard has over his disciples, consider the following incident. In September 1967, Hubbard cabled the personnel at his Saint Hill headquarters in England that they had been declared, as a penalty for some "misbehavior," to be in a "State of Non-Existence" (*op cit* Evans, 1973, p. 107).

*Each of these groups,* as well as the Alamo Christian Foundation, The Way International, the "New Age" at Findhorn (Scotland), and possibly some encounter and therapy groups, *sees its way as the only way to salvation,* a "state of grace," and freedom from the world's evils. Each so dominates its membership that *thinking for oneself is equivalent to mortal sin,* a sure sign that Satan has intruded. Unlike the Amish, Chassidim, Mormons, Jehovah's Witnesses, and other religious sects, the cults urge or require that the individual member contribute all of his/her assets and earnings as well as whatever can be obtained from parents. At the same time, and ironically, members are urged to reject those same parents as non-believers, agents of Satan, and threats to the member's status en route to salvation (Adler, 1978; Edwards, 1979).

Such belief systems, as well as some of the cult conversion practices have resulted in conflicts between non-approving parents, their offspring, and the cults. Parents frequently seek to remove their children forcibly from the cults, usually by kidnapping and then isolating them, and having them deprogrammed. Legal suits initiated by the cult members against the parents have followed such actions, centering on the freedom of religion clause of the First Amendment. Although the legal arguments are clearly beyond the scope of this article, it seems pertinent to note that several of the authors of law review articles are unfamiliar with relevant psychological literature and/or first-hand accounts of the recruiting and conversion techniques employed by the cults that bear on the question of how voluntary and informed is the new member's adoption of and belief in his new faith (Schwartz & Zemel, 1980).

Kelley, for example (1977, p. 301), assumes that new recruits have been ignored by their families and peers, when the evidence cited by psychologists and sociologists is that some were smothered with attention and others were over-protected. Homer states that members have joined the cults voluntarily, having freely chosen to accept the group's teachings, "and when given the choice of repudiating parents and family or leaving the sect, have opted to remain in the sect" (1974, p. 636). Le Moult avers that it is the deprogrammers, and not the religious groups, who engage in "brainwashing" practices (1978, p. 619). Evidence contradicting the last two points appears in Edwards' stirring personal account of his cult experiences and subsequent departure (1979); and in Freed (1978), and Landes (1976). Bates is one of the few who raises the question of the relative cost of subordinating "the welfare considerations of the child to the preservation of religious freedom where it is the mental well-being of the child which is at issue" (1978, p. 311). Delgado's article attributes more weight to the psychological issues and implications for the family than do most of the other legal sources (1977). The discussions of causes of vulnerability and cult conversion techniques place these matters in sharper focus.

### Causes of Vulnerability

It has become abundantly clear that a persuasive speaker or a charismatic figure such as Moon or Maharaj Ji can easily acquire supporters and followers. However, knowing that does not respond to the key question: what makes someone follow such a person? Not all of the identity-seeking, bright, middle and upper-middle-class college youths succumb to the cult recruiter's ploys. Not all of them are so anxious about the present and/or future. Even the "loners" are not willing to surrender their family ties and personal goals for a vague social cause, promised paradise, or a new religion. What, then, are the causes of vulnerability to these persuasions?

The alienated and susceptible youth of the 1970s share several characteristics with their predecessors of the 1960s. Middle-class, intelligent, mostly white, and typically idealistic, these young adults, too, were often lonely, frustrated, depressed, afraid of an uncertain future, and/or dependent in personality. They had, or have, strong needs for affection, a sense of self-worth, feelings of belonging, and a reason for living. In addition, both groups found the freedom and myriad demands of college life perplexing, if not overwhelming, at least boring.

Dr. Seymour Halleck, director of student psychiatry at the University of Wisconsin in the 1960s, said of the alienated youth there that "when confronted with unlimited choice, he refuses to choose. Having failed to develop an internalized value system which allows him to determine his direction in life, he is paralyzed when the external world removes its guidelines and restraints" (Stearn, 1969, p. 80). Stoner and Parks (1977) came to a similar conclusion regarding cult recruits. "They need direction and discipline and a clearly-defined purpose in life. They need to be taught how to think for themselves and to develop their own systems of self-discipline" (1977, p. 75).

The Committee on Adolescence of the Group for the Advancement of Psychiatry found, in its study, that parents, due to a lack of confidence in their own authority, often treated their adolescents as much younger children. "Lacking experience with appropriate levels of shared responsibility, these youths are inadequately prepared to assume appropriate ranges of authority" (1978, p. 174).

Other parents, also unsure of their authority, resort to dictatorial pronouncements in dealing with their adolescents. The danger in parental use of coercive power, if it is successful, is that "it may exaggerate and prolong an adolescent's dependency" (p. 174). In either case, the adolescent/young adult is ill-prepared for decision-making. His or her inability or disinclination to make choices contributes to a willingness to remain in the well-defined confines of a group, such as the cults, where all decisions are made for the members (Schwartz, 1979), and life has predictability and the security afforded by repetitive daily routine.

As Halleck found, these alienated youths fail to develop an internalized value system. This deficiency may be attributed in part to contemporary moral relativity, and in part to the absence of clear role models in the family. They may have low self-esteem and thus "become exceedingly 'field-dependent' and vulnerable to environmental influence" (Chan, 1977, p. 96). In a study of 106 cultists in nine cults, Levine and Slater found that 43 of the subjects had "joined" a cult because "life had no meaning, they were drifting" (1976, p. 413). The cults supplied "answers to identity-related and to existential questions plaguing the members" (p. 415). There are clear rules, rituals, and reinforcements (positive and negative) available in the cults—powerful external sources of control that compensate for the lack of internal controls—that are not present in many families or on many campuses.

Weak or non-existent relations with one's own father contribute also to acceptance of the strong father figure represented by the cult leader (Allison, 1969; Brown, 1977; Salzman, 1976; Spero, 1977; Ullman, 1979; Schwartz and Kaslow, 1979). From a psychoanalytic point of view, such a weak relationship inhibits the development of a strong ego and sense of self, of an adequate body image, and of a healthy super-ego (Galdston, 1969, pp. 31–38). It also suggests that there is probably a deep-seated, almost primitive, longing for the father's attention, approval, and limit setting.

The resulting dependent personality may function, maladaptively, as an "addictive personality." "Rather than developing these internal capabilities when one form of external dependency is not fulfilling her/his needs, the person seeks an alternative source of gratification which appears to meet her/his needs" (Simmonds, 1977, p. 921). The gratifying addiction may be drugs, alcohol, or complete dependency on an authority figure. It has been found that alcoholics and drug addicts have joined religious groups that forbid such indulgences, and have, in so doing, simply exchanged one form of addiction for another (Simmonds, 1977; Peele and Brodsky, 1975). However, a critical factor in vulnerability is not the addictive personality per se, but appears to be the weak father-child relationship cited above which underlies that personality. It is possible that, for some, retreat from reality into psychosis might have occurred if they had not found a niche in the structured, somewhat protected, environs of the cult community.

We have observed that those students who seek therapy on their own for such difficulties as anxiety neurosis or neurotic depression, seem to have their dependency needs met by the therapist and to obtain some sense of structure and direction in treatment. They appear unlikely to gravitate toward a cult. In our research, we expect to ascertain some of the personality variables involved (Kaslow and Schwartz, forthcoming).

Other general characteristics of the vulnerable youth have also been isolated. For example, the idealistic view of the way society *should be*—the equality, brotherhood, honesty, caring, peace among peoples preached to them by parents, teachers, and the clergy—conflict with the realities of society *as it is*. At home, they witness and are the beneficiaries of relative affluence. Although their parents may say that they value learning or art or independent thinking more than money, their actions belie their words in the eyes of their children. The nascent adult resents this hypocrisy. In society, they are aware that while politicians speak of their desire for peace, commitments to the military defense budget far exceed those for the "war on poverty" and to education or for the aged—more hypocrisy. Taught ostensibly in school to cooperate and work for the good of all, in reality, competition is fostered as the parents seek to bask in the reflected glory of their daughter being "first in her class," or their son's achievements on the athletic field or in the classroom. This is perceived as still more hypocrisy. The youth is taught and accepts that "honesty is the best policy" until he finds his parents cheating on their tax return or lying their way out of an uncomfortable situation. The inability to reconcile parental practice and preaching is resented and is conducive to disillusionment.

Another aspect of modern life is the conflict between individualism and the dehumanization wrought by technology and bureaucracy. The reduction of the person to being a student number and little holes on computer cards hits hard at the fragile developing identity of the youth. He feels unknown and uncared for amidst a host of unknowns. Erikson has most clearly discussed the state of identity diffusion, rather than integration, that can occur as a result of "a combination of experiences which demand his simultaneous commitment to *physical intimacy* (not by any means always overtly sexual), to decisive *occupational choice,* to energetic *competition,* and to *psychosocial self-definition*" (1956, p. 79). If the young person is floundering in a sea of diffusion, this further diminution of his individuality may cause him to be in danger of drowning. Perhaps the friendly recruiter from the cult appears as the saviour to the seeker who, consciously or not, is "groping, gravitating, shopping, drifting, browsing . . . on the lookout for change" (Klapp, 1969, p. 41).

As Maslow (1968) has pointed out, needs for affection and a sense of belonging are second only to survival needs as a source of motivation. Despite the abundance of campus organizations, however, these needs are not met in the college setting for many youths. As a result, they feel lonely, sad, and perhaps bewildered. The need for achievement may similarly be unsatisfied through either academic or extracurricular activities, further contributing to depression and even frustration, although academic underachievement is not always present. Cult recruiters are trained to look for individuals displaying manifestations of these feelings because such young people are most vulnerable to the friendly invitation to join a group in doing "good work." Elkind has suggested that "the great appeal of many of the charismatic religious groups is that when young people join, they are assured that support is *not* contingent upon achievement" (1979, p. 42) as it may have been at home and in college. There is evident appeal at being wanted for oneself.

A final characteristic of vulnerable youth is the search for "something" in which to believe. The college youths of the 1960s protested against organized churches, but not religion, which may have accounted for their movement toward Eastern philosophies and primitive forms of Christianity (Stearn, 1969, pp. 52–53). The research conducted for the Roche Report on "Cultism and the young" (1976) and Homer's legal review of first amendment rights as related to the cults (1974) suggest that many of the alienated young adults were disenchanted with organized religion. The cults, however, at least initially, appear to the vulnerable youth as the elusive "something" that will provide the spirituality they desire and satisfy their longing for an idealistic goal to pursue. These are intangibles they feel they cannot find in traditional religion.

In sum, the alienated and vulnerable young person may exhibit any or all of these behaviors and/or emotions.

> The crux of the problem lies in the failure of the young person to be integrated into his society. He feels uninterested, disconnected and perhaps even hostile to the people and activities in his environment. He wants to "do his own thing" but often is not sure what it is or with whom to do it. (Bronfenbrenner, 1974, p. 3)

He or she longs for a simpler, more honest, more straightforward life—one with a clear system of values; wants to be accepted even if his or her identity is still uncertain. And, because the person is unable or unwilling to make decisions, a father figure capable of directing while accepting is sought. By accepting a simple invitation from a new "friend," one can find all that one seeks—and perhaps more than one wants—in a cult.

### Conversion Techniques

The basic recruiting and conversion techniques are very similar in all of the cults with which we have been primarily concerned here. Recruiters within the cults are alerted to the characteristics of "prospects" and taught how to approach them (Stoner and Parke, 1977; Lofland, 1977). Several ex-cult members as well as journalists have testified to the use of seductive techniques, including the use of deceptive appeals in the service of a "great cause" (Edwards, 1979; Freed, 1977–78). For many cults, the typical recruiting scenario begins with the so-called "heavenly deception" and "love-bombing," (described below), which are followed by thought reform techniques, and ends with a strong commitment being made by the new recruit to the cult. From all evidence, it is rare that the youth seeks to join a cult; rather, the cult seeks and entices the youth.

Scene one occurs on a campus street or near a transportation terminal. The recruiter approaches the prospect, engages in casual conversation, and at some point invites the prospect to "come home for dinner with my friends and me so that we can discuss our work for peace (or orphans, or a minority) some more." In the course of that initial meeting, the prospect has begun to reveal something of his attitudes, concerns, longings, likes and dislikes. This information is frequently used later in the conversion process.

Scene two takes place in a house, apartment, or ashram where cult members live. The prospect is greeted warmly, complimented on some aspect(s) of his appearance, and repeatedly told, in many ways, how wonderful he is and how happy the group is that he came to visit. This strongly positive approach is called "love-bombing" (Lofland, 1977, pp. 307–311). It bolsters the potential recruit's weak ego to a point difficult to resist. Conversation during the visit focuses on the uplifting work of the group, with no mention of any church affiliation in most cases. Later in the evening, an invitation is extended to spend a low-cost or free week-end with the group at a lodge, camp, or ranch. Transportation is provided. During the ride, inspirational songs are sung by recruiters and prospects, esprit de corps is fostered, and there is more talk of the group's projects and the prospect's personal assets.

Upon arrival at the destination, usually late at night, each prospect acquires a personal companion. During scene three, this omnipresent escort does not leave the prospect's side, answers (or sidesteps) his/her questions, and seeks to keep his or her charge safely occupied with the business of the week-end. Lectures, group singing, organized games, (directed) discussion, and meals fill the hours, with little time left for sleep and none for privacy. The true nature of the group may or may not be revealed in this scene. The constant activity and companionship leave the prospect with little energy or time to review and digest what is happening (Landes, 1976). Furthermore,

> The vegetarian diet, a staple of many cults, allegedly practiced in emulation of the religiously based vegetarianism of Eastern religions, can produce a rapid weight loss leading to a temporary

state of euphoria which... may foster a heightened state of suggestibility—a state crucial to hypnotic induction. Thus, one can view these diets as designed to bring about psychophysiological change which influences mood; producing the experience of having the "weight of the world lifted off of my shoulders." (Spero, 1977, p. 332)

As Lifton (1961, p. 420) and Holt (1964, p. 295) have indicated in their studies of the "brainwashing" or thought reform practiced by the Communists, the controlled environment of this third scene is crucial to the success of indoctrination techniques.

By cutting off contact with parents, friends, and other social connections, the cult strips the convert of his most vital sources of self-reflection. Isolated in this way and cut off from all external sources of information, an individual may easily be remade by the cult in their own tightly controlled image. Then, once firmly established, this new state of mind becomes self-sustaining. (Conway and Siegelman, 1978, p. 155)

While in the controlled environment, subjected to deprivation of sleep and a normal diet, which in turn affect the efficient functioning of the central nervous system (Sargent, 1957; Meerloo, 1956), faced with unrelenting group pressures to conform, and bombarded with repetitive lectures, the potential convert has little power to retain the ability to think for himself or to maintain his identity (Stoner and Parke, 1977, p. 156; Conway and Siegelman, 1978, pp. 56–57; Edwards, 1979). What Lifton calls "totalist language" is employed by several of the cults. It is "repetitiously centered on an all-encompassing jargon, prematurely abstract, highly categorical, relentlessly judging, and to anyone but its most devoted advocate, deadly dull...." (1961, p. 429). This repetitive use of language is heard in the non-stop chanting of the Hare Krishnas, and the almost automatic, constant recitation of Bible verses by the Children of God or "divine principles" by the "Moonies." Free and reflective thinking is incompatible with this verbal behavior.

Part of the indoctrination process includes the idea that "those who aren't with us are agin' us," whether "those" are parents, peers, or deprogrammers (Adler, 1978; Enroth, 1977; Patrick, 1976). The emphasis is on the idea that "we"—the in-group—are saved, or special in some way, while "they" are not. By stressing and reinforcing this Manichean view, the cult leader(s) further reduces the influence of outsiders on the potential

convert. "The Manichean insists on the need for a decision, but the choice
is loaded and practically makes itself. . . . All good is on one side, all evil
on the other" (Kaufman, 1973, pp. 17-18). Indeed, the recruit is firmly
impressed with the idea that all non-believers are destined to damnation—
as *he* will be if he leaves the sacred confines of the group (Yamamoto,
1977, pp. 63-64).

How is it that the young adult can succumb to these techniques and
become totally committed to a whole new way of life to the point of
seeking to indoctrinate others? "One assumption about compliance that has
often been made either explicitly or implicitly is that once a person has
been induced to comply with a small request he is more likely to comply
with a larger demand" (Freedman and Fraser, 1966, p. 195). This would
account for the prospect's movement from scene one to scenes two and
three. "Given sufficient time, indoctrinated fanaticism, and total control of
the environment, conversion efforts will invariably succeed with a variety
of people, regardless of their age, sex, race, nationality, or personality
makeup" (Hacker, 1976, p. 132). All of the influences coalesce to break
down any resistance to the cult's engulfing practices, resulting in a radical
personality change, dubbed "snapping" by Conway and Siegelman
(1978), that is immediately apparent to parents and friends. This summarizes the effects of scene three.

By surrendering the self to the pressures of the cult, voluntarily or more
often unknowingly, the new convert gains certain advantages. He/she now
has a purpose in life—the mission of the cult, whatever it may be—and is
no longer drifting. There is a strong authoritarian father-figure in the leader
of the cult to replace the weak or absent father in the family. There is no
longer a need to make decisions or even to be concerned about them, for
the cult has clear "do's" and "don't's" to be obeyed. Kaufman has
identified religion as a prime strategy for avoiding decision-making, thus a
good resolution of conflict for what he calls "decideophobics" (1978, p.
8). The recruit is accepted and "loved" unconditionally by fellow cult
members, a welcome change of pace from past feelings of loneliness,
being unwanted or rejected, and alienated. Like any convert, the new
member feels that the joy or wisdom or mission so newly found must be
shared with others. This evangelistic desire to bear witness and proselytize
is regarded as the culmination of commitment.

It should be noted that the employment of these techniques is regarded
by many professionals in a variety of disciplines as a "rape of the mind"
(Meerloo, 1956; Hacker, 1976, p. 135), "internalized coercion" (Reich,
1976, p. 401), or "psychological kidnapping" (Patrick, 1976). The "sudden, drastic alteration of the individual's value hierarchy, including aban-

donment of previous academic and career goals'' (Delgado, 1977, p. 70), and symbolic death and rebirth with a new identity (Lifton, 1961, p. 66) are fundamental causes of anxiety and trauma to the convert's family and form the basis of their reactions which range from attempts to kidnap and deprogram their child to legal suits against the cults (and even a legal defense in the case of Patricia Hearst). In addition, the impact of the physical and psychological debilitation of the youth, the estrangement from the family, and the conversion to another religion are all sources of family stress (Schwartz, 1978, p. 197; Schwartz and Kaslow, 1979).

It should be noted that deprogrammers use some of the same techniques to reach their goals of ''re-opening'' the subject's mind to independent thought as do the cults in the indoctrination process. Total control of the environment, repetitious questioning and quotations from literature to arouse doubts about the cult in the individual, and some manipulation of sleep are practiced. All of these thought reform techniques have been used in other settings, sometimes for goals approved by society and sometimes not. The question of whether the ends justify the means is heatedly debated among mental health professionals and lawyers, parents and civil libertarians.

Bates' argument (1978) about the conflict between the individual's mental health and the preservation of religious freedom (supra) is frequently quoted as justification for such intervention. Despite the illegal nature of the kidnapping by parents or their agents, the courts have tended to empathize with the parents in this action, but to focus in their rulings on the freedom of religion and adult status of the cult member in deciding whether or not conservatorships/guardianships can be awarded to the distraught parents. A ruling in favor of the parents would give them custody of their child, usually for a period of 30–60 days, during which they would have the opportunity to try to counteract the cult's influence. A decision against the parents would result in the further estrangement of parents and child, and probably the removal of the young convert to a site remote from the parents, reducing the possibility of renewed attempts to kidnap or otherwise gain custody.

## *Impact of Cult Membership on the Recruit's Family*

As indicated, the entry into the cults may occur fairly rapidly—taking perhaps a few days to a few months from the time the young person is first approached by a recruiter who has recognized his/her potential vulnerability. From their headquarters near or on a campus, the recruiters are aware of the stress periods in college life and utilize this knowledge in determining when to make overtures. Specific critical periods include the first few months after admission to college, high school or college graduation when a new stage in personal development is approached, and exam weeks. The young person may or may not communicate to his family that he has finally met some people with whom he feels comfortable and compatible and that they have invited him to go away with them for a few days. Most parents, if told, are eager to have their son or daughter make friends and do not probe as to "who" these people are. Frequently they do not hear further from their child for some time and when they call, may learn from their child's roommate that he or she has quit school, moved off campus, and joined a cult.

In our research and clinical practice, we have learned that some parents treat this news casually, believing it is another phase that will pass, a temporary leave of absence from studies. But when the "leave" continues, and the silence persists, they realize it is strange that their youngster remains out of touch with them. Some, whose children previously have been deeply involved in the drug scene, are relieved that their child has joined a group where drugs, liquor, and wild parties are forbidden. They view it as a period of safe respite.

Most parents, however, in this post-Jonestown era where there is a heightened awareness of the cult phenomenon and the control over the minds of members that it can exercise, tend to become very disturbed, angry, and confused. They demand of themselves and anyone who will listen—Why did this happen? What did I (we) do to deserve such punishment? They agonize, lose sleep, and cannot concentrate on anything else. The dilemma is where to turn for help. Often they are unaware of their offspring's whereabouts; the cults are skilled in keeping their fledgling members incommunicado. Families experience a profound sense of loss, of helplessness, and, as time goes on, of hopelessness. Someone they care about has disappeared, often without warning or without giving the parents an opportunity to try to work through the kinds of long-standing problems with their youngster that contributed to his/her vulnerability to the beckoning, warm welcome of the cult. Disbelief, depression, and sadness dominate the family's reaction (see the report by Mr. and Mrs. Hershell in this volume—The experience of one family).

Many parents contact their clergyman. He may suggest prayer and offer words of comfort. Some clergymen by now have worked with many families who have experienced loss of a child to the cults and can provide them with a chance to ventilate their grief and suggest a course of action.

Some clergy believe that part of the attraction of the cults is that they minister to a person's need for commitment that may have been unmet in the family or religious context (McGowan, 1978); they may suggest that the family become more religiously involved and build their spiritual resources while seeking to find a way to have their child leave the cult.

Many families turn to attorneys, hoping to pursue a legal remedy. This has not proven very effective for several reasons. Most lawyers in private practice have had no experience in dealing with the cults, which are formidable adversaries. Turning to the courts is a lengthy and costly process. The cults have amassed great wealth and have seasoned attorneys to plead their cause. Most cases proceed along the lines that a person over 18 years of age has chosen his/her own religion and that parents have no legal right to insist that their child follow their religion or return home or to college.

The argument focuses on freedom of religion. To date the courts have been reluctant to deal with the questions of whether coercive persuasion or "brainwashing" were perpetrated prior to the person's becoming a member of the cult, and if so, if freedom of religious choice was possible under such unusual circumstances (Leahy, 1978). In some cases, courts have appointed parents as "conservators" for young adults on the basis that his/her reasoning is impaired sufficiently that the parents must act in their behalf (Vavuris, 1978). When this has occurred, the cults have been ordered to release the young person to his/her parents. The procedure tends to be traumatic for all.

Unless successful deprogramming occurs following release, the youth still seems possessed by cult ideology and manifests his/her new personality, resenting the intrusion of the parents into his new life. He or she may even bolt and return to the cult. Members of the cult are nearby, eager to re-envelop their "brother" or "sister" with open arms as rapidly as possible. Meanwhile, long smoldering family problems are likely to erupt; the parents are apt to blame each other for their current unhappy plight, and a sense of desperation hovers around everyone.

Some parents seek out parent networks, groups of parents who also have or had children involved in the cults. They offer one another solace and tangible suggestions for action. They exchange information on the pros and cons of "kidnapping," "deprogramming," how to go about the former and who to hire to do the latter. For some, this contact with other parents becomes the major source of strength. They may, if and when their own child returns and is rehabilitated, stay involved in the parent network, providing leadership and endowing their own lives with heightened meaning.

These parent groups have come to resemble other self-help organizations in that they function without professional staff leadership, turn to one another at any time of day or night, and protect the identity of their members. In addition, they may cloak their activities in secrecy to protect themselves from harassment and because often even if one child in the family has been rescued from the cult, a sibling may still be involved or vulnerable. In terms of family therapy, if one child appears to recover, that is, the symptomatology disappears, and yet the family dilemma and need for a scapegoat to bear the burden of their dysfunctioning have not been resolved, the pathology floats and another member becomes the identified patient. Retribution in the form of totally hiding the still-in-the-cult child, or of more aggressive actions is not uncommon (private communications).

Many bring their heartbreak to the therapist's office—to sort out their hurt, confusion, guilt, fury, desperation, anxiety, and the myriad other emotions that engulf them. They need sympathetic, attentive listening; support in looking at how they may have precipitated or contributed to their child's involvement in the cult, realistic responses in the form of therapist knowledge about the cult, and assistance in ascertaining their options and selecting a viable course of action.

The therapist can also focus on problems in the family, conceptualizing the cult member as the identified patient or scapegoat, and helping the parents understand the family dynamics and structure. In this way, during the period of waiting for the child to leave the cult or be removed from it, the parents and their other children can be helped to function in a healthier fashion. Often, marital or family therapy constitutes the treatment of choice at this stage of the process. One cannot minimize the pervasive sense of failure, the anguish, which parents experience when they realize that their child has embraced the cult as a substitute family. The child no longer remains in contact with them as he/she now perceives them as creatures of the devil. Their hopes and dreams for this child have been destroyed, and they may never see their child again. Therapy deals with raw emotions, the grieving process, and then mobilizing for action.

## The Post-Cult Period and Intervention Strategies

In the event that a cult member returns home because 1) he has been kidnapped and deprogrammed, 2) the courts have awarded the parents a conservatorship, or 3) he/she has in some way regained contact with the non-cult world and decided to withdraw from such a circumscribed and totally controlled existence, what then? Shapiro summarizes succinctly in his statement:

> Destructive cultism is a distinct syndrome. It includes behavioral and personality changes, loss of personal identity, cessation of scholastic activities, estrangement from family, disinterest in society and pronounced mental control and enslavement by cult leaders. Management of this sociopathic problem requires confrontation, rehabilitation, sociologic, psychotherapeutic and general medical measures. (1977, p. 80)

If someone has undergone deprogramming, they have generally had a very confrontative experience in which the deprogrammer has sought to undo the mind control exercised by cult leaders. They debunk what the cult stands for, using logic and reason to counter the irrational beliefs which have been instilled. Friends and family are nearby, ready to be called in to reinforce what the deprogrammer is saying and to offer a support network while the person is being worn down. The emotional turbulence, sense of disorientation, fear of going on without the cult peers, while being painfully aware of the threats made in the event of defection, remind us of what happens in those long, grim hours when an addict goes "cold turkey."

As a more benign alternative, we think that if a family can convince their son or daughter to come home from the cult for a visit, and can convene the entire family and many friends, as we do when undertaking network family therapy, (Speck and Attneave, 1972; Rueveni, 1979), that a similar result can be achieved using less drastic and traumatic measures, even if a cult "buddy" is present. Instead of using a deprogrammer, a team of well-qualified network therapists, who are familiar with the various cults and their modus operandi, can be invited to be in charge. Familiarity with the specific cult involved and its jargon would be advantageous. Networks share numerous properties with cults and this should introduce a familiar and treasured part of the cult atmosphere into the session—thus making the transition a little easier. The lead therapist is usually a powerful figure who emits a sense that he can heal those in his charge, and help them garner the strength and motivation to make the requisite changes in their lives.

Promoted is a willingness to volunteer to be in the smaller network which is formed for each member of the nuclear family of the ex-cult member to help them cope with the practical and emotional problems of daily living. Finding a viable balance between togetherness and separateness, and with offering tangible assistance in the form of a job or an invitation to participate in a group activity is emphasized. This appeals to the "good samaritan" instinct in many of those present who are eager to "do something" and provides a sense of purpose and concern for one's fellow human beings that they have been so sorely lacking. In utilizing network therapy in this way, the cult's mainstay of providing a group that offers unconditional love and acceptance, security and continuity, is replaced by a kinship group that has a valuable foundation in the loyalty born of family ties (Boszormenyi-Nagy and Spark, 1973). Such a network can be reconvened periodically as needed; initially fairly often and less frequently as the ex-cult member re-establishes other friendship and anchor points in the community.

In an earlier paper (Schwartz and Kaslow, 1979, pp. 23-25), we dealt with other intervention strategies at some length. Thus, we will summarize those here since our intent is to highlight the new material on the untapped potential of network therapy.

The ex-cultist may be somewhat relieved to be back in the outside world and may wonder how he got "hooked." Initially, he may experience periods of "floating" and altered states of consciousness, or he may yearn to return to an "ashram" or other cult residence and resent his parents' latest interference in his life. Frequently a profound and prolonged depression is experienced; one may feel humiliated over having been duped (Shapiro, 1977, p. 82) and resentful of the time lost in pursuit of career or other life goals. Because of the complexities of these situations, the fragility of the family relationships, the fears and hurts that have been sustained—each case should be carefully evaluated before the treatment of choice is determined and recommended.

Since one's family background and relationships appear to contribute to one's vulnerability to the cult's invitation to join, as well as to one's extrication from the cult, family involvement in the treatment is essential for lasting progress to be made and for family members to attain a better understanding of one another and respect for each other's differences, desires, and goals. Thus, whenever possible, all members of the family unit should be engaged in treatment. If the intensity of the conflict between parents and ex-cult member is very high, it is probable that concurrent treatment will be more feasible, at least at the beginning. The ex-cult member now requires a caring, sensitive therapist all to himself, who may represent, as the cult did, an authority figure and ego ideal outside of the family. This time however it is one who does not demand complete fidelity and renunciation of the parents. In this way, each of the parties can separately receive full attention and concern and have a private time to pour out feelings and clarify thoughts. If each articulates some desire for a rapprochement, then it is likely they can be seen concurrently by the same therapist. However, if the antagonism remains acute and mistrust is rampant, it is advisable that they see different therapists who can collaborate without violating confidentiality. When during the initial family evaluation sessions, it appears everyone is willing to work on the difficulties together, then conjoint family therapy constitutes the most efficacious treatment approach.

Former cult members often suffer something akin to withdrawal symptoms following their exodus, and one of these is the loss of a sense of group belonging and the feeling of identity and purpose the cult provides. Therefore, it is often advisable to involve the young person in a therapy group with other ex-cult members who are facing similar dilemmas and with whom she can sympathize, share, identify, and seek solutions.

Singer (1979, p. 72), a researcher-clinician who has done some of the pioneer work in studying and treating ex-cult members, believes group therapy provides the best context for helping. The therapist must attend to the "content of the (cult) experience" and must understand the fear ex-members have of the cult's power to harm them for being unfaithful and leaving. Participation in group therapy can occur during the same period that the person is involved in family therapy. Healthy peer group ties are fostered to replace those that may have been suddenly ended. Often the ex-cultist feels alienated from his/her pre-cult friends and needs to build new and meaningful friendships. The therapy group provides a transitional place to do this.

Regardless of which treatment modality is selected, it is critical that the therapist be clear about his own views on the cults, be able to articulate his ideas if asked what he really thinks, and that these are consistent with the ethical values and philosophy upon which his/her practice of therapy is predicated. An optimistic outlook is imperative; to convey pessimism is to exacerbate the despair deep within the patients. They long to know if they will ever again function effectively as autonomous, competent individuals not prone to floating and thought disassociations (Singer, 1979).

Given that behaviors are purposive and multi-determined, it is more than coincidence that the ex-cult member had become involved with a group that was quasi-religious in ideology and purported purpose. Following the experience, the young person should be informed about and encouraged to explore non-destructive channels for fulfilling this spiritual quest. This would constitute part of the overall therapeutic package that might also include individual, group, family or social network therapy, vocational rehabilitation, career planning, a return to college if appropriate, and good medical care to rebuild the malnourished body.

## Conclusion

In times of social unrest, economic instability, family disorganization and political uncertainty, some people turn for comfort, security, easy answers, and direction to groups led by an authoritarian and powerful, often charismatic, leader. Often, because the personal and social upheaval contains existential elements related to lack of any sense of purpose and meaning in life, the search for affiliation and direction leads one to a fundamentalist, proselytizing, religious-type organization. Such forces have contributed to the rise and spread of the cult phenomenon in the United States in the past fifteen years. We have attempted to describe the socio-history of some of the more popular contemporary cults, the basis for their appeal, the factors that cause a young person to become and stay involved with them, the impact of a young person's enmeshment in the cults on their personality and on their family members' lives, what routes are possible for extrication from the cults, and intervention strategies that might prove fruitful in the aftermath period following the exodus. Scholarly research into the cult phenomenon is still groping and growing—much more is needed to determine what value cult belonging might have, and temporary and long-range effects of cult membership on both those who stay and those who leave.

A research study on vulnerability and invulnerability to the cults, comparing non-cult and ex-cult members is currently underway and is being conducted by both authors. Preliminary analysis of the data indicates some statistically significant differences in the family dynamics and relationships of these two groups.

## REFERENCES

Adler, Warren. Rescuing David from the Moonies. *Esquire,* (June 6) 1978, *89* (10), 23-30.

Allison, Joel. Religious conversion: regression and progression in an adolescent experience. *J. for the Scientific Study of Religion,* 1969, *8* (1), 23-38.

Bates, Frank. Child law and religious extremists: some recent developments. *Ottawa Law Review,* 1978, *10,* 299-312.

Boszormenyi-Nagy, Ivan, and Spark, Geraldine. *Invisible Loyalties.* New York: Harper & Row, 1973.

Brent, Peter. Why the Guru movement can't succeed here. *Human Nature,* 1979, *2* (2), 30-37.

Bronfenbrenner, Urie. The origins of alienation. *Scientific American,* (August) 1974, *231* (2), 53-61. (Offprint runs pp. 3-9).

Brown, Thomas E. Separation-individuation in development of alternative religious commitments: A psychoanalytic perspective. *Dissertation Abstracts International,* (January) 1977, *37* (7-B), 3598.

Chan, Kwok Bun. Individual differences in reactions to stress and their personality and situational determinants: Some implications for community mental health. *Social Science and Medicine,* 1977, *11* (2), 89-103.

Conway, Flo, and Siegelmann, Jim. *Snapping: America's epidemic of sudden personality change.* Philadelphia: J. B. Lippincott, 1978.

Cox, Harvey. *The Seduction of the spirit.* New York: Simon and Schuster, 1973.

Cultism and the young. *Roche Report: Frontiers in Psychiatry,* 1976, *6* (13), 1-10.

Daner, Francine Jeanne. *The American Children of KRSNA: A study of the Hare Krishna movement.* New York: Holt, Rinehart, and Winston, 1976.

Davis, Rex, and Richardson, James. The organization and functioning of the Children of God. *Sociological Analysis,* 1976, *37,* 321-339.

Delgado, Richard. Religious totalism: Gentle and ungentle persuasion under the first amendment. *Southern California Law Review,* (November) 1977, *51* (1), 1-98.

Denlinger, A. M. *Real People.* Scottdale, Pa.: Herald Press, 1975.

Downton, James V., Jr. *Sacred Journeys.* New York: Columbia University Press, 1979.

Edwards, Christopher. *Crazy for God.* New York: Prentice-Hall, 1979.

Elkind, David. Growing up faster. *Psychology Today,* (February) 1979, *12* (9), 38-45.

Enroth, Ronald. *Youth, brainwashing, and the extremist cults.* Grand Rapids, Mich.: Zondervan Publishing, 1977.

Erikson, Erik H. The problem of ego identity. *American Psychoanalytic Association Journal,* 1956, *4,* 56-121.

Erikson, Erik H. *Identity: youth and crisis.* New York: W. W. Norton, 1968.

Evans, Christopher. *Cults of unreason.* New York: Farrar, Straus, and Giroux, 1973.

Freed, Josh. The Moon stalkers. *The Montreal Star,* (Dec. 31) 1977, (Jan. 3) 1978, (Jan. 7) 1978.

Freedman, J. L., and Fraser, S. C. Compliance without pressure: The foot-in-the-door technique. *J. of Personality and Social Psychology,* 1966, *4,* 195-202.

Galdston, Iago. The psychopathology of paternal deprivation. In Jules H. Masserman, ed. *Childhood and Adolescence.* New York: Grune & Stratton, 1969, 14-45.

Gillin, John Lewis. *Social Pathology,* 3rd ed. New York: D. Appleton Company, 1946.

Glock, Charles Y. The role of deprivation in the origin and evolution of religious groups. In Robert Lee and Martin E. Marty, eds., *Religion and Social Conflict.* New York: Oxford University Press, 1964, 24-36.

Greenfield, Robert. *The spiritual supermarket.* New York: Saturday Review Press, 1975.

Group for the Advancement of Psychiatry (Committee on Adolescence). *Power and authority in adolescence: The origins and resolutions of intergenerational conflict.* New York: GAP Report #101, 1978.

Hacker, Frederick J. *Crusaders, criminals, crazies: Terror and terrorism in our time.* New York: W. W. Norton, 1976.

Holt, Robert R. Forcible indoctrination and personality change. In Philip Worchel and Donn Byrne, eds., *Personality Change.* New York: John Wiley, 1964, 289-318.

Homer, David R. Abduction, religious sects, and the free exercise guarantee. *Syracuse Law Review,* 1974, *25,* 623-645.

Hostetler, John A. *Amish society.* Baltimore: Johns Hopkins Press, 1963.

Kanter, Rosabeth Moss. *Commitment and community: Communes and Utopian sociological perspective.* Cambridge: Harvard University Press, 1972.

Kaslow, Florence W., and Schwartz, Lita Linzer. Vulnerability and invulnerability to the cults: An assessment of family dynamics, functioning, and values. In D. Bagarozzi, ed., *New perspectives in marriage and family therapy: Issues in theory, research, and practice.* New York: Human Sciences Press, forthcoming.

Kaufman, Walter. *Without guilt or justice*. New York: Peter H. Wyden, 1973.
Kelley, Dean M. Deprogramming and religious liberty. *Civil Liberties Review*, 1977, *4*, 23-33.
Klapp, Orrin E. *Collective search for identity*. New York: Holt, Rinehart, and Winston, 1960.
Kuttner, Robert E., and Shaw, Joyce M. Contributions to psychohistory: II. Toynbee's study of history: A contribution to the psychology of crisis cults and religion. *Psychological Reports*, 1977, *41*, 480-482.
Landes, Marie Gisek. Making of a Moonie. *Atlas World Press Review*, (Sept.) 1976, 29-32.
Leahy, John J. On the civil liberties of sect members, Part III. In Irving Louis Horowitz, ed., *Science, Sin, and Scholarship*. Cambridge, Mass.: The MIT Press, 1978, 208-216.
Le Moult, John E. Deprogramming members of religious sects. *Fordham Law Review*, 1978, *46*, 599-640.
Levine, Saul V., and Slater, Nancy E. Youth and contemporary religious movements: Psychosocial findings. *Canadian Psychiatric Association Journal*, 1976, *21*, 411-420.
Lifton, Robert Jay. *Thought reform and the psychology of totalism: A study of "brainwashing" in China*. New York: W. W. Norton, 1961.
Lofland, John. *Doomsday Cult*, enlgd. ed. New York: Irvington Publishers, 1977.
Maslow, Abraham. *Toward a psychology of being*, 2nd ed. New York: Van Nostrand, 1968.
McGowan, Thomas. The Unification Church. *The Ecumenist*, (Jan.-Feb.) 1979, 21-25.
Meerloo, Joost A. M. *The rape of the mind*. New York: World Publishing, 1956.
Mintz, Jerome R. Brooklyn's Hasidim. *Natural History*, (Jan.) 1977, *86* (1), 46-59.
Patrick, Ted (with Tom Dulack). *Let our children go!* New York: E. P. Dutton, 1976.
Peele, Stanton, and Brodsky, Archie. *Love and addiction*. New York: Taplinger Publishing, 1975.
Reich, Walter. Brainwashing, psychiatry, and the law. *Psychiatry*, 1976, *39*, 400-403.
Reuveni, Uri. *Networking families in crisis*. New York: Human Sciences Press, 1979.
Rice, Berkeley. Messiah from Korea: Honor thy father Moon. *Psychology Today*, 1976, *9* (8), 36-47.
Rubin, Israel. *Satmar: An island in the city*. Chicago: Quadrangle Books, 1972.
Salzman, Leon. Types of religious conversion. *Pastoral Psychology*, 1966, *17*, 8-20, 66.
Sargent, William. *Battle for the mind: A physiology of conversion and brainwashing*. London: William Heinemann, 1957.
Schwartz, Lita Linzer. A note on family rights, cults, and the law. *J. of Jewish Communal Service*, 1978, *55* (2), 194-198.
Schwartz, Lita Linzer. Cults: The vulnerability of sheep. *USA Today*, (July) 1979, *108*, 22-24.
Schwartz, Lita Linzer, and Kaslow, Florence W. Religious cults, the individual, and the family. *J. of Marital and Family Therapy*, 1979, *5*, 15-26.
Schwartz, Lita Linzer, and Zemel, Jacqueline L. Religious cults: Family concerns and the law. *J. of Marital and Family Therapy*, 1980, *6*, 301-308.
Shaffir, William. Witnessing as identity consolidation: The case of the Lubavitcher Chassidim. In Hans Mol, ed., *Identity and Religion*. Beverly Hills, Calif.: Sage Publications, 1978, 39-57.
Shapiro, Eli. Destructive cultism. *American J. of Family Practice*, 1977, *15* (2), 80-83.
Simmonds, Robert B. Conversion or addiction. *American Behavioral Scientist*, 1977, *20*, 909-924.
Skinner, B. F. *The Behavior of organisms*. New York: Appleton-Century-Crofts, 1938.
Sontag, Frederick, *Sun Myung Moon and the Unification Church*. Nashville: Abingdon Press, 1977.
Singer, Margaret Thaler. Coming out of the cults. *Psychology Today*, 1979, *12* (8), 72-80.
Speck, Ross V., and Attneave, Carolyn L. Social network intervention. In C. J. Sager and H. S. Kaplan, eds., *Progress in group and family therapy*. New York: Brunner/Mazel, 1972.

Spero, Moshe Halevi. Cults: some theoretical and practical perspectives. *J. of Jewish Communal Service,* (Summer) 1977, *54,* 330-338.

Stearn, Jess. *The seekers.* Garden City, N.Y.: Doubleday and Co., 1969.

Stoner, Carroll, and Parke, Jo Anne. *All Gods children: Salvation or slavery?* Radnor, Pa.: Chilton Publishing, 1977.

Ullman, Chana. Private communication.

Vavuris, S. Lee. On the civil liberties of sect members, Part II. In Irving Louis Horowitz, ed., *Science, Sin, and Scholarship.* Cambridge, Mass.: The MIT Press, 1978, 198-207.

Wallis, Roy. Observations on the Children of God. *Sociological Review,* 1976, *24,* 807-829.

Wallis, Roy. Scientology: therapeutic cult to religious sect. *Sociology,* 1975, *9* (1), 89-100.

Ward, Hiley H. Report on a cult: Children of God. *The Philadelphia Inquirer,* (Dec. 2) 1978.

Yamamoto, J. Isamu. *The puppet master.* Downers Grove, Ill.: InterVarsity Press, 1977.

# THE DYNAMICS OF MASS CONVERSION

## Christopher Edwards

New religions occupy an important place in modern American life. The social scientist who wishes to understand or counsel a devotee or his family will find it useful to explore both the individual's relationship to his family and the technology of conversion and faith maintenance by the group. My own experience as a former cult member, acquaintance of hundreds of members and lay counselor to ex-cultists has taught me that each person's family and group experience must be considered in great detail. Nevertheless, striking similarities can be found in the family histories, conversion technologies, and de-conversion technologies among devotees of a number of popular groups. I would like to explore some of these parallels by examining the experience most familiar to me, membership in the Unification Church.

A number of preliminary studies have shown that the population of Unification Church members, or Moonies, comes from middle class and upper middle class homes (Levine, 1978; Galanter, 1979; Eden, 1979). In the Eden study of 145 ex-Moonies, 98 percent were in this category. Fifty-four percent of all fathers and 32 percent of all mothers were professionals, 36 percent of all fathers were businessmen, 42 percent of all mothers were housewives, and only five percent of all parents were blue collar workers. Seventy-eight percent of these cult members were partially or fully dependent upon their families for financial help at the time of conversion.

The Eden study revealed that 91 percent of the population came from two-parent homes. This study concluded that no single family or other social factor seemed to account for predisposition to cult membership. The Eden study did show that 88 percent of all joiners were facing three or more major life crises simultaneously, including change in job plans, school plans, job/school situations, change in love relationships, uncertainty about future directions, or commencement of career. Forty-seven percent of the

Christopher G. Edwards is an ex-cultist, author of *Crazy for God,* 1979, and currently is editor of *Genetic Technology News.*

*31*

population were facing five or more of these crises at the time of joining. The population is clearly an unstable one at the point of contact with recruiters. This does not, however, account for how and why these people joined this group instead of seeking other opportunities to resolve their conflicts. To begin to answer these questions, we must turn to the nature of group conversion into the Moonies.

The Unification Church practices a technology of conversion. I will outline aspects of this technology so the reader can understand how proselytizers play upon the initiate's family conflicts to effect conversion. A technology of conversion can be defined as an applied method for changing values which encompasses some or all of the following characteristics: careful selection of conversion-prone individuals for indoctrination; the use of interactive techniques designed to rapidly elicit from an initiate his life history information, including goals, fears, basic life conflicts, and emotional needs; the use of a "false" presentation of self or persona accomplished through the control of gesture and speech to facilitate the gaining of trust; the exercise of control over interactions between proselytizer and initiate.

This may be accomplished by varying both the type and amount of information which is exchanged between parties; the presentation of a "group persona" and use of a group persona to create an appealing view of both the group and the individual's relationship to the group. The group persona is a well-established set of interactions between group members which functions to help achieve conversion. It is an advertisement for the group which involves the initiate's participation, an ideal portrayal of the life he could lead with the group; the conversion of the initiate by controlling most or all environmental inputs to the initiate's body, including all inputs for communication of information. This involves control over general level of body activity through alteration of sleep and exercise patterns. It also includes regulation of diet, sexual activity, conversations, books, music, media, telephone use, and location of activities. Recruiters achieve control over perception of time and order by organizing the schedule and rate of activity for each pre-determined activity.

The Unification Church conversion which I experienced in Berkeley and Booneville, California included all of these elements in the order mentioned above. This technology has not changed essentially in the past five years. It is effective to the extent that it can reveal and symbolically resolve early family and peer conflicts. Unification Church members, like new and established religious believers, seek people in crisis during the times and at the places where such a population is likely to be available.

First encounters are often made on campuses or youth hostels where college-age travelers congregate, such as college dormitories or student centers. Examination and graduation periods are critical events for an approach or in lecture halls with a higher degree of success than at other times. Attractive advertisements are used to stimulate the potential novitiate's interest.

Reflecting upon my experiences as a potential member, recruiter, and observer of many attempts at recruitment, I believe that recruiters follow a rigid order of rules for role-playing which increases the recruiter's allegiance while attracting the initiate to the group. A typical pattern would begin with an aggressively friendly greeting, quickly followed by a series of questions which evoke pleasant experiences in the initiate's mind. These are expressed and informed to both initiate and recruiter simultaneously. Recruiters usually reply with distinctly similar stories of their own pleasant experiences. For example, after persuading the initiate to tell him about a favorite subject of study or sport, he will quickly mention a similar life experience in an enthusiastic manner. This is a first step in a group recruiting strategy called "Finding a Common Base," a way for both strangers to perceive each other within a common identity.

When the initiate perceives the recruiter as a peer in an adolescent or young adult group, the recruiter simultaneously perceives the initiate as a person like himself who is about to enter a Unification Church conversion center. This double-mirroring effect is maintained under the control of the recruiter through conversations and friendly non-verbal gestures which elicit a series of pleasant experiences in the mind of the initiate.

In my experience this technique proved most effective when the recruiter could enter a state of ecstasy which he believed to be the result of an externally-directed force. This becomes possible for recruiters after it is learned when numerous ecstatic experiences with other members have occurred. Repeated experiences of this sort which have been made meaningful by lectures on God can be drawn upon by recruiters as a strategy for modifying one's own state to enhance recruitment. This self-stimulation and active retrieval of mental experience is constantly reinforced by daily group experience. From the inside—as a member—it is the power of God.

If the recruiter can induce such a state of mild ecstasy in the initiate and both individuals can deepen a state of ecstasy together, this is labelled a spiritual experience or spiritual relationship by the recruiter. The recruiter begins to perceive the initiate as a different person—as a child who is not yet aware of his desire to be led into Heavenly Father's kingdom by his spiritual parent, the recruiter.

Unification Church recruiters frequently give a selective view of their lives and a limited or deceptive view of their current religious affiliation to initiates, a faithful practice of an informal group doctrine called "Heavenly Deception." If the recruiter can paint a selective portrait of himself (based on information given to him by the initiate) which appeals to early childhood experience of the initiate, the recruiter can exert control over the interaction in a pattern similar to the initiate's early relationship to a parent or older sibling.

This practice of appealing to early childhood experience in a deliberate manner can achieve remarkable effects. After a weekend with the group, for example, I experienced a visual resemblance between my recruiter and my father. Different members of the group looked and acted like significant people from my childhood—my mother, grandmother and brother. As a movement recruiter I noticed that my practice of these strategies could rapidly bring initiates to a similar state of mind. Group members tacitly acknowledge and reinforce these tactics at group meetings where discussions about various new spiritual children are held.

An effective recruiting strategy requires that the group continually strengthen emotional bonds between recruiter and initiate by using powerful but relatively disorganized relationships stored in the minds of the believer. In the Unification Church this begins with the introduction of the initiate to a group of smiling peers over a hot meal in a pleasant, noncombative atmosphere. The initiate is seated with people whom the recruiter believes to share a similar background. Recruiters seated around the initiate will individually ask personal questions about his background before repeating the same process of gaining trust with their pleasing gestures and conversations.

Over the course of the evening, a "group persona" will be presented to the initiate, often based upon routines which several recruiters have used together many times with initiates. The intended message throughout the evening is: we are like brothers and sisters living together and enjoying our life as never before. We want you to get to know us better and let us love you.

The evening is filled with singing, a light-hearted talk by a professorial man who heads the American branch of the group, and a slide presentation of a beautiful farm where happy young men and women are pictured arm-in-arm.

The exchange of information throughout this evening is controlled through the hierarchical structure of the group. No information about the religious nature of the group or their daily practices of proselytizing or money-making is given. All information about the ideals of the group, personal histories of members, or actual relationships established between group members is given only when this matches information which has been volunteered by the initiate about his desires and history. This is in accordance with the information that "no negativity," no negative information, can be expressed during the evening.

If members of higher group status detect negativity, they may communicate this to leaders who will eventually lower the status of the recruiter or punish him with difficult and unrewarding tasks.

The recruiter and other members make a concerted effort at the end of the evening to persuade the initiate to join the group for a "fun weekend." In my case, I was promised the opportunity of a beautiful three days of fellowship, games and discussions about human relationships in the countryside with individuals who want to "build a better world."

If the initiate accepts an invitation for the weekend, he is usually brought to the nearest of a series of camps situated in remote regions of the country. In this camp, the group exercises control of essential environmental inputs including all social data. The camps are usually located in areas too remote to be identifiable to recruits. In my experience in Booneville, California, telephones were locked, no electronic media were allowed, and no time was available during the initiates' days to read any hidden printed matter.

During the weekend, the exchange of social data is strictly controlled by the assignment of initiates to one or more veteran members ideally the recruiter of the initiate. The daily activities take place in a group of ten or twelve led by an experienced member. The leader firmly but enthusiastically tells guests that in order to enjoy warm fellowship and fully participate in the group, the leader will guide all relationships by calling on people who have questions and by making all group decisions. He or she usually asks for "no negativity," explaining that this harmony will make the group more intimate. The leader may state that since the weekend is filled with activity to give a new loving experience to guests, there will be no time for discussion between new initiates. This is firmly enforced by aggressive recruiters who remain with each initiate on a 24-hour basis.

Over the course of the weekend, the group leader directs childlike behavior encouraging initiates to sing children's songs, play children's games, eat children's snacks and voice simplistic statements about peace and love. A group leader might be heard encouraging her members to "melt together like peanut butter and jelly" to be closer together. Childlike behavior is lavishly rewarded with praise, applause, smiles and intense looks of approval directed towards the initiate. Characteristics of adult behavior including detachment, establishment of context, individual decision-making, or individual interpretation are discouraged by group leaders who cheerfully postpone unanswered questions with the promise that they will be eventually answered.

Lectures, games, farm work and other group behavior all take place with familial undertones (Edwards, 1979). The entire weekend is highly ordered, geared towards creating as pleasant a group experience as possible as the initiate is instructed to participate completely under the group's direction.

I feel that my own conversion to the group took place with the acceptance and practice of a group dynamic which allowed me to receive parental and sibling affection from these strangers. Work on the farm, known to the group as "practicing the Principle," reinforced this dynamic and relieved the anxiety I was experiencing in facing adult crises about sexual and family relationships, and future vocational plans.

Religious beliefs of the group are introduced following the weekend, after the initiates have received three full days of close attention with emphasis upon childhood play. The beliefs make the practices of the group intelligible and give guidelines for gaining further acceptance from the group.

As I assumed a more dependent, childlike role in the group, I began to trust the group's perceptions more than my own. The beliefs justified this by teaching that new members of the group become more open to God's truth by trusting like children and leaving fallen thinking behind. The appeal to me was an experimental one, a way of testing this group by accepting their beliefs on an as-if basis. My doubts were resolved by confessing to a woman who resembled my grandmother during my childhood. I accepted some of her interpretations as I once trusted my grandmother and her religious interpretations of life. This began after the love in weekend, despite my lack of religious belief after early adolescence.

Group life reflects the religious belief that individuals enter a spiritual hierarchy by becoming children, siblings, and eventually parents to other spiritual children as they reach a state of perfect identity with Reverend Moon and God. These roles are constantly opposed to the roles converts have experienced during their "fallen" lives. Physical parents, siblings, and their previous childhood roles are disparagingly compared to the simple, perfect spiritual order. Group members learn to idealize their new spiritual family members, expecting the fulfillment of childhood desires for affection without the pain of separation. Older members of the group fulfill the expected parental roles by taking their cues from the initiates. They give gifts of chocolate bars, greeting cards, baubles, or other items in exchange of expressions of loyalty and devotion by new members.

Competition for sexual relationships which would hamper sibling harmony is eliminated by the belief and practice of chastity. Since members believe that sexual relations in the Biblical Garden of Eden is the cause of all man's crimes and misfortune, they wait until Reverend Moon appoints a mate after three years of membership. Three more years of chastity must follow before sexual relations can begin.

Role changes frequently take place in the movement, but only within the unambiguous parent/child/sib triad. The assumption of a group persona and individual persona for witnessing and fund-raising allows Moonies to feel a part of the larger society. As cult businesses have expanded, members have assumed roles as small business executives, public relations people, and salesmen—all within the confines of the group's goals.

Personal goals center upon a simple transformation of the child's desire to grow up and be like his parents, in this case the embodiment of God through the True Parents, Moon and his wife. Nobody has ever been acknowledged by the leader to be a complete adult, a person who would be perfect and on an equal footing with Reverend Moon. A faithful follower, therefore, lives to be a good boy or girl in daily life with the hope that by believing the parents and following their rules, they will learn to completely internalize their perfect parent and become an adult.

## Discussion

Conversion is successful to the degree that recruiters can control the interaction between the individual and the group. They manage to do this by controlling the information in the relationship, particularly by retrieving and exploiting the information stored in the convert's mind about his family relationships.

Purely physiological means can be used to increase control over the relationship. For example, food and sleep deprivation can increase stress reactions, requiring initiates to take anxiety-relieving measures such as confession or commitment to the group (Sargent, 1971; Selye, 1976). This was indicated in my Moonie experience and confirmed by one study reporting an average of 4.9 hours of sleep in the group (Eden, 1979). Conversion occurs more rapidly and completely along with control of this physical environment if the recruit is given limited or false information. This creates confusion of context in the mind of the initiate.

Bateson views cognitive development as the product of a series of experiences which cause the brain to select, sort, and discriminate according to logical hierarchies. Three orders of learning within this hierarchical model would include: receipt of a signal or stimulus, classification of the signal within a meaningful or stable context (arrangement of signals), and classification of this context in relation to other experiences. In a situation where a mother calls her daughter to dinner, the sound of the call would be a signal, the perception that it is time to eat would be the context, and the tone of voice as interpreted by the child would indicate the context of context, i.e., the change in the overall relationship between mother and child. The mother's tone comments upon the relationship as a metacommunicative statement above and beyond the immediate circumstances.

The conversion I experienced seems to fit within Bateson's double bind theory in a very specific way. Bateson's communication theory accounting for schizophrenic and other behavior differences posits three elements: the individual must be involved in an intense relationship requiring accurate discrimination for an immediate response; the individual is involved in a situation where the other person is communicating two orders or logical types of message, one of which denies the other; and the individual is unable to comment on the messages being expressed to correct the discrimination of what order to respond it, i.e., he cannot make a metacommunicative statement (Bateson, 1956).

Initial encounters with group members play upon identity problems by continually shifting the interaction away from examining context and towards "feeling good." By tailoring the presentation to the cues of the initiate about problems in family, peer, and adult relationships, the recruiters can temporarily resolve these problems at a number of levels.

The Eden study revealed the three greatest attractions for initiates in the group were: getting "loved up" or receiving attention; the group's desire to change the world; and the need to find purpose and meaning in life. A common metacommunicative message from the first group weekend could encompass all three of these responses by stating: I am performing well and gaining the approval of these people, and I can make plans to increase this (as peer, child, friend, student and other roles) with them.

Since group members control the interactions, they can confuse context perception while providing clear signals of acceptance of the initiate as child. For example, during the weekend the trainers talk about growing up and forming adult love relationships while they sing children's songs, hold hands by the campfire, speak in stern parental tones to guests, and quickly discourage any attempts at sexual communication. "You must be a child to grow up" is only one of many contradictory messages which exist on both verbal and nonverbal levels. One leader told me sternly: "If you want unconditional love, you have to obey the rules." Another repeatedly stated: "Here you have free will, but once you have heard the Principle, you have no choice."

Bateson (1956) states that double binds exist when both conflicting orders of communication are enforced by punishment. Although the first weekend in the Moonies is primarily oriented towards establishing a positive identity as a child in the group, the indoctrination of the following week focuses on prohibition against any thoughts, feelings, or actions dissonant to the life of the group.

The first weekend redefines the signals into the context: you must be the heavenly child, your true self. The following week's activities emphasize: you must not be a child of fallen parents, a student with individual goals, or a friend of people outside the group who lead you away from God, and you must not play any roles in society which you personally desire. This message is established with a communication context in which the initiate is responding to a "parent" who helps by scolding, encouraging painful confessions about the evils of sex, and counseling to help him overcome the "selfish ways" of extra-cult life. If initiates object, recruiters withdraw their affection, communicate both verbal and nonverbal gestures of intense disapproval, and accuse the initiate of not loving them and not loving the Father in Heaven. The initiate may come to believe that they are being helped and loved by this context and that they can only be helped and loved by this context.

The logic of the group message to converts, as explained above, would be:

1. You must be who you really are (Heavenly Child) through group participation. (Primarily nonverbal)
2. You must not be who you are (Fallen Child of God) through group confession. (Primarily verbal)
3. You must be who we tell you to be (to become your true self).

Individuals are not free to comment on this interaction because of the rigorous schedule, lack of privacy, and silencing of all communication between new initiates. Such an inability to comment is characteristic according to Bateson, of double bind interactions. In fulfillment of Bateson's final requirement for the double-bind to be effective, there is no perceived opportunity to escape. The gates are simply locked for the week.

All of the double-bind behavior is repeated on a daily and weekly basis, ensuring that people begin to adapt to the double-bind conflicts and accept those behaviors which are highly rewarded before they are allowed to leave the farm and work in the city.

If the Moonie indoctrination does create double-bind situations which return people to childhood experience, it would be reasonable to expect that this would have temporary positive effects upon individuals raised in this atmosphere. Several psychiatrists who have treated patients from these training centers (Clark, 1980; Sukhdeo, 1979) have found that their patient diagnosed schizophrenic often improved temporarily during their group membership while other young adults seemed to function poorly in cult life.

Treatment of the Moonie experience as a double-bind may hold promise for further study. It may also aid in the development of therapies which can help the ex-member understand this confusing experience. The value of the double-bind model can be assessed if researchers are willing to gather data through extensive interviews with present and former members and begin to map the cult's communication system. The model and the methodology developed in this research could aid in understanding the structure and function of involvement in a number of other new religious movements.

## REFERENCES

Bateson, Gregory; Jackson, Don; Haley, Jay; and Weakland, John. Toward a theory of Schizophrenia. *Behavioral Science*, 1 (4), 1956. Rep. in *Steps to an Ecology of Mind*. New York: Chandler, 1972.

Clark, John. Personal communication, 1980.

Eden, Eve. The Unification Church: A study of structure and conversion. Unpublished thesis, University of Michigan, 1979.

Edwards, Christopher. *Crazy for God: The Nightmare of Cult Life*. Englewood Cliffs, N.J.: Prentice-Hall, 1979.

Galanter, Marc, et al. The Moonies: a psychological study of conversion and membership in a contemporary religious sect. *American Journal of Psychiatry*, 136 (2), 1979, 165-170.

Levine, Saul. Alternative life styles: the dilemmas of contemporary religious movements. *Adolescent Psychiatry*, 6, 1978.

Sargent, William. *Battle for the Mind*. New York: Harper and Row, 1971.

Selye, Hans. *The Stress of Life*. New York: McGraw Hill, 1976, 405-426.

Sukhdeo, Hardat. Personal communication, 1979.

# A TYPOLOGY OF FAMILY RESPONSES
# TO A NEW RELIGIOUS MOVEMENT

James A. Beckford

Among the reasons given for the intensity of feelings widely elicited by new religious movements[1] in the West is that their recruits are predominantly young people for whom parents and other close relatives still feel a strong measure of responsibility. The modal age of present-day members of such movements as the Unification Church, the Family of Love, the Divine Light Mission or the ISKCON (devotees of Krishna) is probably mid-twenties. The vast majority are unmarried, and many were still undergoing higher education or training courses at the time of recruitment. What is more, these movements offer communal living in which the family is effectively replaced by the religious group. Another obvious, but commonly overlooked aspect of today's new religious movements is that members are usually recruited as individuals. Very few family units have been recruited. This contrasts sharply with the situation prevailing in most "mainstream" Christian churches. Understanding the new religious movements must therefore take account of the special implications which they have for their members' families. (See Kaslow and Schwartz, 1980; Schwartz and Kaslow, 1979.)

The aim of this article is to examine in detail one aspect of the complex connections between one particular new religious movement and its members' families. It reports on research on the ways close relatives of members and ex-members of the Unification Church (U.C.) in Britain responded to the recruits and to their movement.[2] (On the U.C. in Britain see Barker, 1978; Beckford, 1973 and 1975; and Cozin, 1973.) It was conducted mainly by in-depth interviews between 1976 and 1979 with forty-four relatives of U.C. members and twenty ex-members of the movement.[3] Additional information was obtained from discussions with twenty-six activists in the anti-cult movement in Britain. (See Beckford, 1978a.)

After a brief comment on the sociological nature of "accounts" arising

James A. Beckford is Senior Lecturer in Sociology at the University of Durham, England.

from interviews, three types of accounts provided by the relatives of U.C. members are analyzed. The structure of each type of account reflects the character of social relationships prevailing within the families when affiliation to this movement took place. Finally, the particular circumstances surrounding affiliation to the U.C. elicit from families distinctive patterns of action corresponding to their typical ways of explaining membership.

## Accounts

Research into family processes connected with responses to a family member's affiliation to a new religious movement usually calls for a method involving interviewing people about the past. The interview method produces results which are consequently "constructed" in some sense. In other words, people are under pressure during interviews to give an account of their past experiences which will gather together ideas, feelings, hunches and facts in a fairly coherent way. "Accounts" are what is required by this research method, and accounts by definition present an ordered (if not always orderly) version of events and states of mind. This does not, of course, mean that accounts cannot be trusted. It indicates that the conditions in which they are produced must be borne in mind when their meaning is analyzed. One of the tasks of analysis is therefore to "unpack" the order lying beneath accounts and to expose the connections which enable the hearer (as well as the speaker) to make sense of the past and of what is being said about it (Beckford, 1978b).

My interviews with some of the close relatives of recruits to the Unification Church (see Sontag, 1977; Bromley and Shupe, 1980) have produced accounts which display several basic devices for ordering the past in a coherent fashion. The intention behind the following analysis is not to discredit or debunk such accounts. Rather my aim is to reveal the typical processes whereby people produce distinctive explanations for phenomena associated with affiliation to new religious movements. For their accounts are far from being arbitrary or idiosyncratic. They actually display patterned characteristics which tell a great deal about informants' changing sense of the meaning to be found in their experiences. What are the main patterns of account?

## Three Types of Response

### (i) Incomprehension

The first type of family response, as reflected in the account provided of events leading up to, and culminating in, affiliation to the U.C. by a member of the family, can be characterized by a pervasive sense of incomprehension and bewilderment. The recruit's relatives were usually in no doubt about the timing of crucial events or the meaning of his or her significant attitudes and actions, but they consistently gave the impression of being unable to make sense of them as a coherent development. This was sometimes made apparent in correspondence even before the interview had taken place. They expressed doubts, for example, about the usefulness of an interview in view of their allegedly poor grasp of the situation. They typically confessed themselves to be incapable of explaining why their relative had joined the U.C., and their incomprehension was in some cases aggravated by embarrassment.

Relatively few families in my sample fell into this category but they constituted a distinctive category by virtue of several unique characteristics. Social relationships with the recruit prior to affiliation were usually characterized as basically sound but lacking in emotional warmth. The recruit was said to be an independent person who had "grown away" from the family and whose outlook or style of life had occasionally puzzled other family members. Bonds with siblings were described as weak, though not antagonistic.

The recruit's style of life was said to have displayed one or more unexpected, radical transformations in the period prior to affiliation to the U.C. And in recognition of this some parents, like the mother of a former Hippie who had earlier contemplated suicide, grudgingly admitted that the U.C.:

> may be better than what he might have got into otherwise, you see . . . I don't think it's the best thing, but he could easily have got involved with drugs or something and really gone downhill. He could even have jumped off that bridge that he was talking about by now. . .

In other cases ambitions and aspirations for the recruit's career and personal development appeared to have been disappointed, and feelings of frustration were strong in some parents. These feelings were not, however, expressed in dogmatic or self-assertive condemnations of the recruit. Rather, they seemed to express a diffuse inability to predict or to control events which bordered, in some cases, on an attitude of resignation.

The typical response of relatives in this category was to regret the fact that a member of their family had joined a new religious movement but to eschew any idea of trying to remove him or her from it. Affiliation was apparently treated as yet another event in a series which had already weakened family ties, and it was considered no more and no less incomprehensible than any of the earlier events.

From the relatives' point of view the recruit's outlook, actions and intentions were a closed book which defied understanding. Consequently, relatives refused to be unduly alarmed or intrigued by the latest turn in the recruit's biography, nor did they take many steps to find out more about the U.C. They were, of course, aware of the adverse publicity surrounding the movement, but since their primary concern was the "waywardness" of the individual recruit, they were not impelled to campaign against it. It simply represented the latest "thing" which their errant relative had taken up.

There were suggestions in the accounts of some relatives in this category that they would not have been strongly averse from the idea that, provided the recruit settled down to a period of stable participation in the U.C., the movement might actually be beneficial to him or her. Some were clearly impressed by claims that their formerly foot-loose and irresponsible relative had found a vocation and was actually undertaking responsible tasks and commitments. A good case in point was that of David, a drop-out from university, drama school and journalism, whose Welsh working-class father was clearly impressed that, since belonging to the "Moonies," his son had dined at the Savoy Hotel in London, travelled extensively and delivered public lectures:

> He's getting a bit of limelight, you know—like doing what he's wanted to do, acting somehow. After all, when he stands up he's the centre of attraction.

Others admitted more grudgingly that a strong commitment to a religious life, however questionable, was at least preferable to the possible or actual alternatives entertained by the recruit in the past. In neither case was it felt necessary to lodge more than a faint protest at the possibility of continuing involvement in the U.C. On the other hand there was no enthusiasm for the kind of public relations work carried out by the movement among the close relatives of its members. They maintained a neutral stance towards both pro- and anti-cult lobbies.

## (ii) Anger

The second type of family response is much more sharply defined in all respects. It is best characterized by an all-pervading sense of anger and urgency which some relatives had managed to maintain over long periods of time. In the sample of people interviewed, this response was statistically the most frequent, but some echoes of it were also perceptible in the other two types of response. Moreover, this particular response has virtually monopolized the accounts given in the mass-media of reactions to new religious movements; indeed, it has approximated to the status of a stereotype.[4]

The dominant tone of this response was one of anger. The rage of some informants was visible as well as audible, and outbursts of shouting, swearing and crying were not uncommon during interviews. There is no doubt that the kind of emotional animus against the new religious movements portrayed in mass-media stereotypes of the family response is well-founded. What cannot be grasped from the media accounts is the extent to which some relatives have sustained a high level of anger and indignation over many years. The "snapshot" approach of journalists fails to capture the deeply-rooted character of the emotions which drove some family members not only to angry recriminations against new religious movements but also to an all-consuming and constant determination to suppress what they considered to be the evil activities of such movements. A good insight into the tragicomic aspects of this response was provided by a woman who had set aside an "operations room" in her house from which she had been conducting an unrelenting campaign to secure her daughter's "release" from the U.C. for several years. This was her "work":

> I say I do my crying before seven o'clock in the morning, and after that I've got to get on with the day's work, and sometimes, really, if it weren't so tragic, it would be funny. But this is real life.

Not all relatives in this category, however, had been hostile to the U.C. from the very beginning of their association with it. In some cases the relatives' feelings of anger had grown out of frustration engendered by repeated failures to secure any recognition of their claims for privileged access to, or communication with, recruits. In other cases relatives had gradually come to regard the movement as evil because of what they had learned about it in the mass-media or in the literature published by anti-cult organizations. Nor would it be true to say that feelings of anger were equally strong or constant among all informants. Some made it plain that their attitude towards the U.C. was variable and dependent on circumstances.

What was constant in this type of response, however, was an inner connection between hostile feelings towards the movement and various "justifications" or pieces of "evidence" (Beckford, 1979). The most powerful element in their accounts was the conviction that recruits had been manipulated unfairly at all stages of the affiliation process and during subsequent involvement in the U.C.'s activities. This encapsulated "theory" of manipulation was expressed in such accusations as that of "brainwashing," "mind control" or "enslavement." Appropriate evidence in support of the accusations usually referred to sudden changes in the recruit's cognitive performance, emotional balance, attitudes towards kin, and interest in current affairs. Such accounts also made use of before-and-after contrasts in various states of mind, body and social relationships.

It was equally clear from informants' accounts that the theory of manipulation had unambiguous implications for practical action. Above all, it was assumed to justify urgent and drastic action in defence of the U.C.'s "victims" and in prevention of further "outrages" against human freedom of the will. Unconventional and even criminal actions were presented in this framework of thought as necessary, smaller and temporary evils whose justification derived from the urgent necessity to counter an allegedly unnecessary, greater and possibly long-term evil.

The logic which bound all the strands of this response together presupposed a view of human beings as relatively mechanical, yet fragile, people who might be deliberately manipulated by unscrupulous others. Not only was this an internally consistent argument: it was also congruent with the social settings in which it was used. The manipulation argument, far from being an arbitrary or entirely abstract construction, was actually grounded in the social experience of the people who used it. How can this experience be characterized?

Those of my informants who displayed this type of response described their relationship with the U.C. recruit prior to his or her recruitment as affectionate and strong. Typically, the family unit was characterized as close-knit and warm in emotional tone. Family members were said to have enjoyed relaxed relationships which allowed everyone to speak their mind freely and to be respected for their personal views and qualities. Concern for each was apparently strong and each person's affairs were of interest to the others. It was not uncommon for leisure pursuits to be enjoyed together in these families and for personal happiness and unhappiness to be shared. In short, the U.C. recruit was typically presented in such accounts as a member of a close-knit, caring family.

Additionally relevant characteristics of these families included a very limited number of strong links between individual members of the family and outside groups or agencies. It was repeatedly stressed that the home was the centre of activity and interest. Moreover, the authority of parents was "taken-for-granted" and unambiguous. Terms such as "firm" and "disciplined" were applied to child-rearing practices, and evidence of rejection of parental authority was rare. This was a cause of both satisfaction and surprise to some parents. They could not understand, without recourse to notions of brainwashing, how all their best efforts to bring up children in what they regarded as a firm and fair fashion had resulted in an apparently sudden and unexpected rejection of the parental home and of all that it represented. In the words of a woman whose two privately-educated children had both joined the U.C.:

> You cannot believe that all the sacrifice in years is just tossed lightly on one side and nobody's the slightest bit concerned. . . . Here are two parents, and many others like us, that have done without to give their children a good start in life and it's tossed on one side; and they are told that colleges and universities are satanic. It's nonsense and very wrong.

This kind of description of family life is congruent with the theory of manipulation since, from the point of view of my informants, no other explanation of affiliation to the U.C. was conceivable in the case of their particular relative(s). Their only possible explanation was one which constituted the recruit as not-the-same-person who had previously enjoyed such a supportive and relatively problem-free upbringing. The relatives could point to no circumstances in the family which could have made sense of the recruitment. The only feasible alternative was to look for factors outside the family and outside the recruit's personality and character which might have solved the puzzle.

In addition, such a search for external factors was congruent with the family's normal practice of regarding each member's experiences as continuous with those of other members. In other words, it had not been normal to isolate an individual from the family group and to consider him or her as an independent agent; nor had it happened that any individual had tried to resist, let alone reject, the group's norms. The shock of realizing that a formerly close relationship had ostensibly been dissolved was consequently all the more profound. The sense of urgency running through their thinking about how to respond to the shock was therefore understandable in terms of the pattern of social relationships prevailing within the family.

It is worth noting at this point that the strength of commitment to the "anger" response varied directly with the degree to which the recruit was believed to have severed communication with the family. In cases in which affiliation to the U.C. had been a visible and lengthy process which had not involved a sudden and total break with close relatives, their feelings of anger and urgency were relatively weak. But hostile feelings were usually strong in the case of sudden and total "disconnection" from the family unit. It should be added that many ex-members of the U.C. insisted that it had never been their intention to offend their families in this way but that the act of affiliation had nevertheless been felt to be deeply offensive to these families.

A less predictable aspect of the "angry" type of response and of its associated theory of manipulation was the readiness to extend the scope of recrimination well beyond any given family's private quarrel with the U.C. The logic of this position seemed to demand that an all-out attack on the movement, if not on *all* comparable groups, was felt necessary. This was another facet of the disposition to locate the causes of affiliation to the new religious movement outside the individual recruit's own mind, for it represented a further stage in the process of extending the attribution of blame to ever wider sets of external agents. And, given that the recruit was virtually absolved from blame in this view, it made sense for the relatives to be as energetic as possible in their attempts to track down and stamp out the agents of manipulation. Some informants also revealed that active participation in an organization attacking new religious movements in general had helped them to cope with their feelings of anger and frustration. There was the implication that, if they had been unable to obtain the "release" of their own relative, there might have been a greater chance of success in "scoring hits" against the movement as a whole because, as a target, it was more visible and vulnerable. "At least we're doing something" was a common claim.

### (iii) Ambivalence

The third type of family response is the most difficult to characterize partly because it is more elusive and subtle than the others but also because in some respects it represents a residual category for responses which do not fit into them. There is no doubt in my mind, however, that it is necessary to construct a third type in view of the material generated during interviews. For many informants clearly responded in ways which revealed a delicate mixture of ambivalence, hesitancy and indecisiveness mainly lacking in the accounts of others.

The dominant characteristic of this response was the underlying sense that, try as they might to resolve their doubts and misgivings, relatives were uncertain about the overall meaning of their experiences. Many were obviously torn between competing loyalties and emotions, and they felt a strong need to suspend judgment in the hope that more convincing evidence would be forthcoming. Above all, a desire to be fair to all concerned with new religious movements, as well as with anti-cultism, was uppermost in their consideration, and this was said to entail frequent shifts of opinion and mood in accordance with changing information, events and influences.

Like most of the relatives who responded with anger, those in this category were also assiduous in collecting information about the U.C. and about its implications for the recruit known to them personally. They were, for the most part, less demonstrative and open about their connection with the movement but they made no secret of it and were consequently supplied by friends and neighbours with relevant press-cuttings and snippets of hearsay information about it. But it was unusual for them to give wholehearted support to anti-cultism for its own sake; their interest remained largely confined to the case of their own relative(s).

My interviews with these relatives left me in no doubt about their reluctance to make an unqualified judgment about the U.C. They were, or had been, mostly in sufficiently close communication with the recruit from their own family to have been exposed to arguments in favour of the movement and in defence of its integrity against outsiders' attacks. It was also quite common for them to read literature disseminated by the U.C., and a considerable number of them had attended one or more of the functions organized by the movement in an attempt to improve its public image. In short, they were better informed about the U.C. than were most of the relatives displaying other responses to it.

In addition, they were unlikely to explain recruitment in terms of brainwashing, manipulation or mind-control. Their views, which were varied and not all consistent with one another, implied that they were prepared to take seriously the recruits' claims for joining the movement. They were not prepared, by contrast, to consider their own relative as someone who was likely to be duped by a manipulator, nor were they disposed to contemplate overriding the recruit's stated intentions or wishes. Rather, they maintained an image of the recruit as a responsible, though unfortunate and ill-advised, individual whose competence as a self-directing being was not in question. It was entirely consistent with this attitude towards the recruit's integrity that relatives in this category should express sadness at the feeling of being excluded from the recruit's new-found life, interests and values. The feeling of no longer being a party to their relative's most precious and meaningful experiences was painful and distressing as was the allied regret that his or her special skills, talents and endearing qualities might be abandoned in the U.C.

As in the case of the other family responses it is possible to see in this response a logic of congruence between the manner of responding to the U.C. and the reported character of social relationships prevailing within the family before, and after, recruitment. This was indicated by the importance placed on the actual, as well as the idealized, relaxed and open nature of family relationships. Great stress was usually put on the free interchange of ideas and feelings in the atmosphere encouraging independence and experimentation. Relatives were quick to draw attention both to the U.C. recruit's previous signs of independent interests and skills and to the positive encouragement given within the family to fresh projects of various kinds. There was obvious pride and delight when describing the recruit's former idiosyncracies and talents, but no indication of possessiveness.

Given this type of account of family relationships, many relatives found themselves in a grave quandary when faced with the question of how to respond when a family member had joined the U.C. On the one hand, they were accustomed to offering support and encouragement for independence of mind and action, but on the other, they were disturbed by the nature and suddenness of the changes which had taken place in the recruit's lifestyle and outlook. The dilemma was not novel but it was no less painful.

It raised moral issues about the possible limits of toleration in the best interests of freedom, the wisdom of unsolicited intervention in another person's affairs and the long-term consequences of treating a person as irresponsible. Finally, relatives also agonized over the question of whether their already tenuous, but existing, relationship with the recruit would be jeopardized if they persisted in refusing to accept without protest the fact that he or she had freely made a commitment to the U.C. which could not be lightly abandoned.

Inaction or an uneasy resignation were common responses to the dilemma in which these relatives found themselves. At all costs they wished to avoid doing irreparable damage to the relationship which most of them still enjoyed with the U.C. recruit. Some feared deliberate retaliation from the movement if they were perceived as too hostile towards it, but the majority were more anxious to preserve the moral basis of trust in which a continuing and future relationship could be grounded. Under these circumstances, support for anti-cult organizations was only half-hearted, and some of my informants were positively antagonistic towards the very idea of a concerted opposition to all allegedly "destructive" new religious movements. In their opinion it was essential to the interests of a healthy society that religious freedom should be preserved and it was only minor problems of insensitivity which rendered the controversial new religious movements problematic. Only time would solve such problems in their view.

## Practical Responses

I have argued elsewhere (Beckford, forthcoming) that it is not difficult to understand why some close relatives of U.C. recruits have responded in the ways which have just been described. Moreover, there are certain social circumstances surrounding the typical pattern of recruitment to the U.C. which lend further intelligibility to all three types of response. The rest of this article confirms the validity of the three-fold typology of family accounts of affiliation to the U.C. by showing that the circumstances surrounding the process of affiliation were "refracted" by each set of families in distinctive ways. The analysis will show that there was a high degree of coherence running through each type of family response and that the relatives' actions were no less coherent than their interpretations of events.

a. The first important circumstance concerns my informants' evident lack of information about the U.C.—in many cases amounting to total ignorance. Those who *did* try to improve their knowledge experienced considerable frustration.

b. An allied circumstance was the difficulty, if not impossibility, of communicating directly with the recruit in a manner and setting entirely of the relatives' choosing. Ironically, those recruits who did try to communicate personally with their family usually succeeded in communicating only their unreserved enthusiasm and commitment, and this tended to aggravate already strained relationships. The result was not so very different from what had happened when recruits either refused to communicate or acted entirely defensively.

c. The third circumstance was the invisibility to most relatives of the affiliation process. The first inkling that many of them had had of the recruit's interest in the U.C. was a firm statement of his or her commitment to it and the corresponding abandonment of jobs, educational courses, travel plans, accommodation and social relationships. There was usually no "probationary" period and no indication that the commitment was anything other than total and irrevocable.

In combination, these circumstances (ignorance, deficient communication and being confronted with a *fait accompli*) put pressure on close relatives of U.C. recruits to respond practically in some way or other.

Inaction is the key to the first response. In the view of relatives who adopted this response the recruit was largely confirming existing suspicions that he or she was liable to do something bewildering and inexplicable. The facts that the group was unknown, that the recruit was to all intents and purposes *incommunicado* and that an unbreakable commitment had already been made were felt to have been only expected—given the recruit's personality and family-relationships. Active intervention was therefore felt to be out of the question, although it was common for relatives to feel regret and anxiety about what had happened. They did not think it necessary, however, to search for an explanation in terms of "brainwashing" or "manipulation."

By contrast, those who displayed the "angry" response were incensed by the three circumstances surrounding affiliation to the U.C.: each one spurred them on to more energetic and more extensive counter-action. My interviews with ex-members of the movement whose close relatives had responded in this way also underlined the point that each aggressive counter-action had been, in turn, met by a correspondingly, and sometimes deliberate, infuriating response from the recruit. Family accusations of secretiveness for example, had invariably provoked the recruit to even greater reluctance to discuss the U.C. with relatives. A vicious spiral in their deteriorating relationships had quickly been established in many cases, with each side growing progressively more convinced that its worst suspicions and fears were being substantiated by the other's actions. The family, accustomed to being party to each member's "private" life, could only explain the breakdown in relationships with the recruit as a sign of "brainwashing," while the recruit, from an unaccustomed position of detachment, could only interpret the relatives' actions as "to be expected" from people like them.

The "ambivalence" response took account of the three circumstances by viewing them as an expression of the recruit's need to establish a fresh basis for life including family relationships. This point was frequently conceded by my informants, but, as was mentioned earlier, they usually qualified it by adding that they were nevertheless saddened by the feeling that they had apparently been excluded from experiences and events which were obviously significant and valuable to the recruit. The "problem" was therefore seen as one embracing the recruit in his or her relations with significant others rather than a manifestation of psychological idiosyncracy or an outrage against free-will.

For relatives in this category this problem of relationships assumed special importance, and they showed considerable anxiety about the effects on the U.C. recruit's siblings of all the fuss surrounding his or her membership of the movement. Again, their liberal inclinations were in conflict with their view that joining the movement had been ill-advised and possibly harmful. At all costs they wanted to avoid both alarming other siblings who were still living in the parental home and underplaying what they saw as the potential dangers in the movement. It was part of the ethos of such families that problems should be discussed openly, but many parents admitted that they had forsaken their principles in this matter in order to forestall the possibly greater evil of inadvertently encouraging another child to join the U.C. In some cases there was even a transfer in the object of anxiety from the U.C. member to "vulnerable" siblings.

With the exception of anxiety about siblings, however, most of the relatives displaying the "ambivalent" response were agreed that social relationships within the family had on balance been strengthened by the experience of coping with all the problems created by affiliation to the U.C. And, unlike relatives in the other two categories, they did not believe that the problems had aggravated pre-existing tensions and divisions. Rather, the experience had reinforced their practice of dealing with problems as a social-interactional phenomenon; not as matters of individual psychology.

## Conclusion

This article has tried to show that among families faced with the problem of how to respond to a person who had joined the U.C. there was a basically three-fold pattern of response. The responses reflected pre-existing patterns of social relationships and the social circumstances surrounding the affiliation process. In combination, these two factors helped relatives to produce distinctive ways of seeing affiliation to the movement as a particular kind of problem. Further, the responses included distinctive courses of action or inaction designed to modify the recruit's commitment which made sense in the context of their "theories" about affiliation to new religious movements. Each of the three responses was found to be coherent in its own terms, although they each depended heavily on sources of information external to the family.

These findings underscore the importance of going beyond the all-too-common tendency to understand affiliation to new religious movements exclusively in terms of individual psychology. The "career" of recruits is influenced by complex conditions including, *inter alia,* the response of close relatives. And the relatives' responses are themselves conditioned by factors associated with the dynamics of family relationships and the social circumstances bearing on affiliation to the movement.

A further implication of my analysis is that it is futile to search for one single factor in the family background of U.C. recruits which could explain their recruitment. Conventional wisdom expects them to come from broken or unhappy homes, but there is no clear evidence to support this view. Rather, my findings emphasize the variety of family backgrounds and the consequent complexity of family responses which have been reduced here, for the purpose of exposition, to three basic types.

Finally, on a practical note, I would draw attention to the need for family counsellors and others who practise therapeutic intervention in the area of cult-related difficulties to take due account of the wide variations in family responses to cult-recruits.

## NOTES

1. For the purposes of this article the term "new religious movement" may be taken as practically synonymous with "cult." I have preferred the former term because it lacks the kind of value-laden connotations which might be an obstacle to unprejudiced understanding of my analysis.

2. I am grateful to the Social Science Research Council of Great Britain for the grant which enabled me to carry out most of the research on which this article is based.

3. My informants constituted a "snowball" sample in the sense that, in the absence of reliable sampling frames, I was forced to rely on personal contacts and recommendation. In the circumstances this probably means that people hostile to the U.C. are over-represented, but, as I hope the article will make clear, the spectrum of opinions was nevertheless quite wide. In order to preserve their anonymity, the identity of the informants referred to in this article has been concealed.

4. Examples of mass-media use of the stereotype are too numerous to list, but for representative instances, see Freed, 1978; Methvin, 1980; and Carroll & Bauer, 1979.

## REFERENCES

Barker, E. V. Living the Divine Principle. Inside the Reverend Sun Myung Moon's Unification Church in Britain. *Les Archives de Sciences Sociales des Religions,* 1978, *45* (1), 75-93.

Barker, E. V. (Ed), *Society from the Perspective of the New Religions,* forthcoming.

Beckford, J. A. A Korean Evangelistic Movement in the West. In *The Contemporary Metamorphoses of Religion?* Lille: Editions CISR, 1973.

Beckford J. A. Two contrasting types of sectarian organization. In R. Wallis (Ed. *Sectarianism.* London: Peter Owen, 1975.

Beckford, J. A. Cults and cures. *Japanese Journal of Religious Studies,* 1978a, *5* (4), 225-257.

Beckford, J. A. Accounting for conversion. *British Journal of Sociology,* 1978b, *29* (2), 249-262.

Beckford, J. A. Politics and the anti-cult movement. *The Annual Review of the Social Sciences of Religion*, 1979, *3*, 169-190.

Beckford, J. A. "Brainwashing" and "deprogramming" in Britain: the social sources of anti-cult sentiment. In J. T. R. Richardson (Ed), *The Deprogramming Controversy: Sociological, Psychological, Legal and Historical Perspectives*, forthcoming.

Bromley, D. G. and Shupe, A. D. *The Moonies in America*. London & Los Angeles: Sage, 1980.

Carroll, J. and Bauer, B. Suicide training in the Moon cult. *New West*, (January 29) 1979, 62-63.

Cozin, M. A millenarian movement in Korea and Great Britain. *A Sociological Yearbook of Religion in Britain*, 1973, *6*, 1-36.

Freed, J. Living bodies, dead minds. Inside the Moon cult. *Express and News*, (March 6) 1978.

Kaslow, F. W. and Schwartz, L. D. Vulnerability and invulnerability to the cults: an assessment of family dynamics, functioning and values. In D. Bagarozzi, (Ed), *New Perspectives in Marriage and Family Therapy: Issues in Theory, Research and Practice*. New York: Human Sciences Press, 1980.

Methvin, E. Scientology. Anatomy of a malignant cult. *Reader's Digest*, (U.K. edition) (May) 1980, 141-146.

Schwartz, L. D. and Kaslow, F. W. Religious cults, the individual and the family. *Journal of Marital and Family Therapy*, (April) 1979, 15-26.

Sontag, F. *Sun Myung Moon and the Unification Church*. Nashville: Abingdon, 1977.

# CULTS, CULTURE, AND COMMUNITY

Thomas Robbins
Dick Anthony

## Introduction

A vast amount of research has now developed in connection with the emergence of "new religions" in the late sixties and seventies. Although the spectacular tragedy of The People's Temple community at Jonestown has given a strong impetus to research on "cults," studies of unconventional religious movements have been proliferating in the sociology of religion since the early seventies. Much of this research has appeared or has been reprinted in a number of important anthologies (Heenan, 1973; Zaretsky and Leone, 1974; Glock and Bellah, 1976; Needleman and Baker, 1978; Horowitz, 1978; Richardson, 1978a; Robbins and Anthony, 1981; Long and Hadden, forthcoming). A number of special journal issues devoted to new religious movements have also appeared (*American Behavioral Scientist*, 1977; *Society*, 1978; *Sociological Analysis*, 1978; 1980a; 1980b; *Review of Law and Social Change*, 1980). Two newsletters or mini-journals devoted to discussing unconventional religious and therapeutic groups have emerged (*New Religions Newsletter*, *The Advisor*).

As Richardson (1977) has commented, the general public has been concerned:

> not so much... about societal conditions that led to the new movements... Instead attention at the popular level has focused on the organization of recruitment efforts by the new groups. This is understandable from the human point of view, parents and friends of thousands of converts to the new movements are genuinely con-

Thomas Robbins, a sociologist, is a fellow at the Center for the Study of New Religions, Graduate Theological Union, Berkeley, California. Dick Anthony is a member of the staff at the Center for the Study of New Religions, Graduate Theological Union, Berkeley, California.

cerned about the welfare of converts, and are puzzled and alarmed at
their affiliation with new and strange groups (Richardson, 1977:80).

The overriding focus of public and media concern has influenced scholarly
research, which has dealt primarily with *conversion and commitment processes* (e.g., Richardson, 1978; Snow and Phillips, 1980; Stark and Bainbridge, 1980; Lofland and Skonovd, 1980). The present review will be
primarily concerned with (1) the social and historical sources of the current
upsurge of deviant groups, and (2) social processes and structures within
novel movements, although there is relatively little research in this latter
area, excluding studies focusing primarily on conversion and indoctrination. Our aim is to present a sociologically oriented overview of the
emergence of "alternative religions" in the latter half of the twentieth
century and the sociological and cultural issues which this phenomenon
presents. A concluding section will spotlight lacunae in contemporary research and offer suggestions for future studies.

## Typologizing Cults

Much of the writing on contemporary marginal religions implicitly attributes an illusory homogeneity to "cults," which are typified as authoritarian, centralized, communal and "totalistic"—on the model of
Jonestown or Hare Krishna. Richardson (1980) points to significant organizational differences between Jonestown and other authoritarian groups
such as The Unification Church. A recent study (Pilarzyk, 1978a) of the
controversial Divine Light Mission of Guru Maharaj-Ji indicates that the
DLM is distinctly less communally insulated and disciplined than The Hare
Krishna sect. A large proportion of DLM members reported the maintenance of pre-conversion bonds with relatives and friends. Some groups,
such as Meher Baba (Robbins, 1969; Robbins and Anthony, 1972; Anthony and Robbins, 1974) are far less centralized, authoritarian and
bounded than either Hare Krishna or the DLM. To complicate matters
further, many groups appear to have a concentric ring structure entailing
"core" participants (Bird and Reimer, 1976) and outer layers of individuals with "limited liability" involvements. The properties of the
movement and of its devotees will look differently to an observer depend-
ing upon which layer is taken to demarcate the group "boundary."

The term "cult" is increasingly used by both scholars and popular
writers to refer to marginal or deviant spiritual movements, yet the term
*has no precise consensual meaning*. The allegation that cults tend to per-

petrate violent acts is true by definition since any esoteric group "whose members commit violent acts is likely to be subsequently labeled a cult" (Anthony and Robbins, 1980b:9).

A number of scholars have attempted to distinguish between cults and *sects* and assimilate the concept of cult to the corpus of "church-sect theory" in the sociology of religion (Nelson, 1968; Wallis, 1975a, b; Campbell, 1977). Considering both scholarly and popular writings, three somewhat incompatible concepts of *cult* can be discerned involving three distinct defining characteristics:

(1) *Authoritarianism,* and the related notion of "totalism" appears to be the defining property of "cults" in much of the popular and journalistic literature. *Charismatic leadership* is a further specification which crops up frequently in implicit and explicit definitions of cult rendered by non-sociologists (e.g., Lifton, 1979). It is worth noting that these conceptions of *cult* converge in some respects with sociological concepts of *sect.*

(2) *Looseness and diffuseness of organization* and an absence of clear "boundaries" is identified as the defining property of cults (as opposed to authoritarian and clearly bounded sects) by some scholarly typologists (Eister, 1972; 1974; Wallis, 1974; 1975a, b). In this conception, cults are viewed as lacking centralized leadership, clear organizational boundaries, and standardized doctrine. Such groups are presumed to be ephemeral, e.g., a "Ouija board cult" (Quarentelli and Wenger, 1973), although they may persist, e.g., Meher Baba (Robbins 1969; Anthony and Robbins, 1974). According to Wallis (1977), Dianetics, a diffuse cult of the 1950s, was re-organized by its founder, L. Ron Hubbard as a centralized, authoritarian sect called Scientology. Pilarzyk (1978b) has applied Wallis' schema to the DLM, which he identifies as an intermediate entity: a "centralized cult" with a partly centralized authority structure but without a standardized doctrine. Hare Krishna is deemed by Pilarzyk to fit Wallis' concept of a *sect,* with centralized, authoritarian leadership, standardized dogma or interpretive frameworks obligatory for all devotees, and clear-cut boundaries differentiating insiders from outsiders. According to Wallis, diffuse cults must either evolve into more tightly knit sects or else disappear.

(3) *Deviancy* seems to be a criterion utilized to define or identify cults (Lofland, 1978; Dohrman, 1958). A related approach specifies a cult as a group which makes a *radical break with the dominant religious culture,* whereas a sect is seen as a subdivision of a larger, dominant tradition (Richardson, 1978b; Stark and Bainbridge, 1979) e.g., Hare Krishna would be in the American context a cult, while The Children of God would

be a christian sect. One problem arising here is the difficulty of specifying precisely *how much* deviance or discontinuity with larger traditions is required to identify a cult.

Several years ago, Robbins et al. (1975; Robbins and Anthony 1978) attempted to distinguish between two divergent patterns for new movements in terms of the consequences of membership for the integration of members into conventional social processes. *Adaptive* movements promote the assimilation of converts to conventional vocational, educational and familial roles, and are often associated with other "integrative" outcomes such as drug rehabilitation. In contrast, *marginal* movements are associated with patterns of "dropping out" of conventional structures. Marginal movements tend to be characterized by self-sufficient and authoritarian communal institutions, which often evoke hostility from relatives of converts. Beckford (1978a) has criticized this distinction. Wallis' (1979) distinction between "world-accepting" and "world-rejecting" movements converges in a number of respects with the Robbins-Anthony dichotomy. Also relevant here is Enroth's (1977) distinction between cults and "extreme cults" which practice brainwashing.

Bird (1980) and Anthony and Robbins (1977; Robbins et al., 1978; Anthony, 1980) have developed typologies of contemporary religious movements which focus primarily on the *moral ideologies* of different movements. Bird focuses on "the extent to which and ways in which new religious movements encourage among their adherents a reduced sense of moral accountability" (Bird, 1980:335). This sense is produced in a different manner and with different consequences in *devotee, discipleship* and *apprenticeship* groups. The Anthony-Robbins typology is derivitive from the distinction between "monistic" and "dualistic" responses to a pervasive climate of moral ambiguity (see below) arising in part from the erosion of a cultural tradition of dualistic moral absolutism (Robbins, et al., 1978). Two subdivisions of monistic movements have been elaborated involving distinctions between "technical" vs "charismatic" groups and "one-level" (literal) and "two-level" (symbolicist) conceptions of monistic enlightenment (Anthony and Robbins, 1977).

There is some evidence that movements embodying mystical or monistic meaning systems, e.g., oriental guru and meditation groups and avant garde therapeutic movements, tend to appeal to highly educated, culturally sophisticated and politically liberal individuals (Wuthnow, 1976; 1978; Stone, 1978). These individuals have often been influenced by countercultural values associated with the nineteen sixties (Tipton, 1977; 1979; 1981; Foss and Larkin, 1978).

In contrast, converts to dualistic evangelical movements (e.g., "Jesus movement" groups of the early seventies) tend to be less educated and from less affluent backgrounds (Wuthnow, 1976; 1978; Judah, 1977). They are more likely to be "returning fundamentalists" who come originally from conservative Christian homes (Gordon, 1974; Richardson, 1977; Judah, 1977). Dualistic groups tend to be associated with social and political conservatism, anti-communism and patriotism (Adams and Fox, 1972; Harder et al., 1972; Anthony and Robbins, 1978; 1981b; Horowitz, 1978). In general, however, emerging typologies have not yet proved useful in predicting the traits and backgrounds of members.

## Religious Movements in a Secular Culture

It is frequently assumed among students of religion that the present upsurge of new religions constitutes a prima facie refutation of what Andrew Greeley has labeled "the secularization myth" affirming the *declining significance of religion in modern western society.* "With the resurgence of all kinds of weird forms of religions . . . one can even be more confident than one was five years ago when one says that religion is likely to be around in the foreseeable future" (Greeley, 1972:155). Nevertheless, a number of interpretations have identified today's profusion of "cults" as a consequence and indicator of growing secularization. Thus, for Daniel Bell, cults appear "when religions fall . . . when the institutional framework of religions begins to break up, the search for direct experience which people can feel to be 'religious' facilitates the rise of cults" (Bell, 1977:443).

The decline of religious commitment in a society may temporarily *increase* the number of spiritual groups and the range of religious variation and opportunity. According to Bryan Wilson (1976) the dominance of impersonal bureaucratic and technological modes of social control precludes an authentic "great awakening" which might transform culture and social institutions. The "new religions" of today reduce religion to an exotic consumer item; they "add nothing to any prospective reintegration of society, and contribute nothing towards the culture by which a society might live."

A growing class of spiritual dilettantes adorn themselves with exotic mystiques, which they select in today's "supermarket of faiths," but their choices produce no vital consequences "for other social institutions, for political power structures, for technological constraints and controls" (Wilson, 1976:20). In today's "spiritual supermarket" diverse and exotic structures of meaning co-exist precisely "because the wider society is so secular, because they are relatively unimportant consumer items" (Wilson, 1975:80).

There is one additional way in which ongoing secularization enhances religious diversity and produces novel religious movements. Richard Fenn (1978) argues that secularization has produced a *diffusion of the sacred* in modern society. In the modern world, "the sacred becomes so widely dispersed and the boundary between the sacred and the profane so uncertain that societies develop acute uncertainty about the nature and location of any social authority." This uncertainty arises in part because:

> the process of secularization increases the likelihood that various institutions or groups will base their claims to social authority on various religious grounds while it undermines the possibility for consensus on the meaning and location of the sacred . . . as political authority becomes secularized various individuals, groups, and institutions turn to religious culture for support in their claims to increased social authority (Fenn, 1978:55).

Fenn's thesis may be relevant to controversies over the "religious" status of deviant "pseudoreligions" (West, 1975; Shupe et al., 1977) and over the increasing tendency for social movement organizations to appropriate the labels of "religion" and "church" as a device for insulating various practices from governmental scrutiny and regulation (Ofshe, 1980a; 1980b; Robbins, 1980).

### Cults and Cultural Confusion

A pervasive theme running through much scholarly journalistic writing on cults has attempted to analyze the present American religions in terms of a normative breakdown involving an erosion of value complexes such as "civil religion," patriotism, "cold war" anti-communism, traditional morality, "protestant ethic" values, and "liberal" christian modernism. An incisive formulation by Appel (1980) relates the upsurge of small messianic sects to the decay of consensual messianic "Americanism." According to Appel, *messianic anti-communism* has operated as a unifying religio-political ideology in mid-twentieth century America.

> The war against communism ceased to be holy in Vietnam. That war, at least, temporarily, separated church and state. Messianism

and nationalism were sundered and patriotism debunked as a false religion. The obsessive searching for new religions which characterized much of the 70s, has been the consequence of our political fall from grace. The cult phenomenon has substituted a myriad of fragmented visions for the central messianism we once called Americanism (Appel, 1980:A19).

Appel's analysis seems particularly applicable to The Unification Church of Reverend Sun Myung Moon, which Robbins et al. (1978a) view "as a revitalization movement that attempts to reconstitute and recombine declining theistic and anti-communist partriotic values in a context of pervasive politico-moral secularization" (1978a:67). Anthony and Robbins (1978) and Robbins et al. (1978) see the ideology of the Moon movement "as a sectarian version of the disintegrating 'civil religion'" which revitalizes both the American tradition of "dualistic moral absolutism" and the anti-communist "cold war ideology." Similar points might be made concerning the evangelical resurgence and its conspicuous right-wing politicization (Lorentzen, 1970).

The relationship between the upsurge of new spiritual movements and discontinuities in "American civil religion" has been stressed by several other writers (Heenan, 1973; Bellah, 1975; 1976; Hammond and McCutcheon, 1980). While Robbins et al. (1978) and Anthony and Robbins (1978) stress the decline and reconstruction of the theme of America as a "chosen people," other writers emphasize the consequences of the undermining of civil religion for the weakening of the *linkage between private and public value systems* (Johnson, 1981; Anthony and Robbins, 1980a; 1981a). Johnson (1981) argues that the radical differentiation of private and public realms in modern American society creates a disjunction between personal expressiveness and broader social and civic concerns, thus producing a proliferation of privatized and "narcissistic" religiotherapy groups promoting self-actualization (see also Marx and Holzner, 1975). Extrapolating from Johnson's argument, Anthony and Robbins (1980a) argue that the differentiation of public and private spheres and the associated erosion of civil religion has produced two contrasting responses: (1) authoritarian "civil religion sects" such as The People's Temple and The Unification Church, whose meaning systems respond to cultural fragmentation by *synthesizing political and spiritual elements,* and (2) "narcissistic" mystical and therapeutic movements such as Arica or *est,* which reject the explicit infusion of civic-political values into spirituality.

According to Robert Bellah (1975) and others, American civil religion involves a complex of shared religio-political meanings which articulate a sense of common national purpose. But in his prize-winning work, *The Broken Covenant* (1975) Bellah comments, "Today the American civil religion is an empty and broken shell" (1975:145). In Bellah's view, the present spiritual ferment attempts a "birth of new American myths" as a response to the decay of civil religion (Bellah, 1975:139–163). Bellah (1976) views the new religions which flourished in the 1970s as "successor movements" to the "crisis of meaning" of the late sixties, which entailed a revolt against the moral and cultural hegemony of utilitarian individualism, materialism and "technical reason." Steven Tipton (1977; 1979; 1981) has extrapolated Bellah's analysis in field studies of Zen devotees (1979), *est* participants (1977) and Jesus converts (1981). Tipton interprets the role of these movements as mediating between resurgent utilitarian individualism and the opposing value-orientations of countercultural "situational-expressivity" and fundamentalist biblical literalism. Through participation in *est*, individuals are "saved from the sixties" through the acceptance of the subtle moral ideology of "rule egoism," which accommodates the sixties' ethos of expressive spontaneity to conformist utilitarian individualism (see also Stone, 1981).

Charles Glock (1976) highlights the erosion of traditional notions of *personal autonomy and mastery* as the essential cultural transformation of the sixties and seventies, which has produced a search for new forms and structures of meaning. Glock's view of contemporary value shifts are supported by recent survey research on popular notions of causation in social and individual experience by Glock and Piazza (1981) and Wuthnow (1975b), which has revealed a significant movement away from individualist-voluntaristic orientations toward both "mystical" and "scientific" orientations. Wuthnow (1976b; 1978) has suggested interesting convergences between these cultural shifts and emerging patterns of religious "populism." The erosion of the cultural belief in personal responsibility also contributes to controversies over alleged cultist brainwashing and enhances the popular appeal of deterministic "mind control" conceptions of conversion to deviant religious sects (Robbins, 1979; Hargrove, 1980).

Both cults and anti-cult groups thus benefit from the consequences of various sociocultural trends in undermining the subjective plausibility of traditional notions of personal autonomy and responsibility. The decline of traditional voluntaristic assumptions enhances the appeal of the medical model of deviance and the imputation of involuntary pathology to exotic or subversive orientations (Robbins and Anthony, 1978:82-83).

Finally, Anthony and Robbins (1980b; 1981 a, b; Robbins et al., 1978) have identified the source of the present spiritual ferment in an *emerging climate of moral ambiguity,* reflecting the rapid decline of a cultural tradition of dualistic moral absolutism which incorporates a presumption of personal responsibility and mastery. The pervasive moral confusion has produced comprehensive resolutions on the spiritual level. *Monistic* worldviews extrapolate relativistic and subjectivistic tendencies in cultural modernism and elaborate systematic worldviews grounded in assumptions of metaphysical unity ("oneness") and the illusory quality of the phenomenal world (i.e., the primacy of consciousness). *Dualistic* worldviews stridently reaffirm themes of ethical dualism, moral absolutism and millenarianism from American evangelical and puritan traditions. Both perspectives—systematic relativism and stridently resurgent absolutism—provide a basis for constructing meaning in the face of apparent moral chaos (Anthony and Robbins, 1981; McGuire, 1981).

This section can be summarized by evoking Eister's (1972; 1974) view that the current proliferation of cults is linked to "dislocations in the communicational and orientational institutions of advanced societies" (1974:612). This dislocation adds up to a "culture crisis" in which structures for articulating meanings and values have broken down, with consequent normative and spiritual confusion.

## Cults and Community

Much of the literature which seeks to explain the present spiritual ferment has focused on the decline of *mediating structures* or:

> those institutions that stand between the individual in his private life and the large institutions of modern society . . . These institutions offer the opportunity for close, face-to-face contact with people with whom one shares a sense of belonging; they shape and support personal values, which are almost always, communal values . . . Mediating structures provide a moral foundation in their ability to generate and sustain values where the megastructures offer mainly impersonal processes" (Kerrine and Neuhaus, 1979:11).

Traditional mediating structures such as extended family patterns, homogenous "folksy" neighborhoods, personalistic work settings or conventional churches are being undermined by a pattern of social changes involving increased geographical mobility, bureaucratization of vocational structures, and social policies promoting "governmental displacement of mediating structures" (Berger and Neuhaus, 1977; Kerrine and Neuhaus, 1979).

The decline of traditional mediating structures raises the prospect of pervasive atomization and widespread "homelessness" or loss of social rootedness (Berger and Neuhaus, 1977). In fact, however, there is some tendency for declining mediating collectivities to be replaced by emergent "social inventions" (Coleman, 1970) and encounter groups, cults and communes, which operate to detach young persons from exclusive reliance upon the nuclear family for interpersonal relationships and value transmission. Such groups create settings for "extended communal relations transcending kinship ties" and thus constitute "contemporary attempts to create new intermediate relations between individuals and primary groups on the one hand, and traditional . . . secondary groups on the other, through extended primary relations" (Marx and Ellison, 1975:455). Religious movements are particularly useful here because of their *capacity to create universalistic values and symbols which legitimate new patterns of interpersonal relationships and communal interaction.* Devotees of contemporary religious movements often believe that they partake of a special fellowship in which "loving" relations among spiritual brethren are derivative from each devotee's inner affective liaison with Jesus, the Holy spirit, an exalted spiritual master or an immanent mystical entity (Robbins and Anthony, 1972; Robbins, 1973; Anthony and Robbins, 1974; Petersen and Mauss, 1973; Bradfield, 1976). Gratifying interpersonal relationships among devotees in a cult crystallize a legitimating "plausibility structure" for the symbol system of the movement, which in turn provides a symbolic mystique which enhances the perceived "loving" quality of the spiritual fellowship (Barker, 1979). Although the relationship between the belief system and the interpersonal matrix can be viewed as mutually reinforcing and reciprocal (Anthony and Robbins, 1974) recently it has been forcibly argued that indoctrination into a belief system is a delayed secondary process grounded in prior assimilation to a *community,* to a *life-style* and to the *role* of a convert (Bromley and Shupe, 1979a; 1980; Balch, 1980).

Religious and ideological movements are able to crystallize communal fellowships which combine the diffuse affectivity or "loving" quality of familial roles with universalistic symbols and meanings. Such movements or "ideological primary groups" (Marx and Holzner, 1975) may thereby sometimes be able to play a mediating role between nuclear families (see below) and the larger society. "Social inventions" such as cults, communes and encounter groups operate as extended family surrogates and "part-time quasi-collectivities" which "resocialize the individual away from familial norms and values, wean him away from dependence on the nuclear family" (Marx and Ellison, 1975:452). These movements partly reconstitute "intermediate collectivities" between primary groups and the larger society. As a critic of The Unification Church has conceded, The Church as surrogate family ". . . does provide an effective therapeutic setting that offers linkage to the larger society without its turmoils" (Horowitz, 1981:165).

The current proliferation of esoteric movements as well as the evangelical resurgence can be viewed as part of a broader "sectarian reaction to mass society," which is providing an impetus for the emergence of a variety of movements. These groups qua mediating structures have been depicted as performing a variety of adaptive and therapeutic functions for individual devotees (Snelling and Whitely, 1973; Petersen and Mauss, 1973; Marx and Seldin, 1973; Gordon, 1974; Zaretsky and Leone, 1974; Robbins et al., 1975; Bradfield, 1976; Anthony et al., 1977; Anthony, 1980; Galanter and Buckley, 1979), as well as integrative and tension-management functions with respect to the social system (Robbins, et al., 1975; Robbins and Anthony, 1978). However, much of the literature delineating the therapeutic and integrative consequences of contemporary deviant sects appeared in the early and middle seventies. More recently a flood of literature has appeared identifying the pathological consequences and significance of involvement with what Shapiro (1977) labels "destructive cultism" (Shapiro, 1977; Enroth, 1977; Delgado, 1977; Singer, 1979; Levine, 1980). The consequences of involvement in stigmatized "cults" can thus be both (and perhaps simultaneously) integrative and disintegrative, adaptive and maladaptive.[1] This paradox is most poignant with respect to the relationship between cults and the nuclear family.

## Cults and Families

The decline of mediating structures is ultimately interrelated with another tendency: the increasing *isolation of the nuclear family*. Our society is characterized by a high degree of structural differentiation: kinship roles are increasingly segregated from occupational and educational roles, residential land is segregated from business land, young persons are increasingly involved in peer contexts (e.g., schools, colleges) detached from parental supervision. Extreme structural differentiation is the core of the isolation of the family, which is reinforced by the decline of mediating structures such as extended family systems, "folksy" neighborhoods, or conventional churches, which provided supports and services for nuclear families. Contemporary families are thus in a precarious situation and require new supports (Keniston, 1977).

The structural isolation of the family entails a sharp discontinuity between the diffuse-affectivity or "loving" quality of familial roles and the "impersonal" quality of "adult" roles in educational and occupational milieux. This discontinuity produces a search for *surrogate families* in extrafamilial relationships. "Families sanctified by Eastern gurus and Western psychopaths [have] offered multiple possibilities for alternative kinship promising unequivocal acceptance, warmth and structure. The unconditional welcome ("we love you," "God loves you," "Jesus loves you") made the order imposed by even the most disordered of minds seem appealing. More sophisticated or traditional-minded Americans have found surrogate fathers (seldom mothers) and siblings in therapies like *est* or in evangelical religions. These are generally less demanding families than the ones developed by Jim Jones and Reverend Moon, but they provide structure, meaning, and a full schedule of family activities" (Gordon, 1980:10).

The isolation of the nuclear family makes it difficult for the family to fulfill all of the expressive needs of young post-adolescents. As previously stated, religious movements can offer alternative "familial" milieux and wean young persons away from exclusive affiliative and valuative dependence upon the nuclear family of origin. On the other hand, religious movements can provide a congenial context for the development and stabilization of new nuclear families. Religious movements can provide services and supports for families, including jobs, day care for children, medical assistance, welfare and shared value commitments. These supports are only viable, however, if a family *becomes part of the movement.* If such assimilation is resisted by one or more members of the family, the impact of the cult on the family may be *disintegrative,* especially if the movement is close-knit, militant and "totalistic."

An eminent sociologist of religion has written a remarkable sympathic account of marital and familial patterns in The Unification Church (Fichter, 1979). Professor Fichter makes some important points; however, some qualifications will be entered below.

Fichter notes that the theology of the church sacrilizes the nuclear family as the fundamental spiritual unity:

The family is the foundation for understanding the love of God . . . The pure and perfect relationship with God helps to establish the perfect relationship between husband and wife, and then between parents and children. The spiritual and physical Kingdom of God, the total salvation that God intended in sending the Messiah, will be achieved by the ever expanding network of such God-centered families" (Fichter, 1979:226-7).

While the spiritual vocation of Catholic monasticism entails celibacy,

the totally committed member of the Unification community is being prepared for marriage and the family. The individual is spiritually incomplete until joined to a spouse in holy matrimony, and participating in a blessed family. Single persons who are converted to the church . . . soon learn the spiritual importance of family life, for which they are destined . . . there is not much future for a celibate in The Unification Church" (Fichter, 1979:226).

Fichter notes that the norm which forbids marriage outside of the church "is the same strict rule that governs the marriage of Salvation Army Officers and the mate selection of Israeli Jews. It was the same rule against mixed marriages which has gradually lost its effectiveness in the Catholic Church" (Fichter, 1979:226-7). Mate selection by the spiritual leader is not compulsory for devotees, however, many devotees "have a deep trust in Mr. Moon as the voice of God for them." One engaged devotee told Fichter, "You try to have confidence in your prayer life that God knows what is best for you, that He will work through Reverend Moon to suggest the proper match for you."

Fichter concludes that:

the Moonies have come upon a family program that works. While marriage counselors and parish priests are wringing their hands over the breakdown of family life, The Unification Church is doing something about it. The [Moonist] God-centered family is not merely a nice slogan or a spiritual ideal . . . it is also a deeply motivated system for restoring marital fidelity and family stability to modern society" (1979:228).

Perhaps Professor Fichter is overlooking the fragility of the Moonist "God-centered family," which depends for its viability upon the permanent assimilation of each member to a narrow, dogmatic and esoteric belief system. When one family member leaves a cult, the family often breaks up and sharp custody disputes ensue (Singer, 1979; Robbins, 1979; 1980).

While the Unification community can under some conditions be a supportive context for family stability, it is also a surrogate family for devotees. As such it is often in conflict with the non-God-centered (i.e., non-Moon-centered) original families of devotees (Bromley et al., 1980). The present authors have studied the Unification movement and observe:

> A close-knit solidarity develops among Unification converts. Reverend Moon and Mrs. Moon are referred to as "our true parents," and Reverend Moon is frequently called "father." According to Divine Principle, familial relations can be harmonious only if they are "God-centered"; non-God centered familial and conjugal relations are spiritually harmful. Thus, it is fairly common for members to sever relationships with parents and spouses to join the movement. (Robbins et al., 1978:54–55).

In a recent study of conflicts between The Unification Church and parents of devotees, Bromley et al. (1980) note that joining The Unification Church "involved a fictive kinship system in which all members were designated as 'true parents' (as opposed to biological parents). Moon's charismatic status as a messianic figure accorded him moral authority over UC 'family members' superior to that of biological parents" (Bromley et al., 1980:4). This replacement of the biological family by the "true family" constituted a fundamental source of strain generating tension between parents and the church. A second major source of strain emerged when children "radically re-oriented their life-styles and values and concomitantly rejected those career/domestic aspirations which until that time they had shared in common with their parents, the latter were predictably distraught" (1980:4).

The Unification Church confers a sacred significance on family life, but has a divisive and destructive impact on many actual families. It is worth noting, however, that the Moonist sacrilization of the family, so admired by Professor Fichter, does not hold for all controversial cults. According to a journalist (Noonan, 1977:7) who has studied The Hare Krishna sect, "Members of the movement admit that for them the traditional concept of family, as it is understood in this country, is alien and unnecessary. Leaders admit that contact with family is not encouraged, and a number of sources say it is actually discouraged." The journalist was told by a devotee:

that as a result of the increase in deprogramming attempts . . . a plan is underway to increase contact between Krishna members and the people they left behind on the 'outside.' But even with that effort, he said, the family concept is still, and will remain, irrelevant to Hare Krishna members, and will probably never get much of their energy (Noonan, 1977:7).

Conflict between families and militant, close-knit sects is hardly a new development. Consider Matthew 10:35, "For I have come to part assunder a man from his father, and a daughter from her mother . . ." Messianic impulses will always be to some degree divisive in its impact on conventional institutions. In evaluating these conflicts, it will be necessary to question the premise of many polemics: *The integrity of families is the highest or only fundamental value.* Often value conflict is obscured through the assumption that the messianic commitment which challenges the family is an inauthentic and artificial product of "mind control." However, conflict is not the whole story with regard to the relationship between cults and families. There is a vital need for more research on the formation, consolidation and breakup of families *within* cults.

## Conclusion

The imperative need with respect to sociological research on controversial religious movements is for *longitudinal* studies. There is a conspicuous dearth of such studies. The dominance of social psychological perspectives and conversion research in cult studies has already been noted (see Introduction); however, studies of institutions, ideologies and life-styles within deviant spiritual movements have generally involved "snap-shots" of patterns dominant at transitory moments in time.

The substance of this essay and other essays in this volume raise important issues which can only be resolved through longitudinal studies which follow the evolution of sectarian organizations and individual sectarian "careers" within deviant movements over a significant time period. A few of these issues and issue clusters are listed below:

(1) Do converts remain indefinitely ("trapped") in cults or is there in fact the rapid turnover and revolving door effect which a number of scholarly and journalistic observers have inferred (Welles, 1978; Ofshe, 1976, Shupe et al., 1977; Lofland, 1979; Skonovd, 1979; 1981; Beckford, 1978b)? In contrast Conway and Siegelman (1978: 36) "found very few people who got out of The Unification Church or any other cult on their own." This view is supported by the clinical sample of ex-converts studied

by Singer (1978) in which approximately 75 percent of the sample had undergone deprogramming and/or had been forcibly removed. There is no reason to expect that this sample is representative; indeed it may be statistically biased from the effects of referrals to the clinician, a supporter of legal deprogramming, from parents and countercult groups involved in the removal and deprogramming of cultists. Representative samples and precise statistics are understandably hard to come by but long range observational studies of given movements could clear up matters somewhat.[2]

(2) Various contradictory hypotheses have been put forward regarding whether persons who are removed from cults have more or less difficulties in adjustment relative to persons who spontaneously drift away or leave voluntarily (Singer, 1979; Thomas, 1979; Solomon, 1980). There are indications that voluntary leavers or drifters are more likely to enter another deviant group (Downton, 1979; Thomas, 1979), an outcome which is negatively evaluated in many quarters. In this connection longitudinal follow-up studies of ex-converts may be revealing, although the criteria for evaluating the psycho-social adjustment of ex-converts contain elements of subjectivity, e.g., is it "poor adjustment" for one who leaves one communal movement to move into another such group.

(3) Longitudinal research on converts who remain for long periods in cults is equally vital. Do long-term devotees conform indefinitely to the cult convert stereotype (e.g., Singer, 1979) involving communal encapsulation, stringent regimentation and exclusive involvement in menial and unskilled tasks? Or do long-term devotees tend to gravitate toward more skilled and demanding tasks, e.g., working in newspapers such as The New York *Newsworld* controlled by The Unification Church or occupying social leadership or commercial managerial roles within sectarian organizations. The development of "careers" within cults is a key issue and may be related to patterns of defection from cults and to adjustive techniques whereby converts "covertly strategize" to manipulate and obtain rewards within sectarian movement organizations (Strauss, 1980). The emergence of profitable commercial and financial operations operated by sects may lead to the exodus of converts who lack business skills or proper attitudes (Cawley, 1979; Ofshe, 1980a). There are some indications that the encapsulation or regimentation of devotees tends to diminish as long-term devotees make adjustments involving the articulation of "outside" vocational and recreational involvements and even a continuing overarching commitment to esoteric religiosity (Anthony and Robbins, 1974; Anthony et al., 1977). This observation has not been validated with respect to the more authoritarian and totalistic groups. Indeed a contrasting "total institutionalization" hypothesis positing increased encapsulation and

"bridge burning" associated with longer involvements seems plausible for some groups. Clearly the degree of encapsulation may vary from group to group (Pilarzyk, 1978a) as well as within a group at different phases of its development (Downton, 1979). Longitudinal research is thus "essential for validating propositions regarding the 'integrative' (or conversely, the disintegrative) consequences for individuals of involvements in today's religious movements" (Robbins and Anthony, 1979:85).

(4) The evolution and institutionalization of sectarian movements is another area requiring longitudinal research. Richardson et al., (1978) have made a start in this area and have applied propositions from the study of "movement organizations" to the evolution of a communal Jesus sect. A sequence of studies of "Jesus Freaks" in the Seattle and Spokane (Petersen and Mauss, 1973; Mauss and Petersen, 1974) provides some support for the proposition advanced by Robbins et al. (1975; Robbins and Anthony, 1978) that retreatist "marginal" movements evolve over time in the direction of worldly "adaptive" movements. A contrasting pattern can be extrapolated from the pioneering study of Dohrman (1949) of a movement which reacted to the apparent failure of its messianic mission by re-locating in an isolated communal enclave, a pattern somewhat similar to the trajectory of the ill-fated People's Temple community at Jonestown. Lofland (1978) plots the trajectory of The Unification Church in America (see also Bromley and Shupe, 1979b) and anticipates a retreatist sequence convergent with Dohrman's model. Wallis' (1977) describes the evolution of Scientology from a loosely run *cult* (its "Dianetics" phase) into a tightly centralized *sect*. Bainbridge and Stark (1980b) anticipate a future evolution of Scientology's "magical" incentive system in a supernaturalist or "religious" direction, thus further insulating Scientology from disconfirmation of its claims. The "managerial strategy of organizational transformation" of the Synanon movement has been analyzed cogently by Ofshe (1980a) who depicts the evolution of the movement from a therapeutic community into an alternative society and finally into a religion. Downton (1979) briefly describes the stages through which the Divine Light Mission of Guru Maharaj-Ji has developed. A more formal treatment of the evolution of the DLM derived from Wallis' cult/sect schema has been provided by Pilarzyk (1978a; 1978b). Finally, Cawley (1978) has described the increasing commercial involvement of the Brother Julius sect, which has been associated with a shrinkage of membership and a decrease in active proselytization. There are indications that this pattern of *commercialization plus retrenchment* is currently a general pattern for cults in the United States (U.S. News and World Report, 1978; 1980; Richardson, 1981).

The above findings notwithstanding, most of the existing longitudinal research is unsystematic and theoretically inconclusive. No single unified theoretical structure has emerged and there has been no incisive specification of the conditions under which different evolutionary paths manifest. In the subarea of movement evolution as in the broader area of deviant religious movements, there is a need for more research and a need for more theoretical integration of disparate observations and inferences.

## NOTES

1. See Beckford (1978a; 1979) for critical comments regarding the analyses of religious movements in terms of positive or negative "functions."

2. Trudy Solomon (1980) doubts whether a simple dichotomy of voluntary and involuntary exodus is viable. In her sample some form of "intervention," i.e., "deprogramming," "therapy" or "rehabilitation" was fairly ubiquitous. Dr. Solomon makes two interesting observations: (1) therapeutic assistance is readily available, indeed eagerly offered, to persons who leave cults; and (2) ex-devotees who left cults voluntarily are hard to track down because they are less likely to have had contact with the network of ex-members which is associated with counter-cult groups. It can be inferred from this view that samples of ex-cultists will tend to systematically underrepresent "voluntary" leavers, thus enhancing the importance of longitudinal studies of a given movement. One such study, being conducted with regard to a Moonist group in England by Dr. Eileen Barker, reports a remarkably high attrition rate (personal communication from Dr. Barker).

## REFERENCES

Adams, Robert and Robert Fox. Mainlining Jesus: The New Trip. *Society,* 1972, *9,* 50–56.

*The Advisor: Journal of the American Family Foundation.* P.O. Box 343, Lexington, Mass.

Anthony, Dick and Thomas Robbins. The Meher Baba movement: its effect on post-adolescent youthful alienation. In Irving Zaretsky and Mark Leone, (Eds), *Religious Movements in Contemporary America.* Princeton: Princeton University Press, 1974, 479–501.

Anthony, Dick and Thomas Robbins. A typology of non-traditional religious movements in contemporary America. Presented to the American Association for the Advancement of Science, Denver, 1977.

Anthony, Dick and Thomas Robbins. The effect of detente on the growth of new religions: Reverend Moon and the Unification Church. In J. Needleman and G. Baker (Eds), *Understanding the New Religions.* New York: Seabury, 1978, 80–100.

Anthony, Dick and Thomas Robbins. Religious movements and legitimation crisis. Presented to the International Society for Political Psychology, Boston, 1980a.

Anthony, Dick and Thomas Robbins. A demonology of cults. *Inquiry,* (September 1) 1980b, 9–11.

Anthony, Dick and Thomas Robbins. Contemporary religious ferment and moral ambiguity. *Journal for the Scientific Study of Religion,* 1981a, forthcoming.

Anthony, Dick and Thomas Robbins, Spiritual innovation and the crisis of American civil religion. *Daedalus,* 1981b, forthcoming.

Anthony, Dick; Robbins, Thomas; Curtis, Thomas; and Doucas, Madalyn. Patients and pilgrims: changing attitudes toward psychotherapy of converts to Eastern mysticism. *American Behavioral Scientist,* 1977, *20* (6), 861–86.

Appel, Willa. Satanism in politics. *New York Times,* Op-ed. (January 15) 1980, A19.

Bainbridge, William. *Satan's Power: A Deviant Psychotherapeutic Cult.* Berkeley: University of California Press, 1978, 312 pp.

Bainbridge, William and Rodney Stark. Scientology: To be perfectly clear. *Sociological Analysis,* (Summer) 1980, *41* (2), 128-136.

Balch, Robert. Looking behind the scenes in a religious cult: implications for the study of conversion. *Sociological Analysis,* (Summer) 1980, *41* (2), 137-143.

Barker, Eileen. Whose service is perfect freedom: the concept of spiritual well-being in relation to the Reverend Moon's Unification Church. In D. Moberg (Ed), *Spiritual Well-Being.* Washington, D.C.: University Press, 1979, 153-172.

Beckford, James. Cults and cures. *Japanese Journal of Religious Studies,* 1978a, *5* (4), 225-257.

Beckford, James. Through the looking glass and out the other side: withdrawal from the Rev. Moon's Unification Church. *Les Archives de Sciences Sociales des Religions,* 1978b, *45* (1), 95-116.

Beckford, James. Politics and the anticult movement. *Annual Review of the Social Sciences of Religion,* 1979, *3,* 169-190.

Bell, Daniel. The return of the Sacred? The argument on the future of religion. *British Journal of Sociology,* 1977, *28* (4), 419-44.

Bellah, Robert. *The Broken Covenant.* New York: Seabury, 1975.

Bellah, Robert. The new religious consciousness and the crisis of modernity. In C. Glock and R. Bellah (Eds), *The New Religious Consciousness.* Berkeley: University of California Press, 1976, 335-52.

Berger, Peter and Richard J. Neuhaus. *To Empower People: The Role of Mediating Structures in Public Policy.* Washington, D.C.: American Enterprise Institute, 1977.

Bird, Frederick. The pursuit of innocence: new religious movements and moral accountability. *Sociological Analysis,* (Winter) 1980, *40,* 335-346.

Bird, Frederick and William Reimer. A sociological analysis of new religious and para-religious movements. In *Canadian Religion.* Crusade: MacMillan Press, 1976.

Bradfield, Cecil D. Our kind of people: the consequences of neo-penecostalism for social participation. Paper presented to the Association for the Sociology of Religion, 1976.

Brainwashing. *Society* Magazine, (April/June) 1980, *17* (3).

Bromley, David and Anson Shupe. 'Just a few years seem like a life-time': A role theory approach to participation in religious movements. In L. Kriesberg (Ed), *Research in Social Movements, Conflict and Change.* Greenwich: JAI Press, 1979a, 159-185.

Bromley, David and Anson Shupe. *The 'Moonies' in America.* Beverly Hills: Sage, 1979b.

Bromley, David, Bruce Busching and Anson Shupe. The Unification Church and the American family: strain, conflict and control. Presented to the Society for the Scientific Study of Religion, Cincinnati, (October) 1980.

Campbell, Colin. Clarifying the Cult. *British Journal of Sociology,* 1977, *28* (3), 375-388.

Cawley, Patrick. God's little acres. *Connecticut Magazine,* (August) 1979.

Coleman, James. Social inventions. *Social Forces,* 1970, *49,* 163-173.

Conversion and Commitment in American Religion. *American Behavioral Scientist,* (July/August) 1977, *20* (6).

Conway, Flo and Jim Siegelman. *Snapping: America's Epidemic of Sudden Personality Change.* New York: Lippincott (Delta Pb), 1978.

Delgado, Richard. Religious totalism. *University of Southern California Law Review,* 1977, *15* (1), 1-99.

Dohrman, H. T. *California Cult.* Boston: Beacon, 1958.

Downton, James. *Sacred Journeys: The Conversion of Young Americans to the Divine Light Mission.* New York: Columbia University Press, 1979.

Eister, Allan. An outline of a structural theory of cults. *Journal for the Scientific Study of Religion,* 1972, *11,* 319-334.

Eister, Allan. Culture crises and new religious movements: a paradigmatic statement of a theory of cults. In I. Zaretsky and M. Leone (Eds), *Religious Movements in Contemporary America*. Princeton: Princeton University Press, 1974, 612-627.

Enroth, Ronald. *Youth, Brainwashing and Extreme Cults*. Grand Rapids, MI: Zondervan, 1977.

Fenn, Richard. *"A Theory of Secularization."* Ellington, CT: Society for the Scientific Study of Religion Monograph Series, 1978.

Fichter, Joseph. Marriage, family and Sun Myung Moon. *America*, (October 27) 1979, 226-228.

Foss, Daniel and Ralph Larkin. Worshipping the absurd: the negation of social causality among followers of Guru Maharaji-ji. *Sociological Analysis*, 1978, *39* (2), 156-164.

Galanter, Marc and Peter Buckley. Evangelical religion and meditation: psycho-therapeutic effects. *Journal of Nervous and Mental Disease*, 1979, *166* (10), 685-691.

Glock, Charles. Consciousness among contemporary youth: an interpretation. In Charles Glock, Robert Bellah (Eds), *The New Religious Consciousness*. Berkeley: University of California Press, 1976, 353-366.

Glock, Charles and Thomas Piazza. Exploring reality structures. In T. Robbins and D. Anthony (Eds), *In God We Trust*, New Brunswick, N.J.: Transactions, 1981, 67-84.

Gordon, David. The Jesus people: an identity synthesis interpretation. *Urban Life and Culture*, 1974, *3* (2), 159-179.

Gordon, Suzanne. You can't go home again. *Working Papers for a New Society*, 1980, *7* (4), 10-12.

Greeley, Andrew. *The Demoninational Society*. New York: Scott, Foresman & Co., 1972.

Hadden, Jeffrey and Theodore Long. *The New Relevance of Religion*, forthcoming.

Hammond, Phillip and Robert McCutchen. Cults and civil religion: a tale of two centuries. Presented to The Society for the Scientific Study of Religion, Cincinnati, (October) 1980.

Hargrove, Barbara. Evil eyes and religious choices. *Society*, 1980, *17* (3), 20-24.

Heenan, Edward. *Mystery, Magic and Miracle*. Englewood Cliffs, N.J.: Prentice-Hall, 1973.

Horowitz, Irving. *Science, Sin and Scholarship*. Cambridge, MA: MIT Press, 1978.

Horowitz, Irving. The politics of new cults. In T. Robbins and D. Anthony (Eds), *In Gods We Trust*, Transaction, 1981, 161-170.

Johnson, Benton. A sociological perspective on new religions. In T. Robbins and D. Anthony (Eds), *In Gods We Trust*, Transaction, 1981, 35-50.

Judah, J. Stillson. *Hare Krishna and the Counterculture*. New York: Wiley, 1974.

Judah, J. Stillson. Attitudinal change among members of the Unification Church. Presented to a conference on religion at the Toronto School of Theology, 1978.

Kelley, Dean. *Why the Conservative Churches are Growing*. New York: Harper and Row, 1972.

Keniston, Kenneth. *All our Children: The American Family Under Siege*. New York: Norton, 1977.

Kerrine, Theodore and Richard Neuhaus. Mediating structures: a paradigm for democratic pluralism. *The Annals*, (Nov.) 1979, *446*, 10-18.

Levine, Edward. Rural communes and religious cults: refugees for middle class youth. *Adolescent Psychiatry*, 1980, 7.

Lifton, Robert. The appeal of the death trip. *New York Times* Magazine, (January 7) 1979.

Long, Theodore and Jeffrey Hadden. *The New Relevance of Religion*, forthcoming.

Lorentzen, Louise J. Evangelical life style concerns expressed in political actions. *Sociological Analysis*, (Summer) 1980, *41* (2), 144-153.

Marx, John and David Ellison. Sensitivity training and communes contemporary quests for community. *Pacific Sociological Review*, 1975, *18*, 442-60.

Marx, John and Burkhart Holzner. Ideological primary groups in contemporary cultural movements. *Sociological Focus*, 1975, *8*, 312-29.

Marx, John and Joseph Seldin. At the crossroads of crisis: therapeutic sources and quasi-therapeutic functions of post-industrial communes. *Journal of Health and Social Behavior*, (March) 1975, *14*, 39-52.

Mauss, Armand and Donald Petersen. Les 'Jesus Freaks' et retour a'la respectabilite'ou la prediction des fils prodiques. *Social Compass,* (Summer) 1974, *41* (2), 144–153.

Needleman, J. L. and George Baker. *Understanding New Religions.* New York: Seabury, 1978.

Nelson, Geoffrey. The spiritualistic movement and the need for a redefinition of cult. *Journal for the Scientific Study of Religion,* 1968, *8,* 152–60.

*New Religions Newsletter.* Center for the Study of New Religions, Graduate Theological Union, Berkeley, California, 1979.

Noonan, David. The Hell of Hare Krishna. *Soho Weekly News,* (January) 1977, 6–7.

Ofshe, Richard. Synanon: the people's business. In C. Glock and R. Bellah (Eds), *The New Religious Consciousness.* Berkeley: University of California, 1976.

Ofshe, Richard. The social development of the Synanon cult: the managerial strategy of organization transformation. *Sociological Analysis,* (Summer), 1980a, *41* (2), 109–127.

Ofshe, Richard. Shifts of opportunities and accountability and the regulation of religious organizations. Presented to the Association for the Scientific Study of Religion, New York, (August) 1980b.

Peterson, Richard and Armand Mauss. The cross and the commune: an interpretation of the Jesus people. In C. Glock (Ed), *Religion in Sociological Perspective.* Belmont, CA: Wadsworth, 1973, 261–79.

Pilarzyk, Thomas. Conversion and alternation processes in youth culture: a comparative analysis of religious transformations. *Pacific Sociological Review,* 1978a, *21* (4), 379–405.

Pilarzyk, Thomas. The origin, development and decline of a youth culture religion: an application of sectarianization theory. *Review of Religious Research,* 1979b, *20* (1), 23–43.

Quarantelli, E. and D. Wenger. Characteristics and conditions of the emergence of a Ouija board cult. *Urban Life and Culture,* 1973, *1,* 379–400.

*Review of Law and Social Change.* Colloquium: Alternative Religions: Government Control and the First Amendment, 1980 *9,* 1.

Richardson, James. Conversion and commitment in contemporary religion: an introduction. *American Behavioral Scientist,* (July/August) 1977, *20* (4), 799–804.

Richardson, James. Conversion careers: in and out of the new religions. Beverly Hills: Sage, 1978a.

Richardson, James. An oppositional and general conceptualization of cult. *Annual Review of the Social Sciences of Religion,* 1979a, *2,* 29–52.

Richardson, James. From cult to sect: creative eclecticism in new religious movements. *Pacific Sociological Review,* (April) 1979b, *22* (2), 139–166.

Richardson, James. The people's temple and Jonestown: a corrective, comparison and critique. *Journal for the Scientific Study of Religion,* 1980, *19* (3), 235–259.

Richardson, James. Economic policies and practices of new religious groups, 1981. Unpublished Manuscript.

Richardson, James, Mary Stewart and Robert Simmonds. *Organized Miracles: A Sociological Study of a Fundamental Youth Communal Organization.* New Brunswick, N.J.: Transaction, 1978.

Robbins, Thomas. Eastern mysticism and the resocialization of drug users: the Meher Baba cults. *Journal for the Scientific Study of Religion,* 1969, *8* 308–17.

Robbins, Thomas. Even a Moonie has civil rights. *The Nation,* 1977, *224* (8), 238–241.

Robbins, Thomas. 'Cults' and the therapeutic state. *Social Policy,* 1979, *10* (1), 42–46.

Robbins, Thomas. Religious movements, the state and the law. *Review of Law and Social Change,* 1980, *9* (11), 33–50.

Robbins, Thomas and Dick Anthony. Getting straight with Meher Baba: a study of drug-rehabilitation, mysticism, and post-adolescent role-conflict. *Journal for the Scientific Study of Religion,* 1972, *11* (2), 122–140.

Robbins, Thomas and Dick Anthony. New religions, families and brainwashing. *Society,*

(May/June) 1978, 77–81. Reprinted in T. Robbins and D. Anthony (Eds), *In Gods We Trust,* Transaction, 1978.

Robbins, Thomas and Dick Anthony. The limits of coercive persuasion as an explanation for conversion to authoritarian sects. *Political Psychology,* 1980a, *2* (2).

Robbins, Thomas and Dick Anthony. The medicalization of deviant religion: preliminary observation and critique. Working paper, Yale University Sociology Department, 1980b.

Robbins, Thomas and Dick Anthony. *In Gods We Trust: New Patterns of Religious Pluralism in America.* New Brunswick, N.J.: Transaction, 1981.

Robbins, Thomas; Dick Anthony; Thomas Curtis; and Madalyn Doucas. Youth culture religious movements. *Sociological Quarterly,* 1975, *16* (1), 48–64.

Robbins, Thomas; Dick Anthony; Madalyn Doucas; and Thomas Curtis. The last civil religion: Reverend Moon and the Unification Church. In Irving Horowitz (Ed), *Science, Sin and Scholarship.* Cambridge: MIT Press, 1978, 46–73.

Shapiro, Eli. Destructive cultism. *American Family Physician,* 1977, *15* (2), 80–83.

Shupe, Anson; Roger Spielmann; and Sam Stigall. Deprogramming: the new exorcism. *American Behavioral Scientist,* 1977, *20* (6), 941–956.

Shupe, Anson and David Bromley. *The New Vigilantes: Deprogrammers, Anti-Cultists and The New Religions.* Beverly Hills, CA: Sage, 1980.

Singer, Margaret. Coming out of the cults. *Psychology Today,* 1978, *12* (8), 72–82.

Skonovd, L. Norman. Apostasy: a model of religious defection. Paper presented at the annual meeting of the Pacific Sociological Society, 1979.

Skonovd, L. Norman. Apostasy: the process of defection in religious movements. Dissertation in progress, Sociology, University of California, Davis, 1981.

Snelling, Clarence and Oliver Whitely. Problem-solving behavior in religious and parareligious groups. In Allan Eister (Ed), *Changing Perspectives in the Scientific Study of Religion.* New York: Wiley, 1974, 315–334.

Snow, David and Cynthia Phillips. The Lofland-Stark conversion model: a critical assessment. *Social Problems,* 1980, *27,* 430–47.

*Sociological Analysis.* (Special issue on Religious Movements), (Summer) 1978, *39* (2).

*Sociological Analysis.* (Special issue on Sects, Cults and Religious Movements), (Summer) 1980, *41* (2).

Solomon, Trudy. Integrating the 'Moonie' experience: a survey of ex-members of the Unification Church. In T. Robbins and D. Anthony (Eds), *In Gods We Trust.* New Brunswick: Transaction, 1981, 275–296.

Stark, Rodney and William Bainbridge. Of churches, sects and cults: preliminary concepts for a theory of religious movements. *Journal for the Scientific Study of Religion* 1979, *18,* 117–131.

Stark, Rodney and William Bainbridge. Networks of faith: interpersonal bonds and recruitment to cults and sects. *American Journal of Sociology,* (May) 1980, *85* (6), 1376–1395.

Stone, Donald. New religious consciousness and personal religious experience. *Sociological Analysis,* 1978, *38,* 123–34.

Stone, Donald. The social consciousness of the human potential movement. In T. Robbins and D. Anthony (Eds), *In Gods We Trust.* New Brunswick: Transaction, 1981, 215–228.

Straus, Roger. Becoming a scientologist: a case study of career development in a cult-like social world. Presented to the American Sociological Association, New York, (August) 1980.

Thomas, Patricia. Targets of the cults. *Human Behavior,* (March) 1979, *8* (3), 58–59.

Tipton, Steve. EST and ethics: rule-egoism in middle class culture. Presented to the American Psychological Association, 1977.

Tipton, Steve. New religious movements and the problem of a modern ethic. In Harry Johnson (Ed), *Religious Change and Continuity.* San Francisco: Jossey-Bass, 1979, 286–312.

Tipton, Steve. *Getting Saved from the Sixties.* Berkeley, CA: University of California Press, 1981.

Ungerleider, J. Thomas and David K. Wellisch. Coercive persuasion (brainwashing), religious cults and deprogramming. *American Journal of Psychiatry,* 1979, *136* (3), 279–282.

U. S. *News and World Report.* Religious cults: is the wild fling over? (March 27) 1978, 44–45.

U.S. *News and World Report.* Comeback for religious cults? (November 24) 1980, 73–74.

Varieties of Religious Experience. *Society* Magazine (May/June) 1978, *15* (4).

Wallis, Roy. Ideology, authority and the development of cultic movements. *Social Research,* 1974, *41* (2), 299–327.

Wallis, Roy. The cult and its transformation. In Roy Wallis (Ed), *Sectarianism.* New York: Halstead, 1975a, 35–49.

Wallis, Roy. Scientology: therapeutic cult to religious sect. *Sociology,* 1975b, *9* (1), 89–99.

Wallis, Roy. Observations of the Children of God. *The Sociological Review,* 1976, *24* (4), 807–828.

Wallis, Roy. *The Road to Total Freedom: A Sociological Analysis of Scientology.* New York: Columbia, 1977.

Wallis, Roy. The elementary forms of religious life. *Annual Review of the Social Sciences of Religion,* 1979, *3,* 191–212.

Welles, Chris. The eclipse of Sun Myung Moon. *New York* Magazine, (September 27) 1976.

West, W. In defense of deprogramming. Arlington, TX: International Foundation of Individual Freedom, (Pamphlet), 1975.

Wilson, Bryan. The secularization debate. *Encounter,* 1975, *45* (4), 77–83.

Wilson, Bryan. *Contemporary Transformations of Religion.* Oxford: Oxford University Press, 1976.

Zaretsky, Irving and Mark Leone. *Religious Movements in Contemporary America.* Princeton: Princeton University Press, 1974.

# CULTS VERSUS FAMILIES:
# A CASE OF MISATTRIBUTION OF CAUSE?

Brock K. Kilbourne
James T. Richardson

## Introduction

Is conversion to new religious groups a threat to the institution of the family? More than a few observers seem to think so (see Levine, 1980a, 1980b; Schwartz and Kaslow, 1979; Delgado, 1980; Clark, 1976, 1978, 1979a, 1979b) and feel justified in publicizing their fears. Some who share this view are members of the "anti-cult movement," described recently by Shupe, Spielman, and Stigall (1980). While the threat of new religious groups to the structure and cohesiveness of the family unit may not be self evident, it is apparent that much of the anti-cult leadership has arisen out of affected family units. Shupe et al. have examined the structure and ideology of the anti-cult movement, a major proponent of those fearing cult influences may weaken the family unit, and have found up to 80–90% of the anti-cult's constituency was made up of immediate family and friends of members of the newer religions. Moreover, some members of various professions whose livelihood depends upon a certain conception of the family (clergy, psychiatrists, physicians, social workers, and educators) tend to perceive many new religions as threats to both the physical/mental health of adherents and to the "ideal family" they promote and service.

It has also become apparent in recent years that a number of recurrent themes of detrimental influence to the family have surfaced to instil among laymen and professionals a conscientious concern with, if not outright suspicion of, the proliferation of new religious groups. The main thrust of this shared concern appears to evolve around the following allegations and

Brock K. Kilbourne is a graduate student in the Department of Social Psychology, and James T. Richardson is professor of sociology at the University of Nevada at Reno. This paper was completed while the second author was a Fulbright Fellow at the Psychology Laboratory, Catholic University, Nijmegen, The Netherlands. Gratitude is expressed for his support.

accusations: 1) membership in newer religions leads to reduced commitment to and communication with the family, 2) parents may be redefined as the incarnation of evil and as the agents of Satan, 3) the biological family is often given new meaning in light of the establishment of surrogate parents as new objects of affection, 4) the parent-child bond is generally weakened or severed, 5) church elders are often responsible for mate selection, 6) infants and children may be raised communally and not considered the personal property of their biological parents, 7) children may not receive benefits of middle class health care and education, and 8) the new religions sometimes practice strange sexual behaviors.

Taken together, these accusations tend to paint a vivid picture of atrocity, even though the evidence to support such claims is clearly mixed and inconclusive. The general impression of such a listing of characteristics assumes a homogeneity among the newer religions that is not defensible. Indeed, certain of the newer religious groups go directly counter in their practices and teachings to most of the "anti-family" characteristics just listed (see Richardson et al., 1978a for an example of a strongly "pro-family" group).

However, atrocity tales of the nature depicted by the eight anti-family characteristics sometimes function to authorize punitive actions against new religious groups, to motivate anti-cultists to take specific actions authorizing "rescue" attempts, and to encourage a variety of other attacks against newer religions (see Robbins and Anthony, 1978 and Bromley, Shupe and Ventimiglia, 1979). Because of such atrocity tales, immediate family and friends of cult members may feel justified in taking drastic action against new religious groups without fear of guilt or legal sanctions. In response to such actions, some individuals not entrenched in the anti-cult movement or personally involved with children of their own have expressed concern that in our haste we may be unwittingly creating an institution of informal and formal practices with the potential for impeding, and conceivably suppressing, the growth of other new movements in the future (Robbins, 1977).

The present review examines the familial effects of conversion to new religious groups with the explicit intent of proffering a "corrective view" of what may be an "overreaction" to the contemporary cult phenomenon. A more neutral assessment of so-called cult membership appears to be warranted by an appreciation of the following: 1) the sociological literature on contemporary conversion to the newer religions contravening the "worst" of some family's fears, namely, the possibility of brainwashing by the newer religions, 2) the historical forces and stresses having impacted upon the institution of the family in American society, 3) the diversity of familial forms in American society, and 4) an overview of extant research investigating the specific impact of new religious groups upon the family.

## A Sociological Perspective

The *sine qua non* of family fears concerning membership in the newer religions appears to be the possibility that certain unscrupulous techniques have been employed to gain the allegiance of the young and unsuspecting (see Schwartz and Kaslow, 1979, for an example of this position). The absence of coercion found by most researchers in new religious groups (see Richardson, Simmonds and Harder, 1972; Solomon, 1978; Balch and Taylor, 1978; Robbins and Anthony, 1979; Ungerleider and Wellish, 1979; Barker, 1978; and Anthony, Robbins and McCarthy, 1980) has generally been ignored and has served, in part, to confirm this belief in unscrupulous tactics. Such beliefs have often been rationalized in terms of either an "evil eye" theory of bewitchment (Cox, 1978; Hargrove, 1980) or on the basis of metaphors of mind control and brainwashing (Szasz, 1961).[1] The logic of this reasoning rests upon the assumption that the young and naive have been hypnotized and/or seduced by evil-intending "Pied Pipers" and surreptitiously separated from their families. Packaged treatments of group pressure, isolation, fatigue, and induced dissociative states are then supposedly administered to the young in such a fashion as to disrupt, confuse, and obliterate their natural ties to family and community.

Robbins and Anthony (1979a, 1979b, 1981), in response to these and similar family fears, have noted how the metaphor of brainwashing is best understood as a conceptual and social weapon. In this capacity the brainwashing metaphor can function to justify the suppression of unpopular social movements and ideas by implying authorities are not trying to suppress opinion, just the way it has been induced. They also point out that the applicability of brainwashing, relative to free will, can never be disproven and that the use of the brainwashing metaphor suggests religious devotees

---

[1]In relation to those instances in the newer religions involving deception, allegations of brainwashing have been preferred to the more scientific concept of misattribution (Storms & Nisbett, 1970; Valins & Ray, 1967; Ross, Rodin & Zimbardo, 1969; Loftis and Ross, 1974)—the process whereby individuals are made information dependent and social cues are manipulated to insure a certain label will be assigned by the individual to his/her experience—and the absence of informed consent procedures in other socially legitimate pursuits, e.g., clinical psychology (Everstine, Everstine, Heyman, True, Frey, Johnson & Seiden, 1980) have been overlooked.

are passive recipients of social conditioning, rather than volitional seekers of religious meaning and commitment. Building upon the work of Robbins et al. in an attempt to identify the motivational antecedants of the use of the brainwashing metaphor (Meerloo, 1956; Sargant, 1957; Lifton, 1961; Schein, Schneier, and Barker, 1961; Verdier, 1977; Conway and Siegleman, brainwashing metaphor (Meerloo, 1956; Sargant, 1957; Lifton, 1961; Schein, Schneier, and Barker, 1961; Verdier, 1977; Conway and Siegleman, 1978; Patrick, 1976; Delgado, 1980; Lifton, 1979, 1980; Stoner and Park, 1977; Singer, 1979a, 1979b; Enroth, 1977; Levine, 1980a) to share to varying degrees the common ideological bias of anti-totalism and anti-collectivism in relation to the plainly preferred values of individualism and democratic capitalism. This ideological bias of the brainwashing models, while consonant with many of our cultural assumptions about human nature as well as our value preferences, cannot it appears be justified on empirical grounds alone and must rely to a disproportionate extent upon its social control function for legitimation.

One body of empirical evidence supporting this view and with negative implications for the application of the brainwashing model to membership in the newer religions can be derived from the combined sociological concepts of role and seekerhood. These two concepts provide us with the basis for reconceptualizing the apparent sudden changes in behavior and attitudes subsequent to membership in a new religious group. From this perspective, rapid behavioral and attitudinal transformations are not seen to be indicative of radical personality change per se, and thus confirmative of the brainwashing metaphor, but more likely to be indicative of a person's change in social role and/or his/her seeking proclivities.

For instance, in an early paper on role theory and conversion Zetterberg (1952) claimed religious conversion proper entails the sudden acceptance of a social role advocated by a religious group and not the transformation of a person's personality. Religious conversions mostly occurred, according to Zetterberg's findings, in group settings. Bromley and Shupe (1979) have adopted this general approach to the study of participation in the new religious movements. Bromley et al. present an alternative conception to the dominant motivational perspective of conversion by placing commitment in a social context and by eschewing the theoretical predilection of many to treat conversion in psychological reductionist terms, to equate affiliation with attitude change, and to overemphasize the contribution of predisposing motives.

Essentially the motivational model explains new religious group membership on the basis of the "match" between the group's new beliefs and the predisposing needs or motives of the new recruit. Role theory, on the other hand, focuses on *how* and not why people join new religious groups. This shift in focus allows us to construe affiliation as a social process whereby the group functions to meet both the individual's needs and to shape those needs. In lieu of attributions of pathology and necessary predisposing states, role theory contends changes in a person's status and role often result in attitudinal changes which create the public appearance of personality transformation.

Bromley and Shupe have in fact reported empirical support for the role theory approach in their study of the Unification Church. In general, their findings indicated the predisposing motives of new recruits were too varied to be accounted for by a simplistic motivational model, that many individuals eventually found their interests broadened in the church, the assumption of active membership most often led to dramatic changes in the new recruit's behavior prior to belief changes and the development of commitment, and lastly, value and goal commitment to the church usually emerged out of active role performance.

Balch (1980) has similarly reported evidence supporting this view. In a study of a UFO cult using an investigative reporting procedure, Balch found that "playing the role" of a convert was a powerful explanation of sudden behavior change and generally involved the social requirements of limiting oneself to certain explicit activities, developing certain kinds of relationships, learning a special vocabulary, and learning appropriate public displays.[2] Most importantly, new recruits willingly adopted the convert role upon entering into the UFO camp and manifested, in many instances, dramatic changes in behavior and verbal reports *prior* to acquiring the appropriate cult beliefs and even concurrent with their self doubts. Interestingly, many members learned to conceal their self doubts and disillusionment from their partners and cohorts. Thus members learned to act like a convert by outwardly conforming to the role expectations of the group while quietly keeping to themselves or in some cases only disclosing to their most trusted confidants their personal concerns. This finding is directly analogous to early laboratory research on conformity behavior (Festinger, 1953; Jahoda, 1959 and Kelman, 1958) which drew a distinction between public conformity and private disagreement. Balch also contends the UFO members in this study deliberately adopted, along the lines of

---

[2]From an interactionist perspective (Sampson, 1976), we should recognize, of course, that roles and "vocabularies of motives (Mills, 1940)" are negotiated within a context of individual skills and attributes, situational demands, third parties, and broad cultural constraints (McCall and Simmons, 1966; Secord and Backman, 1974).

Goffman's (1959) distinction between front stage and backstage performances, an expressionless public facade while at large and "once back in
the safety of their own camps, they would start acting like real people
again."

These findings by Bromley and Shupe and Balch are, of course, consistent with previous findings on role playing and role enactment. For instance, Janis and Gilmore (1965) found role players were adept and convincing at selecting good arguments for their positions and, according to
Sarbin and Allen (1968), the process of taking on a new role entails
improvising arguments and aspects consistent with it, which in turn increases a person's commitment to the role. Additionally, Lieberman (1956)
has shown how change in occupational role can account for both a change
in expressed attitudes and the reversion to one's original positions upon
returning to the original role. More recently, and supportive of a role
theory approach to new religious group membership, Jellison and Arkin
(1979) have presented evidence that oftentimes the attitude of a person is a
response intended to maximize reward and minimize punishment in the
immediate and similar situations. An expressed attitude, from this perspective, represents the person's response to the reinforcement contingencies in
the social environment and is by no means indicative of permanently internalized beliefs, attitudes, or values.

A related line of empirical evidence at odds with the presumption of the
brainwashing prowess of the newer religions can be seen in the systematic
work of some conversion researchers on the themes of "active agency"
and "seekerhood" (Straus, 1976, 1979a, 1979b, 1979c, 1979d; Balch and
Taylor, 1978; Richardson, 1979, 1980; Balch, 1980). Most exemplary of
this perspective is the work of Roger Straus on scientologists, who has
concluded that conversion is most productively viewed as an *accomplishment* (1979a) on the part of a seeker. Seekers are individuals striving and
strategizing to achieve quantum change in their life experience. And collectivities are viewed in terms of their capacities to offer seekers the hope and
opportunity for resolving their quests for meaning and for their desired
identity changes. The focus in studying conversion shifts from a concern
with passive personality systems to an investigation of how competent
social actors construct and reconstruct their respective social and
phenomenological realities.

Straus (1976) contends seekers manage their conversions through a
series of specific strategies. Seekers generally begin with a process of
"creative bumbling" by which they comb through various social networks, chance encounters, and the media for prospective leads to lifestyles

and groups. As seeking continues, the individual develops specialized search tactics for recognizing a "find," "checking it out," exploiting the collectivity, and finally "pulling it off." Pulling it off ranges from entrance requirements, through transforming oneself, to the realization and public announcement of life change. We can also conceptualize this seekerhood pattern in terms of *conversion careers* or the active sampling of identity sequences that can be viewed as cumulative (Richardson, 1980) and in terms of self efficacy motivation to produce desired outcomes in one's life (Gecas, 1979).

Hence the aforementioned research on the role theory and seekerhood conceptions of conversion clearly suggests, at least for many converts to new religious groups, just how difficult it really is to accept uncritically the claims by some of the purported brainwashing of "children" by the newer religions. However, even in the face of this growing "subject centered" literature on seekerhood and role playing, the anti-cult movement and related groups have successfully revived the brainwashing metaphor of the fifties, which was originally implemented to discredit the validity of communism as a viable system of thought, and have directed their efforts toward characterizing all new religions in a generally threatening manner to family life. This organizational strategy has succeeded to some extent and has allowed the anti-cult movement to: 1) define appropriate and inappropriate behavior; 2) misattribute new values and ideas to personal pathology and anomie; 3) isolate "deviant individuals" from sources of group support; and 4) suppress experimentation in family life. Lastly the brainwashing metaphor provides the victims, the errant family member and his/her family, with an excusatory account (Taylor, 1976; Beckford, 1978; Scott and Lyman, 1968) to deny responsibility for former actions. Actions which in the case of the convert may have appeared unintelligible and inexplicable are explained, and in the case of the convert's family, actions which may have actually contributed to the convert's decision to join a new religious group are rationalized away.

## The Weakening of the Institution of the Family

A majority of contemporary textbooks on marriage and the family either begin or end with a discussion of the future of the family in today's rapidly changing society. Few experts on the family would dispute either that the form of the family is changing or the reality of multiple familial forms. Much fewer in number would be inclined to agree concerning the positive or negative impact of these sources of change or the evolving outcome of familial forms in contemporary American society. Concerning the changing form, role, and functions of the family, however, the following has been fairly well substantiated empirically: 1) Many traditional functions of the family (reproduction, biological maintenance, socialization, work, education, social control, status placement, sexual gratification, and emotional maintenance) have been transferred to or are shared with other institutions in society (Romanyshyn, 1971); 2) there is evidence of increasing change in the roles of men and women in today's society as more women are entering into the labor force, seeking higher education, and functioning as the head of single households (U.S.D.L., 1976; U.S.D.L., 1979; U.S. President, Council of Economic Advisors, 1973; Magarrell, 1978); 3) the divorce rate continues to climb (U.S.N.C.H.S., 1979; U.S.B.C., 1976); 4) the sophistication of birth control devices reduces the need to marry in order to satisfy sexual needs (Makepeace, 1975); 5) there has been a significant increase in the incidence of teenage premarital sex and pregnancies, out of wedlock (*Newsweek*, Sept., 1980); 6) there has been a significant increase in the numbers of people who live together but do not marry (Glick and Norton, 1978; Macklin, 1978); 7) there has been an alarming nationwide rate, and in some instances significant increases, of child abuse (Bakan, 1971; Gil, 1970; Stolk, 1974) and adolescent suicide (Cantor, 1977); 8) more individuals today practice co-marital sex (Athanasiou; Shaver, & Tavris, 1970; Smith and Smith, 1979; Johnson, 1974); 9) between 1970 and 1975 the fertility rate in the United States fell to the lowest in the nation's history, (Melville, 1977); 10) there is a general increase in the visibility of group and communal family styles (Fairfield, 1972; Ramey, 1972, 1975, 1978; Zablocki, 1971); 11) the rate of remarriage continues to edge upwards (Furstenberg, 1979); 12) the steady rise in the numbers of singles continues (Stein, 1975, 1978; Interchange 6, 1977; C.P.R., 1978); and 13) abortion rates continue to climb (Weinstock, Tietze, Jaffee, and Dryfoos, 1976) and to receive widespread support (Arney and Trescher, 1976).

In order to place the above findings into a coherent and meaningful conceptual framework, a number of researchers and theorists of the family (Clayton, 1979) have emphasized the role of industrialization, urbanization, and secularization to explain both changes in society and in the family system. Simply put, the family has changed because society has changed. Thus changes in sex roles, work experiences, divorce rates, marital styles, etc., are better understood as *covariates* of larger macro-level forces. The processes and structures of industrialization, urbanization, and secularization, along with other changes in our environments, i.e., over-population, place new pressures on traditional marriage and family arrangements.

This is not surprising. After all, it is generally accepted that industrialization tends to differentiate society and to affect substantive changes in its stratification (Rostow, 1960; Tumin, 1967). Trends of mass consumption encouraging the multiplication of products, activities, and lifestyles characteristically evolve in modern industrialized societies. Moreover, the overall expansion of the upper and middle classes, the drastic change in the occupational structure, and the proliferation of institutions and organizations all contribute to make society more complex and to transform the family unit primarily into a unit of companionship (Landis, 1975), mediating between the individual and his society (Romanyshyn, 1971). This latter point has been developed with specific reference to new religions by Robbins and Anthony (1978).

Urbanization (Wirth, 1938) also tends to de-emphasize the importance and autonomy of the family simply by the multiplication of roles and relationships and the segmentation of the majority of relations. People become dependent upon more people for the satisfaction of their needs and membership in highly divergent groups becomes the norm. The accompanying emergence of secularization (Wilson, 1975a, b, 1976; Fenn, 1972), the process by which mankind attempts to control the physical and social environments vis à vis social and rational decision-making, further contributes to the weakening of the family. This is most evidently accomplished in the provision of standardized rational accounts justifying the cost-effective satisfaction and management of needs and goals outside of the family unit.

While the preceding conceptualizes the family to be an essentially passive receiving system, Farber (1964) has also stressed studying the family as an independent variable. This view allows us to examine the extent to which the family may be an active instigator of change. More succinctly, the theme of familial active agency allows us to understand how families, like certain individuals, may strive to transform themselves and to experiment with different relationships, structures, and life styles. We can better appreciate from this perspective that society affects the family and the family affects society. Similarly, the concepts of bidirectionality of influence (Bell, 1968, 1971; and Harper, 1971) and/or reciprocal determinism (Bandura, 1974, 1977) have been used in child and social development research to explicate this two-way process of social influence at the interpersonal level. Thus the role of the meaning of the family to family members, their respective competencies in and out of the family, and the availability of certain opportunity structures may help us to understand how certain families attempt to construct their own behaviors and family situations and to ultimately affect the kind of society they live in.

For it is apparent that some families self-consciously seek desired out-comes in a matter-of-fact and straight forward fashion. Recognition of this fact encourages us to attribute a certain amount of variance in family structure and family behavioral patterns to the family members themselves, over and above what can be attributed to macro-level structures; in addition, there may also be a confluence of effects of these two different perspectives. That is, the structural provision of certain opportunities and resources to certain families in society tends to increase the likelihood of their active role in their own creation. This social psychological level of analysis provides the basis for understanding the relativity of freedom of choice, acquired social competencies, and the overriding importance of meaning within the family system in the everyday affairs of human beings.

## Is There a Universal Family Form?

Sidney Jourard (1970) contends that while we live in a fantastically pluralistic society, there is a general tendency for many of us to restrict legitimacy to the middle class design of the family. Evidently we do this, even though there is a growing awareness of the tremendous diversity of relationships between parent and child, between men and women. Keller (1971), in much the same vein, believes the idea of a universal family is not only highly misleading but tends to deceive us into expecting a single pattern of family life. Keller maintains there are as many forms of the family as there are forms of society. However, single mindedness of thought concerning the family tends to trap us into thinking the kind of family life we enjoy is the universal and natural form of the family. To the consternation of many an expert in family life, many of us continue to think the nuclear family unit is the prototype for all family life. The lens of ethnocentricity, regardless of its cultural grounding, can, it appears, blur our perception of the multiple realities of family living and lead to a state of pluralistic ignorance about the family.

What is the reality of family life in general then and in contemporary American society in particular? Most experts agree the family cannot be characterized by one pattern or form. Crossculturally, diversity is the norm for just about any dimension of analysis. For instance, in relation to free-dom of choice, the joint family system of Asia and the affiliated family system of Latin America contrast markedly with the reduced dominance of individuals found in most contemporary American nuclear families. In fact, the farm family of our not so distant past most clearly resembles in form the "begin-all" and "end-all" attitude of family life in joint and affiliated family systems. Interestingly, Winch and Blumberg (1972), in a study evidencing the continuity between past and present family forms, have demonstrated support for a curvilinear hypothesis of family structure by which larger family systems preponderate in agrarian societies and smaller family systems in more developed societies. It would appear that the independent family, or nuclear family, has attained its "full form" in contemporary American society. Today, separate living arrangements are considered to be a requirement for independence from parents and relatives.

Yet the significance of the diversity of marriage and familial forms is not to be found in the convergence toward the conjugal family (Goode, 1963). Rather the diverse nature of family life is evident in the growing numbers of group and communal marriages, same sex marriages, living togethers, co-marital sex, open marriage, and "swinging," not to mention the large number of singles. Without question, conditions of personal, marital, and family living styles have changed drastically in recent years and has made it nearly impossible to talk about a universal or ideal family form.

## What Is the Evidence?

When the aforementioned is taken into consideration, we must seriously question the usage of the brainwashing metaphor to explain new religious group membership and recognize much of the so-called strain on the institution of the family can be correctly attributed to societal conditions in general instead of misattributed to new religious groups. Most threats to and strains upon the American family are similar to those felt by society as a whole. These strains arise from the social changes associated with industrialization and urbanization. From this standpoint, both the changing family and the emergence of new religious groups are *covariates* of larger macro-forces in society and, in this sense, we need not misattribute cause by blaming one covariate, i.e., new religions, for perceived and experienced strains upon another covariate, i.e., the institution of the family, that would occur in any case but perhaps in a different form. New religious groups appear to be just one of the many ways our social horizons have become increasingly differentiated and compounded. Multiple roles, relationships, identities, and realities are today's norm (Berger, 1963) and accompanying this progressive transformation of society has been the almost incessant change in our relationships with others and in our self identities. This appears to be the case even in those instances of commitment to some totalistic communal sects (see Solomon [1978] for a discussion of high turn-over rates in the Unification Church). Consequently, there is little reason to believe that the American family (regardless of its form) should be otherwise affected by larger societal trends.

Another source of strain upon the institution of the family, independent of macro changes in society, is self induced. That is, some families are more than just passive recipients of change, they are active instigators of their own transformations, and such change sometimes does not come easily and without pain.

In contradistinction to these two apparent strains upon the traditional American family which do not derive from conversion to new religions by family members, there is a growing body of evidence indicating the absence of a clear pattern of relationship between membership in new religious groups and the weakening of family ties. This is indicated by: 1) Some people attracted to new religious groups indicate being dissatisfied with their lives and alienated from their families *prior* to membership (Peterson and Mauss, 1973; Levine and Salter, 1976; Galanter, Rabkin, Rabkin, and Deutch, 1978; Richardson, Stewart, and Simmonds, 1978b); 2) many individuals who join new religious groups are seekers who attempt to try out various organizations that can provide them with differential opportunities by which to manage their own self transformations (Gerlach and Hine, 1970; Holloman, 1974; Gordon, 1974; also, see previous citations on seekerhood for Straus, Balch and Taylor, Richardson, and Balch); 3) a large proportion of members in new religious groups, prior to their membership, have already experienced a number of non-conventional life-styles and value systems (Nicholi, 1974; Richardson, et al., 1978b; Austin, 1977; Pilarzyk, 1978) at odds with middle class norms of family life; 4) some families contend the new religious experiences of their children are growth experiences consistent with the family's general philosophy of life (Richardson, et al. 1978a; Heirich, 1977; Beckford, 1981); 5) recruitment into some new religious groups proceeds through established social networks, i.e., the family, and attempts to absorb the entire family unit, intact, into its community and not to disintegrate the family (Stark and Bainbridge, 1980; Snow and Phillips, 1980); 6) some affiliations with new religions actually *increase* affective ties between the individual and family members (Snow and Phillips, 1980 and Richardson, Stewart, and Simmonds, 1978b); 7) forceful removal of individuals who have established families *within* new religious groups is often destructive of those family ties (Robbins and Anthony, 1978); and 8) de-programming efforts in some cases have apparently brought about more, not less, animosity between the subject of the deprogramming and the family members involved (Robbins and Anthony, 1978).

However, from another perspective, Bromley, Bushing, and Shupe (1980) have found two sources of strain arising within individual families[3] which were directly related to a family member joining a new religious group, the Unification Church. These two major sources of strain were attributed to: 1) the new religious group's competition with the family's goal of preparing offspring for participation in the economic order, and 2) the challenge posed by the new religious group to the titular leadership status of the parents and the continued membership of their offspring in the family unit. Beckford (1981) has also explored the patterned responses of parents to the membership of their children in new religious groups and has found three typical responses—incomprehension, anger, and ambivalence. Of these three types of parental response, Beckford contends the anger response is statistically most frequent and is usually characterized by parental recriminations against the new religious group (also see Schwartz and Kaslow, 1979: 20-21, for a discussion of individual family reactions to a member joining some new religious groups).

Considered together these results are especially noteworthy. In one sense the findings by Bromley et al. are not in and of themselves particularly damaging to the status of new religious groups. Any group, and there are many in contemporary American society, has the potential for competing with the values and norms governing family life. Yet the actual preponderance of angry recriminations by many parents toward certain new religious groups (Beckford), understood in relation to the Bromley et al. findings, suggests that some parents are very sensitive to the *Zeitgeist* of their culture and are henceforth especially deserving of our attention. In other words, some parents appear to recognize that generally it would be inappropriate to accuse a ski club or a surf club (both of which offer the young competing allegiances and sometimes competing values to those of the middle class family) of interrupting their child's preparation for adulthood or thwarting the family's authority (although some youngsters would debate this latter point). Most likely such vilifications would fall upon deaf ears. On the other hand, similar allegations against new religious groups, especially communal ones, are culturally more appropriate because in our culture, at least, it is permissible to believe in God, but not too much. Individuals in our culture are encouraged to be "part time" believers in

---

[3]In this respect, we should distinguish between threats and strains to individual families and those to the institution of the family.

God but not to be full time believers and adherents, as is the case in some communally organized groups.

Some parents appear to have responded to their children's "over-religion" by calculatively employing their own angry recriminations as self presentation strategies (Averill, 1974) in an attempt to convince others of the seriousness of the situation and to further justify their actions in relation to allegations of brainwashing and coercion. These parents are unquestionably experts in the common stock or knowledge of our culture. Their self presentational emotional displays are legitimate accounts and constitute the stuff of which social influence theorists write volumes (Mills, 1940; Goffman, 1967; Scott and Lyman, 1968; Harre and Secord, 1973; Harre, 1979).

Ironically, there is some evidence that in certain circumstances the recruitment of a family member into a new religious group sets the stage for the eventual *strengthening* of the family unit. This can occur in at least two ways. First, eventual strengthening may occur in those instances where the family is internally torn and perhaps on the verge of disintegration. The "rescue" and/or "accommodative" response of certain parents in certain familial contexts may serve a reintegrative function by "bringing back together" the otherwise alienated family members. This phenomenon appears to be analogous, in part, to Laing's (1970, 1971) description of the pathological or schizophrenic family. For example, Laing suggests the pathological family may use the labeled schizophrenic member: 1) to conceal the family's pathological condition, 2) for purposes of boundary maintenance to define normal and abnormal behavior, 3) in order to scapegoat, and 4) literally to hold the family together. In the case of a troubled family unit confronting a new religious group, it may be that reintegration evolves around "rescue" attempts and results in the family "side-stepping" their own problems. There are, in fact, a number of reports suggesting the reuniting and/or strengthening of certain families following the "rescue" attempts and/or accommodations by the family (Patrick, 1976; Stoner and Parke, 1977; Beckford, 1981; Ungerleider, 1980).

This "reintegration hypothesis" can be, in turn, extended beyond the context of the troubled family. Membership in some new religious groups may provide a basis for certain alienated and uncommitted youth to overcome their sense of alienation (Kim, 1976) and to begin to make the first meaningful commitments of their lives to themselves, their families, and their communities (Robbins, Anthony, Curtis, 1975; and Richardson, et al. 1978a: 97-99). Thus for the divided family and for some alienated youth, involvement with a new religious group may function therapeutically to strengthen the family unit as a whole or to further the religious member's commitment to self, family, and community.

Interestingly, some of the new religious groups actually stress traditional American family values of monogamy, fidelity, and the raising of children (see Richardson et al., 1978). And on a more symbolic level, many new group's use of familial terminology (father, mother, brother, sister) in addition to their self conscious efforts to build family-like communal forms (Kanter, 1972) indicates an acceptance of familial values and an attempt to promote such values.

In conclusion, the present review proffered a "corrective view" to counter the growing tendency by some families and professionals to possibly "overreact" to the proliferation of new religious groups. An alternative conception to the brainwashing metaphor, one based upon empirical studies of role change and seekerhood, was used to explicate sudden behavior change subsequent to membership in new religious groups and with the sole intent of placing into perspective familial fears of harmdoing to family members. Furthermore, strain upon the institution of the family was in large part accounted for by structurally induced changes in American society and a review of extant empirical research in this area indicated the lack of a causal relationship between membership in new religious groups and the weakening of family ties. To the contrary, evidence was discussed indicating the "reintegrative" function of membership in some new religious groups in relation to self, family, and community, and to the symbolic and actual support of family values by many such groups.

## REFERENCES

Anthony, D., Robbins, T., and McCarthy, J. Legitimating Repression. *Society*, 1980, *17* (3), 39–42.

Arney, W. R. and Trescher, W. H. Trends in attitudes toward abortion, 1972–1975. *Family Planning Perspectives*, (May–June) 1976, *8*, 117–124.

Athanasiou, R., Shaver, P. and Tauris, C. "Sex." *Psychology Today*, (July) 1970, 37–52.

Austin, R. Empirical adequacy of Lofland's conversion model. *Review of Religious Research*, 1977, *18* (3), 282–287.

Averill, J. R. An analysis of psychophysiological symbolism and its influence on theories of emotion. *Journal for the Theory of Social Behavior*, 1974, *4* (2), 147–190.

Bakan, D. *Slaughter of the Innocents*. Toronto, Ont.: CBC Learning Systems, 1971.

Balch, R. and Taylor, D. Seekers and Saucers: the role of cultic milieu in joining a UFO Cult. In J. R. Richardson (Ed), *Conversion Careers: In and Out of the New Religions*. Beverly Hills: Sage Publications, 1978, 43–64.

Bandura, A. Behavior theory and the models of man. *American Psychologist*, 1974, *29* (12), 859–869.

Bandura, A. Self efficacy: toward a unifying theory of behavioral change. *Psychological Review*, 1977, *84* (2), 191–215.

Barker, E. Confessions of a Methodological Schizophrenic: Problems Encountered in a Study of the Rev. Sun Myung Moon's Unification Church. Research Bulletin, Institute for the Study of Worship and Religious Architecture, 1978, University of Birmingham, England.

Beckford, J. A. Accounting for Conversion. *British Journal of Sociology,* (June) 1978, *29* (2).

Beckford, J. A. Family responses to new religious movements. *Marriage and Family Review, 4* (3/4), 41–55.

Bell, R. Q. A reinterpretation of the direction of effects in studies of socialization. *Psychological Review,* 1968, *75,* 81–95.

Bell, R. Q. Stimulus control of parent or caretaker behavior by offspring. *Development Psychology,* 1971, *4,* 63–72.

Berger, P. L. *Invitation to Sociology.* Garden City, N.Y.: Anchor Doubleday, 1963.

Bromley, D. G. and A. D. Shupe. "Just a few years seem like a lifetime," a role theory approach to participation in religious movements, research in social movements, conflicts and change. *JAI Press, Inc.,* 1979, *2,* 159–185.

Bromley, D. G. Shupe, A. D. and Ventimiglia, J. C. Atrocity tales, the Unification church, and the social construction of evil. *Journal of Communications,* 1979, *29* (3).

Bromley, D. G. and Shupe, A. D. The Tnevnoc Cult. *Sociological Analysis,* 40 (4), 361–366.

Bromley, D. G., Busching, B. C., and Shupe, A. D. The Unification Church and the American family: strain, conflict, and control. In E. Barker (Ed), *Society From the New Religious Perspectives.* Cambridge: Cambridge University Press, 1980.

Cantor, P. Suicide and attempted suicide among students: problems, prediction and prevention. In P. Cantor (Ed), *Understanding a Child's World.* N.Y.: McGraw Hill, 1977.

Clark, J. An unpublished paper presented to the Vermont Legislature, 1976.

Clark, J. We are all cultists at heart. *Newsday,* (November) 1978.

Clark, J. Sudden personal change and the maintenance of critical government institutions. Paper presented at the Annual Meeting of the International Society for Political Psychology, Washington, D.C., 1979a.

Clark, J. *Journal of the American Medical Association,* (July 20) 1979b, *242* (3).

Clayton, R. R. *The Family, Marriage, and Social Change.* Second Edition, MASS: D. C. Heath and Company, 1979.

Conway, F. and Siegleman, J. *Snapping.* New York: Delia Book, 1978.

Cox, Harvey. Deep structures in the study of new religions. In J. Needleman and G. Barker (Eds.), *Understanding the New Religions.* New York: The Seabury Press, 1978, 131–137.

Current Population Reports Series No. 323, (April) 1978, p. 20.

Delgado, R. Limits to proselytizing. *Society,* (March/April) 1980, *17* (3).

Enroth, Ronald. *Youth, Brainwashing, and the Extremist Cults.* Grand Rapids, Michigan: Zondervan, 1977.

Fairfield, R. *Communes U.S.A.: A Personal Tour.* Baltimore: Penguin Books, 1972.

Farber, B. *Family Organization Interaction.* San Francisco: Chandler, 1964.

Fenn, R. K. Toward a new sociology of religion. *Journal for the Scientific Study of Religion,* 1972, *11,* 16–32.

Festinger, L. An analysis of compliant behavior. In M. Sherif and M. O. Wilson (Eds), *Group Relations at the Crossroads.* New York: Harper, 1953, 232–256.

Furstenberg, F. F. Recycling the family: perspectives for a neglected family form. *Marriage and Family Review,* 1979, *2* (3).

Galanter, M. Psychological induction into the large group: findings from a modern religious sect. *American Journal of Psychiatry,* 1980, *137* (12), 1574–1579.

Galanter, M., Rabkin, R., Rabkin, J., and Deutch, A. The "Moonies," A Psychological Study, Paper for 131st Annual Meeting of the American Psychiatric Association, Atlanta, 1978.

Gecas, V. Beyond the "looking glass self": toward an efficacy-based model of self esteem. Paper presented at a Roundtable Session of the Annual Meetings of the American Sociological Association, Boston, 1979.

Gerlach, L. and Hine, V. *People, Power, Change: Movements of Social Transformation.* Indianapolis: Bobbs-Merrill, 1970.

Gil, D. G. *Violence Against Children: Physical Child Abuse in the United States.* Cambridge, Mass: Harvard University Press, 1970.

Glick, P. C. and Norton, A. J. Special Report, "Couple Households." U.S. Bureau of the Census. Washington, D.C.: Government Printing Office, 1978.

Goffman, I. *The Presentation of Self in Everyday Life.* New York: Doubleday, 1959.

Goffman, I. *Interactional Ritual.* New York: Doubleday, 1967.

Goode, W. J. *World Revolution and Family Patterns.* New York: The Free Press, 1963.

Gordon, D. Identity and social commitment. In H. Mol (Ed), *Identity and Religion: International, Cross-Cultural Approaches.* Beverly Hills, CA: Sage Publications.

Gordon, D. The Jesus people: an identity synthesis. *Urban Life and Culture,* 1974, *3,* 159-178.

Hargrove, B. Evil eyes and religious choices. *Society,* (March/April) 1980, *17* (3), 20-24.

Harper, L. V. The young as a source of stimuli controlling caretaker behavior. *Developmental Psychology,* 1971, *4,* 73-88.

Harre, R. and Secord, P. F. *The Explanation of Social Behavior.* Totowa, N.J.: Littlefield, 1974.

Harre, R. *Social Being: A Theory for Social Psychology.* Basil Blackwell: Oxford, 1979.

Heirich, M. Change of heart: a test of some widely held theories about religious conversion. *American Journal of Sociology,* 1977, *83* (3), 653-680.

Holloman, R. Ritual opening and individual transformation: rites of passage at Esalen. *American Anthropologist,* 1974, *26,* 265-289.

Interchange 6. Population Reference Bureau, (May) 1977, 2-3.

Jahoda, M. Conformity and independence: a psychological analysis. *Human Relations,* 1959, *27,* 239-247.

Janis, I. L. and Gilmore, J. B. The influence of incentive conditions on the success of role playing in modifying attitudes. *Journal of Personality and Social Psychology,* 1965, *1,* 17-27.

Jellison, J. and Arkin, R. Social comparison of abilities: 'a self presentation approach to decision making in groups.' In J. Suls and R. Miller (Eds), *Social Comparison Processes: Theoretical and Empirical Perspectives.* New York: Halstead Press, 1979.

Johnson, R. Study of Extramarital Sex. In L. G. Smith and J. R. Smith (Eds), *Beyond Monogamy.* Baltimore: John Hopkins University Press, 1974.

Jourard, S. M. Re-inventing marriage: the perspective of a psychologist. In Herbert Otto (Ed), *The Family in Search of a Future.* New York: Appleton Century Crofts, 1970.

Kanter, R. M. *Commitment and Community: Communes and Utopias in Sociological Perspective.* Cambridge, Mass: Harvard University Press, 1972.

Keller, S. Does the family have a future? *Journal of Comparative Family Studies,* (Spring) 1971, 1-14.

Kelman, H. C. Compliance, identification, and internalization: three processes of attitude change. *Journal of Conflict Resolution,* 1958, *2,* 51-60.

Kim, B. Conversion and faith maintenance: the case of the Unification Church of Rev. Sun Myung Moon. Paper presented at the Annual Meeting of the Society for the Scientific Study of Religion, 1976.

Laing, R. D. and Easterson, A. *Sanity, Madness, and the Family: Families of Schizophrenics,* 2nd Edition. London: Tavistock Publications, 1970.

Laing, R. D. *The Politics of the Family and Other Essays.* New York: Pantheon Books, 1971.

Landis, P. H. *Making the Most of Marriage,* 5th Edition. New Jersey: Prentice Hall, Inc., 1975.

Levine, S. and Salter, N. E. Youth and contemporary religious movements: psychological findings. *Canadian Psychiatric Association Journal,* 1976, *21,* 411-420.

Levine, E. Deprogramming without tears. *Society,* (March/April) 1980a, *17* (3), 34-38.

Levine, E. Religious Cults: their implications for society and the democratic process. Paper presented at Annual Meeting of the International Society for Political Psychology, 1980b.

Lieberman, S. The effects of changes in roles on the attitudes of role occupants. *Human Relations,* 1956, *9,* 385-402.

Lifton, R. J. *Thought Reform and the Psychology of Totalism.* New York: Norton and Company, Inc., 1961.

Lifton, R. J. The Appeal of the Death Trip. *New York Times* magazine, (January 7) 1979.

Lifton, R. J. Lifton finds adolescents vulnerable to cult recruiting. *Journal of the American Family Foundation,* (February) 1980, *2* (1).

Macklin, E. D. Nonmarital heterosexual cohabitator. *Marriage and Family Review,* 1978, *1,* 1-12.

Magarrell, J. Women account for 93% enrollment gain. *Chronicle of Higher Education,* (January 9) 1978, 7-11.

Makepeace, J. M. The birth control revolution: consequences for college student life styles. Unpublished Ph.D. dissertation, Washington State University, 1975.

Meerloo, J. *The Rape of the Mind.* New York: Grosset and Dunlap, 1956.

Melville, K. *Marriage and Family Today.* New York: Random House, 1979.

Mills, C. W. Situated actions and vocabularies of motive. *American Sociological Review,* 1940, *5,* 904-913.

Miller, D. Deprogramming in historical perspective. In J. T. Richardson (Ed), *The Brainwashing/Deprogramming Controversy.* New Brunswick, N.J.: Transaction Books, forthcoming, 1980.

Nicholi, A. M. A new dimension of the youth culture. *American Journal of Psychiatry,* (April) 1974, *131* (4), 396-400.

Patrick, T. *Let Our Children Go.* New York: E. P. Dutton & Company, Inc., 1976.

Petersen, D. W. and Mauss, A. L. The cross and the commune: an interpretation of the Jesus people. In Glock (Ed), *Religion in Sociological Perspective,* Wadsworth Publishing Company, Inc., 1973.

Pilarzyk, T. Conversion and alternation processes in the youth culture: a comparative analysis of religious transformations. *Pacific Sociological Review,* (October) 1978, *21* (4), 379-405.

Ramey, J. W. Communes, group marriage and the upper-middle class. *Journal of Marriage and the Family,* 1972, *34,* 647-655.

Ramey, J. W. Intimate groups and networks: frequent consequences of sexually open marriage. *The Family Coordinator,* 1975, *24,* 515-530.

Ramey, J. Experimental family forms: the family of the future. *Marriage and Family Review,* 1978, *1* (1), 1-9.

Richardson, J. T., Simmonds, R. B., and Harder, M. W. Thought reform and the Jesus Movement. *Youth and Society, 4,* 185-200.

Richardson, J. T., Stewart, M., and Simmonds, R. B. *Organized Miracles.* New Brunswick, N.J.: Transaction Books, 1978a.

Richardson, J. T., Stewart, M., and Simmonds, R. B. Conversion to fundamentalism. *Society,* 1978b, *15* (4), 46-52.

Richardson, J. T. A New Paradigm for Conversion Research. A paper for the International Society for Political Psychology, Washington, D.C., 1979.

Richardson, J. T. and Kilbourne, B. Classical and contemporary brainwashing models: a comparison and critique. Presented at the International Society of Political Psychology Third Annual Meeting, (June 4) 1980.

Richardson, J. T. Conversion Careers. *Society,* (March/April) 1980, *17* (3), 47-50.

Robbins, T., Anthony, D., and Curtis, T. Youth culture religious movements: evaluating the integrative hypothesis. *Sociological Quarterly,* 1975, *16* (1), 48-64.

Robbins, T. 'Brainwashing' and religious freedom. *The Nation*, (April 30) 1977.

Robbins, T. and Anthony, D. New religions, families and brainwashing. *Society*, 1978 *15* (4), 77-83.

Robbins, T. and Anthony, D. Cults, brainwashing, and counter-subversion. *The Annals of the American Academy of Political and Sociological Science*, (November) 1979a.

Robbins, T. and Anthony, D. The limits of "Coercive Persuasion" as an explanation for conversion to authoritarian sects. Paper presented to the International Society of Political Psychologists, (May) 1979b.

Robbins, T. and Anthony, D. The "brainwashing metaphor as a social weapon": a new conceptual tool for the therapeutic state. To be published in J. Richardson (Ed), *The Brainwashing/Deprogramming Controversy: On Joining and Leaving New Religious Groups*, forthcoming, 1981.

Romanyshyn, J. M. Social Welfare: *Charity to Justice*. New York: Random House, 1971.

Rostow, W. W. *The Stages of Economic Growth*. New York: Cambridge University Press, 1960.

Sarbin, T. R. and Allen, V. L. Role Theory. In G. Lindzey and E. Aronson (Eds), *Handbook of Social Psychology*, 2nd Edition. Cambridge, Mass: Addison-Wesley, 1968, *1*.

Sargant, W. *Battle for the Mind*. Garden City, N.Y.: Doubleday, 1957.

Schein, E., Schneier, I., and Barker, C. H. *Coercive Persuasion*. New York: Norton, 1961.

Schwartz, L. L. and Kaslow, F. W. Religious cults, the individual and the family. *Journal of Marital and Family Therapy*, (April) 1979, 15-26.

Scott, M. B. and Lyman, S. M. Accounts. *American Sociological Review*, 1968, *33*, 46-62.

Shupe, A., Spielman, R., and Stigall, S. Cults of anti-cultism. *Society*, (March/April) 1980, *17* (3), 43-46.

Singer, M. T. Coming out of the cults. *Psychology Today*, (January) 1979a.

Singer, M. T. Psychological mechanisms of cult affiliation. Paper read to the American Psychological Association, New York, (September) 1979b.

Smith, J. and Smith L. Co-marital sex and the sexual freedom movement. *Journal of Sex Research*, 1970, *6*, 131-142.

Snow, D. A. and Phillips, C. L. The Lofland-Stark conversion model: a critical reassessment. *Social Problems*, (April) 1980, *27* (4), 430-447.

Solomon, T. Programming and Deprogramming the Moonies: brainwashing revisited. Unpublished manuscript, 1978.

Stark, T. and Bainbridge, W. S. Networks of faith: interpersonal bonds and recruitment to cults and sects. *American Journal of Sociology*, 1980, *85* (6), 1376-1395.

Stein, P. J. Singlehood: an alternative to marriage. *The Family Coordinator*, (October) 1975, *24*, 489-503.

Stein, P. J. The lifestyles and life chances of the never-married. *Marriage and Family Review*, 1978, *1* (4), 1-11.

Stolk, M. V. Who owns the child? *Childhood Education*, 1974, *50*, 259-265.

Stoner, C. and Parke, J. *All God's Children*. New York: Penguin Books, 1977.

Straus, R. Changing oneself: seekers and creative transformation of life experience. In J. Lofland (Ed), *Doing Social Life*, Wiley and Sons, 1976.

Straus, R. Religious Conversion as a personal and collective accomplishment. *Sociological Analysis*, 1979a, *40* (2), 158-165.

Straus, R. Inside Scientology: everyday life in a societally deviant world. Paper presented at the Annual Meetings of the Pacific Sociological Association, 1979b.

Straus, R. Becoming an "Insider": Toward subject-centered analysis of participation in Cults and other contemporary social worlds. Unpublished manuscript, 1979c.

Straus, R. Becoming a scientologist: a case study of career development in a cult-like social world. Unpublished manuscript, November, 1979d.

Szasz, Thomas. Some call it brainwashing. *New Republic*, 1961.

Taylor, B. Conversion and cognition: an area for empirical study in the micro-sociology of religious knowledge. *Social Compass*, 1976, *XXIII*, 5-22.

Tumin, M. M. Competing status systems. In Moore and Feidman (Eds.), *Labor Commitment and Social Change,* 1967, 280-282.

Ungerleider, J. T. and Wellisch, K. K. Coercive persuasion (brainwashing), religious cults, and deprogramming. *American Journal of Psychiatry,* (March) 1979, *136* (3), 279-282.

Ungerleider, J. The Programming (brainwashing)/Deprogramming Religious Controversy. Unpublished paper, 1980.

U. S. Bureau of the Census, 1976.

U. S. Department of Labor, Women's Bureau; Women Workers Today, Washington, D.C., 1976.

U. S. Department of Labor, Women's Bureau; Unpublished Data. Washington, D.C., 1979.

U. S. National Center for Health Statistics, (March) 1979.

U. S. President, Council of Economic Advisors, Economic Report of the President. Washington, D.C.: U. S. Government Printing Office, 1973.

Verdier, P. *Brainwashing and the Cults.* Hollywood, CA: Wilshire Book Co., 1977.

Weinstock, E., Tietze, C., Jaffe, F. S., and Dryfoos, J. G. Abortion Needs and Services in the United States, 1974-1975. *Family Planning Perspectives,* (March/April) 1976, *8,* 58-69.

Wilson, B. *The Noble Savage: The Primitive Origins of Charisma.* Berkeley: University of California, 1975a.

Wilson, B. The secularization debate. *Encounter,* 1975b, *45,* 77-83.

Wilson, B. *Contemporary Transformations of Religion.* Oxford: Oxford, 1976.

Winch, R. and Blumberg, R. L. Societal complexity and familial complexity: evidence for the curvilinear hypothesis. *American Journal of Sociology, 77,* 898-920.

Wirth, L. Urbanism as a way of life. *American Journal of Sociology,* 1938, *44,* 1-24.

Zablocki, B. *The Joyful Community.* Baltimore, MD: Penguin Books, 1971.

Zetterberg, H. The religious conversion as a change of social roles. *Sociology and Social Research,* (Jan-Feb.) 1952, *36* (3), 159-166.

# FAMILIES AND CULTS

Teresa Donati Marciano

## Introduction

Cults* have been perceived more or less condemningly as frontal assaults on the prior claims of families to their children's loyalty and beliefs. For those condemning, conversion to cults tends to be seen as a rejection of family religious heritage; because the cults so disproportionately attract youth, conversion is viewed as an often brutal rejection of parental authority.

These perceptions take several overlapping forms: those for whom such conversions are "coercive persuasion," or "brainwashing," with the dangers they hold for a free society (e.g., Conway and Seligman, 1979); ex-cultists who have been "de-programmed" or who dropped out dissatisfied with cult life (e.g., Edwards, 1979; Wood, 1979); and those who see in cults a threat to the longstanding wisdom and stability of Judaeo-Christian traditions (e.g., Rudin and Rudin, 1980; Enroth, 1979).

Jewish reaction has been particularly strong, and understandably so in demographic terms. Low Jewish fertility rates and high degrees of secularism (internally perceived) have evoked concerns over numerical and religious survival. Spero (1977), for example, cites an estimated twelve percent of American membership in the Unification Church (UC, or "Moonies") to be Jewish, a vastly disproportionate overrepresentation. While Christian evangelism is still perceived as a threat to the Jewish community, the cults have been a focus of special alarm (e.g., JCRC, 1978; Schwartz, 1978(a); Spero, 1977). But the clear nature of such evangelistic campaigns as "Key 73" now seem less threatening than the subtle, low-pressure approach that cults are perceived to use. There is also

---

Teresa Donati Marciano is professor of Sociology at Fairleigh Dickinson University, Teaneck, N.J.

---

*The term "cult" is used generically here to denote a variety of departures from "mainstream" religious patterns; the term includes groups holding "Eastern" religious and philosophical beliefs (e.g., Zen, Hare Krishna), and such "radical" Christian forms as Jesus People.

*101*

a sense of shared concern in many of the writings, with Christian families whose children are in cults or felt vulnerable to cult recruitment (e.g., Schwartz and Zemel, 1980).

Anti-cultists attack what they see as an abuse of First Amendment freedoms; there is a "conspiracy" theory of cults, implicit or explicit, in these writings. They contend that the social immaturity of the young leaves them prey to mind control via cult indoctrination; the repetitive preaching and chanting during and after the conversion overwhelms the free will of the convert, with lasting effects even after leaving the cult (e.g., Singer, 1979).

Non-condemning writers and researchers on the cults do not overtly endorse specific cult beliefs, but rather assume a posture of detachment. While some strong rapport can be found between researchers and cultists (e.g., Richardson et al., 1978), there is a sense that the cults' rationality is demonstrated by their providing access to researchers (e.g., Galanter et al., 1979; Judah, 1978, 1974). These writers are more likely to see benefits in cult memberships for those who had unhappy and/or drug-dependent lives before their affiliation with the cults (e.g., Anthony and Robbins, 1974). They see or imply a more fluid cultic process (converts moving into cults, others moving out) while the condemning writers see deception and psychological impairment resulting from membership. At this time, the weight of scholarly opinion seems to have swung against the alarmists.

What is apparent in all the writings is that the researchers, however they view the cults, do not seem to find them personally seductive. The researchers tend to be older than the modal age groups attracted to cults (or at least, the leaders of research teams are so). This in itself is an unexplored area for its implications: our culture may structure its generations so that a point of "immunity" is reached toward cult appeals. That immunity does not seem to hold in the case of the evangelicals, who are not included in the generic term "cults" as used here. Sharper age cutoffs appear where more "extreme" departures from prevalent religious practices occur. Correlates between age-linked susceptibility to cults and opportunity (to be where the cult recruiters are), are apparent throughout the literature, and strikingly so among ex-cultists (e.g., Wood). High rates of geographical mobility among the young, and campus living, are two instances of detachment from family control linked in the writings to cult recruitment. Levine and Salter (1976), for example, studied 106 members of nine groups (Hare Krishna, Divine Light, 3HO, UC, Foundation, Process, Jesus People, Scientology, and Children of God). The ages of respondents ranged from 17 to 30, with a median age of 21.5. The age connection has also been linked to the cults as outgrowths of the 1960's counterculture, though the Beats had made Zen visible a decade before (see, e.g., Prebish, 1978). The counterculture has now waned but the cults continue. If they—and particularly those based in Eastern beliefs—reflected the particular dissatisfactions of America in an unpopular war, a time of upheaval and alienation, what current needs do they meet? They evidently meet needs for many, but nowhere near a majority, of youth. They are also, for many of their members, transitory stages of life, points at which personal needs and group (cult) existence intersect. Some groups in fact invite or permit a type of membership which has the nature of occasional interaction and participation (e.g., Meher Baba—see Robbins, 1969—and the "external community" friendly to the Hare Krishna in New York and elsewhere). For some, then, the cults constitute a stage of more or less intense experimentation, an added step or role in the life sequence.[1]

Through the twenty years that have marked the noticeable rise of cults in the U.S., one characteristic seems to persist: the values they represent continue to be alternative primary values, substituting one kind of "familyhood" (intentional) for that which is biologically based. It is this substitution that is so strongly attacked by the anti-cultists. The major ways in which they support their case against cults include: personal testimony of ex-cultists or family members, which condemn cult tactics and effects (e.g., Wood, 1979; Edwards, 1979; Fraiman, 1979); and clinical samples wherein negative effects of cult membership on personal and family functioning are emphasized. Stressing the seduction of the naive young, these writings do tend to be marked by the absence of control groups, and the bias built into a use of clinical samples where the cult has already been defined as a "problem" (e.g., Schwartz and Kaslow, 1979; Schwartz, 1978 (a) and (b)).

The detached observers examine cult processes in one or more categories: structure (e.g., Eister, 1972; Lemert, 1975; Snow, Zurcher and Ekland-Olson, 1980; Wuthnow, 1980); culture (e.g., Staude, 1972; Roszak, 1973; Judah, 1974; Prince, 1974; Robbins, Anthony, Doucas and Curtis, 1976); and life-stages including the search for identity and answers to alienation (e.g., Levine and Salter, 1976; Wuthnow, 1978; Stone, 1978; Straus, 1970; and Richardson, 1980). Comparison groups for cult effects are found among these (e.g., Galanter et al., 1979), and where comparison samples are not available, these researchers note it as a flaw (e.g., Levine and Salter, 1976).

Cults are addressed from the standpoint of family processes giving rise to cult conversions, and the family is examined as a source of recruits. In this, a minority of youth are addressed, for we do not know why the unsuccess is so great for cults, though Wuthnow (1978) has attempted to distinguish this in his treatment of San Francisco Bay Area data. The difference between interest, participation, and distinterest, their correlates with social variables, remains to be synthesized generally and for the range of cults in America.

It must be remembered that the "vulnerability" of families to their children's involvement in cults, is part of the large pattern of vulnerability in "loss of children" in America. Children depart relatively early for college, and thence careers, learning and adopting norms of neolocality. Schools and jobs are patterned in neolocal expectations, and cults are the structural equivalents: they are neolocal forms of independently-chosen lifestyles.[2]

A family is "vulnerable" insofar as it can or cannot hold its children against other claims made upon them. From that perspective, two issues are examined at the outset: first, the degree to which families have successfully justified their prior claims on their children against claims of such other institutions as religion, or the state; second, the degree to which the cults' attractiveness represents one way of viewing the permeability of family boundaries in a "scientific" age.

## Prior Claims upon the Young

Who "owns" the child? In the West, this question has been moving toward the answer, "children own themselves." Except that they do not. For the movement toward children's rights has been marked by the claims of the state against the family and its parental authority, including the authority to impose or transmit religious beliefs. This has long been the case in the Soviet Union, which represents an example closer to a hypothetical (Weberian) "ideal type" of state claims, than any particular Western case. The Soviet example is therefore considered before the cases of Sweden and the U.S.

After the Bolshevik Revolution, children born out of wedlock were accorded the same legal rights as those born within marriage. Status determination (legitimacy) was therefore removed immediately from the family's traditional capacity to give its members "legal" standing in the national society. The state, rather than the family, conferred "legitimacy." The biological father was separated from the "social father," with the state assuming the latter role. (Legitimacy is no longer a discriminatory case in Sweden, and the U.S. appears to be evolving toward the same point. Once children are granted equality of inheritance, as happens now in the U.S. irrespective of "legitimate" birth, the next step would appear to be a discarding of "illegitimate" status, at least legally, and eventually, socially).

In the U.S.S.R., the Family Code over time very clearly represented the absolute capacity for state definitions within the family, and for state interpositions between parents and children. Parental rights, as explained by Makarenko (cited in Bronfenbrenner, 1968), are *delegated* by the state. (This is actually a logical correlate of the state as "father.") Parents have the joy of their children, but are raising them to be members of the collectivity, the larger society. As a result, prior claims by the state are implicit in all family law, so that children may be removed from their biological parents and placed under the state's "parentage" where there is neglect, alcoholism, drug abuse, where medical problems require special environments for the child, or where the parents live "anti-socially." That last is the strongest prior political claim by the state upon the family unit. Both the Family Code and criminal law can be invoked against parents who in some manner abuse their delegated parental authority.

Specific religious consequences arise from Family Code and criminal law configurations of parental rights. It is forbidden, for example, to send a child to religious instruction in a group setting, though in-family transmissions of religious values are not criminal acts. Any participation in religious groups not approved by and registered with the state, is a criminal act. Taking a child to religious rites not approved by the state, can be and has been interpreted by the courts as constituting moral and physical endangerment of the child. A case against parents would of course be even stronger where religious beliefs prohibited children's participation in the state school system, service in the military, or membership in Komsomol.[3]

Recently, these laws based in the idea of delegation of parental authority have been invoked against Baptists in the Soviet Union. Children have been removed from their parents' custody in an assertion of the rights of the state and the greater society, against the Baptists' claims of rights to teach their religion to their young (see Juviler, 1978; 1977).

While this may be considered an "extreme" case of state interposition, it does not actually differ substantially in result from the many kinds of interposition already in existence in the West. In Sweden, for example, a law was passed three years ago which prohibits the use of corporal punishment by parents against their children. There are no legal sanctions to this law, yet it is an assertion of prior claims of the state to the form of discipline allowed to be exercised on children.

There are no cases in the West, however different the political processes, where courts cannot do what is done in the Soviet Union. The removal of children from neglectful and abusing parents, the rescue of children from moral and physical danger, is if anything often perceived as insufficient in its exercise by the courts. Battered children who die as a result of court inaction, or as a result of untimely return to battering families, are held up as instances of state cowardice, court ignorance, and inadequate exercises of interposition power.

The rights of children to separate themselves from parental authority has also been a recent issue in the U.S. One such case is that of Walter Polvochak, who has sought court and state interposition to prevent his parents from compelling his return with them to the Soviet Union (U.S. News, 1980). While there is also an issue of political refuge here, the courts have held in favor of a child against its parents who were moving to another state and wanted to take the child with them (Castillo, 1980).

If children belong to themselves, they must still find their rights in an authority external to their parents. In the sense that people "belong" to those who have some controls over them, whether of love or law, they "belong" more to the state than to parents, where the generations are adversaries in the courts. It of course raises the question, "Qui custodiet custodiens?"—who will guard the guardians; for in determining children's rights and "best interests," the courts *are* owners of the children's fates, and as such are "alternative parents." (See, e.g., Holgate, 1980, for the ways in which children's rights are weighed against those of parents').

There are many involuntary consequences upon children of religious beliefs that courts will not accept. Compromises over education have been made with Amish and Hutterite communities, but children do have power in the courts. A minor child's "adult" or "rational" decision to abide by the consequences of a religious belief will be upheld, typically, by the courts. Cases involving Jehovah's Witnesses are excellent examples of distinctions the courts have made in this matter. In 1977, for example, a 16-year-old girl was in a coma after an auto accident; her parents, in keeping with their faith, objected to the blood transfusions doctors had ordered for her. The court ordered the transfusions (New York Times, Oct. 25, 1977). But those children not comatose or otherwise adjudged to be incompetent to make their own decisions, have had their religious wishes respected by the courts. In 1978, a 13-year-old girl died of Fanconi's aplastic anemia. She had refused bone marrow transplants from her sister, partly out of fears for possible danger to her sister, partly because of her

Jehovah's Witnesses' beliefs. The court honored her decision over doctors' objections (New York Times, Oct. 26, 1978).

With the cults, the court decision history has been mixed, though now-respectable religions have had their court conflicts in the past.[4] The cults present a case not of the minor child against parents, but of parents against a child who is no longer a minor. The major legal recourse of parents against cults was in the period 1975–1977, when conservatorship (in California) was allowed, so that parents could take custody of their non-minor children. In 1977 the California courts overturned this type of action, though after the Jonestown debacle, new fears arose over cults and conservatorships were once again tested (Robbins, 1979).

Neither the attackers nor defenders of cults see much hope of successful legal recourse against cults today. Schwartz and Zemel (1980) recount cases where, for example, "mind control" arguments against Hare Krishna were not upheld. But these authors do argue for a therapeutic model to be applied to cult converts, to justify the intervention of the courts on the issue of "informed consent."

The attack on the medical model is an attack also on court intervention in cult memberships (Robbins and Anthony, 1980 (a) and (b)). They summarize (1980(b)) the benefits of cult membership revealed by an array of studies as well as their own research. Taking the individual-benefit view against the family-under-attack view of the anti-cult writers, they find cult members to be happier, in drug-free lives, more directed, and with reduced neurotic disorder. They attack retrospective accounts of ex-cultists as a negotiated reconstruction of the past, in parental and therapeutic contexts. While not disputing the possibility of pathology as an outcome of cult membership, they strongly disagree with the view that there is an inevitable relationship between membership and pathology, and the court intervention that results.

While court recourse both against cults and against deprogrammers are now relatively unsuccessful, there was a 1980 case (New York Times, August 29, 1980) in which a Federal court awarded a father monetary judgment against the Unification Church. The court upheld the father's contention that his parental rights had been violated by the UC's recruitment of his daughter five years earlier, when she was sixteen years of age.

The continuing recourse by families to courts, however (un)successful, is an outcome of permeable family boundaries, which are evolutionary, and which in modern times has been shaped by the influence of science upon culture.

## Family Boundaries and the Cults

Not all parents object to their children's joining cults; not all children are dragged away from them, kidnapped, summoned to court, or in other ways forced out of the cults. In fact, deprogrammer attacks upon the cults (such as those made by Ted Patrick, a noted deprogrammer), in the view of Robbins and Anthony (1980(a)), are guilty of the "generic fallacy" which assumes all cult movements to be essentially similar, negative, notorious configurations on the American scene. Not only do they find wide differences among cults, but they show that converts are not "passive victims" in an evil process; they, along with Bromley and Shupe (1979) and Straus (1970) see an active pattern between convert and group, that often benefits the recruit.

In Judah's (1978) data, which he sees as tentative and which are directed toward the question of religious liberty for cults, he notes that for the UC, relatively few who attend weekend workshops are converted or even remain for a longer period beyond the weekend. He sees cult converts as not significantly different from more "mainline" religious conversions, and warns that censure of religions which perform no illegal acts, threaten the religious freedom of all.

There has already been a growth of religious hostility toward law (given the mutually antagonistic claims between them) in industrialized society, and shown by Long (1980). He points to the evangelical response on such issues as abortion and gay rights. Adams (1979) in fact points out that the major First Amendment issue today is not one of establishment, but of the free exercise of religion. Ironically, the evangelicals who strongly object to cult practices are also at risk, then, in terms of their own religious freedoms.

To understand why the evangelicals have apparently had an easier time than cults in obtaining First Amendment guarantees and Fourteenth Amendment equal protection of laws, one need only look at cultural assumptions behind the legal and family systems. Kuhn's (1970) work on paradigms and scientific revolutions, celebrates the triumph of science itself in western culture. The evangelicals have made much more progress in adopting scientific means of defending biblical belief, particularly in showing that the two are complementary rather than contradictory. They have, in Mary Douglas's terms, (1965) moved from a pre-Copernican to a Copernican view of the world (i.e., governed by impersonal scientific laws. See also, Kuhn, 1957). Unless religion learns to function in the language of science, it cannot defend its "rationality" or rightness in modern terms. The idea of "speaking two different languages," out of the two different paradigms of science and religion, is illustrated by Ammerman (1980), who sees conversion to fundamentalism as a process of acquiring a new (archaic) biblical language to support an archaic view of the world. The more scientifically respectable evangelism goes the other way, illustrating biblical truths in the discoveries in psychotherapy, paleontology, and physics.

Just as scientists have gained exclusive judgment over what constitutes rational defense of a given position, within science, the medical profession has gained exclusive power over defining illness. Robbins and Anthony (1980(b)), in showing this, complete the picture of why cult members and families do not seem to "hear" each other, especially at the beginning of deprogramming experiences. The converts are defined as sick (when they often do not feel so), and defend themselves in categories their parents cannot recognize as rational or valid. In upholding any "medical model of cultist pathology" (Robbins and Anthony, 1980(b)), then, the courts become arms of the scientific state, and excercise interposition powers in terms of those understandings.

## Cults and Family Systems

Because not all families oppose their children's cult participation, the conditions of antagonism are of special interest. What generates such bitterness and contention among parents, children, and cults? For the sake of analysis, that contention will be viewed from the perspective of family process dysfunction. It is by no means the only possible approach, but can serve to point out the apparent contradictions (happiness or misery) that show up in various writings. The framework is Murray Bowen's (1976) family systems approach to family process (known officially since 1975 as Bowen Theory).

When a family opposes a cult, it opposes the role of a particular significant other in its physical and mental structure. In any culture, the acceptability of a significant other is value-determined; in a scientific culture, "rational" arguments against a significant other tend to be powerful. Where the cult is viewed as a detrimental significant other, families actually interpret membership as dysfunctional for the convert member. But while membership can be a sign of personal dysfunction (as can a multitude of other actions), there is no proof that cults *cause* dysfunction. They may be causal, or enhance dysfunction, but cult membership is not a predominant sign in the literature of new dysfunctions among members. There is ample evidence that prior experimentation with alternative religions, "intentional families," "alternative lifestyles," characterizes cult members. Even among the anti-cult writers, there is evidence of confusion, dissatisfaction, family problems, and alienation preceding membership for many adherents (e.g., Singer, 1979; Harrison, 1979; Galanter et al., 1979; Levine and Salter, 1976; Robbins and Anthony, 1972, 1980(a) and (b); Sage, 1976; Schwartz and Kaslow, 1979). For the youthful convert, the cult may be a resolution (at least temporarily) of family and personal conflict; the cult may be a way out of a "triangle."

Triangles, in Bowen theory, are expressions of dysfunction: a "triangled" child is one who is acting out the conflicts between two other family members, such as the parents. Gaining control over that process and oneself, is "detriangling." Another group, outside the family, may be necessary to provide support in the child's attempt to gain control. If anything, the descriptions of young cult members coming out of drug-using lifestyles (a possible symptom of triangling) into drug-free cult lives, could be considered a substitution of symptom, but could also be a route to freedom.

The literature shows that cult membership, despite the emotional intensity of religious conversion processes, still involves teaching rules, assumptions, and expectations. Strong rules and strong roles may be found for the first time in the cult. A convert may remain very happy, or find dissatisfaction levels rising (viz. Singer, 1979). Clearly recognizable sources of and reaction to dissatisfactions may thus be apparent for the first time. The very "familyhood" of the various cults may enhance this awareness of problems in one's role as a child in a family. (By way of illustration: Edwards, 1979, reports the use of the term "heavenly kids," i.e., "children" in cult life, by the UC recruiters.) Short of obsessional and constant involvement, there are bound to be periods of letdown, fatigue, and perhaps doubt. Those who drift away or drop out may reflect the process of having to come to terms with sources of their own (un)happiness; and whether in or out of the cult, the (ex)member may finally have an experience not obtainable elsewhere for self-analysis. It is unknown whether, in post-membership therapy, therapeutic definitions of membership exacerbate dysfunction. Especially where a child has been "kidnapped" from a cult, and deprogrammed, there has not been the time to arrive at one's own perspective on the cult, and its long-term value to the member.

This does not mean that the cult is a conscious therapy or necessary phase of growth; it simply points out the latent consequences of cult membership where the member comes out of a dysfunctional family system. It may also have latent consequences for the family, causing them to find a new center around which to organize, displacing inner conflicts on outside entities.

Examples of support for this framework-view of cult membership can be drawn from the findings of Schwartz and Kaslow (1979), who are negative toward cults, and Levine and Slater (1976), who are among the detached observers.

Schwartz and Kaslow (1979) start with structural conditions of adolescence in the U.S., the boredom and difficult relationships with families that abound. Compounding these difficulties, they cite family enmeshment (overinvolvement of family members in each other), in a culture that values personal autonomy. They see the more-enmeshed group, the cult, as a way of resolving that conflict, since it is so strong a resolution. Note that detached observers find the same sorts of family problems (e.g., Galanter et al., 1979; Robbins, 1969; Robbins and Anthony, 1972). Schwartz and Kaslow, however, object to cult life as a resolution of conflict, seeing it as deleterious to individual development. Yet they go on to describe characteristics of cult-vulnerable families: double messages from parents (e.g., avowing love for children but sending them off to camp, school, etc., to free parents from children's demands); poor father-child relationships out of which the cult leader (e.g., Moon) serves as a substitute father figure; loners and depressed children; those conflicted about sexual pressures or the demands of adulthood; those needing affiliation and dependency who had previously used drugs to satisfy these needs. The authors feel that the love and solicitude offered the new recruit ("love bombing"), because the youth are so vulnerable, constitute "coercive persuasion." They draw a specific distinction between such totalistic groups as Mormons, Amish, and Orthodox Jews, and the cults, in the fact that the first three promote full-family participation. But the distinction overlooks the fact that the family is often already troubled when the cult becomes a choice. The idea of the cult as a transitional phase to personal wholeness is rejected out of evidence of physical neglect, poor nutrition, and insufficient sleep. Yet they add data on family impact which shows youth fearing to be entrapped by their biological families once again, and parental fears of renewing family battles. Because the authors view the cults as deceptions, they see validity in the parental view of cult members as children rather than as adults; this is justified by the child-like dependence they see in the member-cult relationship. To their credit, the authors recommend family therapy or concurrent treatment in post-cult dealings with families. But they at no point mention relatively untroubled continuation in the cults, nor voluntary departure from them.

The view of cults as false solutions persists even where studies are cited which show a reduction of earlier psychological problems and distress. Rudin and Rudin (1980) cite Galanter's various studies e.g., of the UC and the Divine Light Mission, showing these positive effects (though the book does not use consistent or scholarly citation). They also cite the cults as caring communities that counter modern isolation and loneliness, but see them as inauthentic substitutes for the family and religion of origin. What Prince (1974) called "cocoon work," religious/mystical practices (rites of passage) bridging the gap between childhood and adulthood, is a positive view of the same outcome of dysfunction.

Levine and Salter (1976) find similar patterns, though not in clinical samples. Most of their respondents reported their parents having an "average or good" relationship, with the exception of the Children of God. (This is particularly interesting because FREECOG—Free Our Children from the Children of God—was the first major anti-cult parents' group, which became the Citizens Freedom Foundation, the largest current anti-cult group. It is a case where degree of antagonism matches reported family dysfunction). Among those reporting a good parental marital relationship, there were still 43 who wanted to get away from the home environment. Reasons for joining the cults ranged from feelings of loneliness, rejection, sadness and non-belonging (46), to those seeking meaning in life (43), to having been impressed by the happiness of the recruiters (32); to unpleasant or disastrous family situations, personal situations, or crises. Intrapsychic and interpersonal benefits from cult membership were reported by 80%, with 77% reporting they felt more secure and self-confident, and 64% reporting greater happiness, calm, and better health. All reported the benefit of closer friends, more and better friends. The authors report diminished anxiety and depression among the members, and conclude that the cults fill personal needs and a social void.

In light of these findings, parental attitudes toward cults and post-cult therapeutic assumptions must be re-evaluated. There are both hints and outright evidence that cults externalize family tensions; and for those who drop out and then recriminate against the cults, Robbins and Anthony (1980(a)) say this may provide the ex-convert with a new sense of identity, purpose, and meaning. Cults thus are an alternative to the family system, leading to a consideration of the deprivation thesis, from the point of view of family deprivation.

## Family Status Deprivation

The "deprivation hypothesis" as presented in the sociology of religion, views religion as possessing special functions for the disinherited (Lanternari, 1965). Liston Pope (1942) in his classic study of working class response to religious messages, advanced the idea of religious status as an alternative or substitute for social status.

The deprivation hypothesis was expanded by the work of Glock and Stark (1965) who set forth five kinds of deprivation which may find religious compensation: economic, social, psychic, ethical, and organizational (or communal). As religious substitutions for worldly deprivations begin to occur, the adherent undergoes a process of resocialization to the new, compensatory values. Lofland (1966) and Lofland and Stark (1965), studying the UC, describe in this process anger and resentment against the secular order, and a renunciation/rejection of the depriving condition (the secular society). As the member becomes more ardently involved, the sense is enhanced of gaining something far better than the world offers.

Anthony and Robbins (1974) found in the Meher Baba movement a compensation for ethical deprivation (a sense of being forced to live according to values one does not truly hold, and of being unable to live in accord with values in which one truly believes). Meher Baba followers work at their jobs in the world, serving others, and realizing their loving feelings toward humankind. Of all types of deprivation in the literature, this seems to fit most closely with the sense of the 1960's era, with its "love" ethic and countercultural pressures. It is also an important study as a jumping-off point from which to view current cult appeals. In a later article, Robbins et al. (1976) found in the UC and activist dimension that compensates for communal deprivation, for the loss of a sense of community.

Religion is not the only means to resolve feelings of deprivation; revolution and madness are two other alternatives. Lofland and Stark (1965) cite these political, religious, and psychiatric alternatives in resolving deprivation. Winter (1977: 146-148) has an excellent review of the literature which has sought clues as to why religion rather than other means, is chosen as an avenue of compensation for deprivation. Where it is chosen, the gap between felt deprivation and compensation would be a predictor of dissatisfaction with, and numbers leaving, the cults. To the extent that cultists seek family status resolutions, they experience "family status deprivation" before joining. The convert may find compensation for specific family roles that were denied, confused, or poorly realized; in the cult there is finally a chance to be a child, and to experience a "normal" sequence of roles leading to spiritual "adulthood."

It may be that the countercultural legacy has been modified or reversed in this process, with "impulse" giving way to "institution" (Turner's (1977) categories) as the locus of self. Turner saw a shift from institution to impulse at the time of his writing, and described the key differences between the two as follows (1977: 992–995): the institutional locus is where the real self adheres to high standards despite temptation or crises; it exists where the individual is in full control of action; failure to live up to internal standards or ideals constitutes hypocrisy; but impulsives reveal the true self in doing what one truly and spontaneously wants to do; true self is discovered rather than created, through the aid of inhibition-reducing drugs and alcohol; hypocrisy consists of living according to externally-imposed standards. These are "ideal types," of course, with most people falling into some combination of the two. And high rates of the formerly drug-dependent, and aimless (time disorientation) among converts would indicate a shift back from impulse, to the curative effect of cultic, institutional goals. Cult rules, often far clearer than family rules, set a new locus of self and compensate for deprivation of family satisfaction.

The cults may have adapted better, then, to the waning of the counterculture, than many who lived in it, and even than many who once denounced it.

## NOTES

1. An increased number of stages or steps in status and role sequences for the young was previously noted (Marciano, 1975: 417), where "communes may serve in the role sequence as future equivalents of monastic retreat houses in the middle ages. They become a place in which to live intensely a certain value-style. . . . As then, so in the future, communes may constitute places of renewal, self-integration, and alternative experience." This holds true as well for the cults, or for any "new" option evolving out of cultural re-formations.

2. An early "cultist" was St. Francis of Assisi, who as a young man had turned back from the Crusades, and who then received a a vision of rebuilding the church. Inspired by his new understanding of Christianity, he gave away his cloth-merchant father's goods, suffered parental displeasure for his impulse, stripped himself naked in front of the local bishop to demonstrate his rejection of earthly claims upon him (including his father's claims), and went on to found an order marked by extreme commitment to poverty, humility, and joy. His "cult" was, however, absorbed in the larger structural framework or "umbrella" of the Roman church, which could set recognizable parameters around his beliefs. Parents were very alarmed over Francis' appeal to their children, and often vehemently opposed their idealistic

determination to join the saint. The common religious backdrop in which all were living, served to help parents reconcile their objections over time. The hegemony of the Roman church raises the issue of scale, with the capacity for a structure of any given size to absorb or integrate variants. It must also be noted that "pure" Franciscan form did give way to far less ascetic practices over time.

3. I am indebted to Wesley Fisher, of Columbia University, and Peter Juviler of Barnard College, for their help in providing materials, comments, and sources for this section of the article.

4. The contrast should not be taken as a necessarily continuing one. Just as Jehovah's Witnesses, and before them Mormons, were once "suspect" in the eyes of the courts, any of the cults may achieve the same type of "religious respectability" over time. In fact there is probably already a gradient of "respectability" among the cults, with Zen among the most relatively respectable.

## REFERENCES

Adams, W.M. An overview of the religious discrimination issue, U.S. Commission on Civil Rights. *Religious Discrimination: A Neglected Issue*. Washington, D.C.(April 9-10) 1979.

Ammerman, N.T. Learning a foreign language—participating in fundamentalism. Paper presented to the Association for the Sociology of Religion, August 1980.

Anthony, D. and Robbins, T.R. The Meher Baba movement: Its effect on postadolescent youthful alienation. In I. Zaretsky and M. Leone (Eds), *Religious Movements in Contemporary America*. Princeton: Princeton University Press, 1974.

Bown, M. Theory in the practice of psychotherapy. In P.J. Guerin (Ed ), *Family Therapy: Theory and Practice*. New York: Gardner Press, 1976.

Bromley, D.G. and Shupe, A.D., Jr. Just a few years seem like a lifetime: A role theory approach to participation in religious movements. In L. Kriesberg (Ed), *Research in Social Movements, Conflicts and Change*. Vol. 2. Greenwich, Conn.: JAI Press, 1979.

Bronfenbrenner, U. The changing Soviet family. In D.R. Brown (Ed), *The Role and Status of Women in the Soviet Union*. New York: Teachers College Press, 1968.

Castillo, A. Children sue parents: Who controls the child's life? *New York Times,*(October 11) 1980, 21.

Conway, F. and Seligman, J. *Snapping: America's Epidemic of Sudden Personality Change*. New York: Delta, 1979.

Douglas, M. *Purity and Danger*. London: Routledge and Kegan Paul, 1966.

Edwards, C. *Crazy For God*. Englewood Cliffs, NJ: Prentice-Hall, 1979.

Eister, A.W. An outline of a structural theory of cults. *J. for The Scientific Study of Religion,* 1972, *11*, 319-333.

Enroth, D. *The Lure of the Cults*. Chappaqua, NJ: Christian Herald Books, 1979.

Fraiman, P.I. I lost my brother to a cult. *Reform Judaism,* 1979, *7*, 1,5,7.

Galanter, M., Rabkin, R., Rabkin, J. and Deutsch, A. The "Moonies": A psychological study of conversion and membership in a contemporary religious sect. *American Journal of Psychiatry,* 1979, *1363*, 165-170.

Glock, C.Y. and Stark, R. *Religion and Society In Tension*. Chicago: Rand-McNally, 1965.

Harrison, B.G. The struggle for Wendy Helander. *McCall's,*(October) 1979, 87-94.

Houlgate, L.D. *The Child And The State: A Normative Theory of Juvenile Rights*. Baltimore: Johns Hopkins Press, 1980.

Jewish Community Relations Committee. *The Challenge of the Cults*. Philadelphia, 1978.

Judah, J.S. *Hare Krishna and the Counterculture*. New York: Wiley, 1974.

Judah, J.S. New religions and religious liberty. In J. Needleman and G. Baker (Eds.), *Understanding the New Religions*. New York: Seabury Press, 1978.

Juviler, P.H. Law and the delinquent family: Reproduction and upbringing. In D.D. Barry, G. Ginsburgs, and P.B. Maggs (Eds), *Soviet Law After Stalin. Part Two. Social Engineering Through Law.* Alphen aan-den-Rijn, The Netherlands: Sijthoff and Nordhoff, 1978.

Juliver, P.H. Women and sex in Soviet law. In D. Atkinson, A. Dallin, and G. Lapidus (Eds), *Women In Russia.* Stanford, Calif.: Stanford University Press, 1977.

Kuhn, T.S. *The Copernican Revolution.* Cambridge, Mass.: Harvard University Press, 1957.

Kuhn, T. S. *The Structure of Scientific Revolutions.* Second Edition. Chicago: University of Chicago Press, 1970.

Lanternari, V. *The Religions of the Oppressed.* New York: Mentor, 1965.

Lemert, C.C. Social structure and the absent center: An alternative to new sociologies of religion. *Sociological Analysis,* 1975, *36,* 95-107.

Levine, S.V. and Salter, N.E. Youth and contemporary religious movements: Psychosocial findings. *Canadian Psychiatric Association Journal,* 1976, *21,* 411-420.

Lofland, J. *Doomsday Cult.* Englewood Cliffs, NJ: Prentice-Hall, 1966.

Lofland, J. and Stark, R. Becoming a world-saver: A theory of conversion to a deviant perspective. *American Sociological Review,* 1965, *30,* 862-875.

Long, T.E. Religion, law and social control in modern society. Paper presented to the Association for the Sociology of Religion,(August)1980.

Malinowski, B. *Magic, Science and Religion.* New York: Free Press, 1954.

Marciano, T.D. Variant family forms in a world perspective. *The Family Coordinator,* 1975, *24,* 407-420.

Pope, L. *Millhands and Preachers.* New Haven: Yale University Press, 1942.

Prebish, C. Reflections on the transmission of Buddhism to America. In J. Needleman and G. Baker (Eds ), *Understanding the New Religions.* New York: Seabury Press, 1978.

Prince, R.H. Cocoon work: An interpretation of the concern of contemporary youth with the mystical. In I.I. Zaretsky and M.P. Leone (Eds), *Religious Movements in Contemporary America.* Princeton: Princeton University Press, 1974.

Richardson, J.T. Conversion careers. *Society,* 1980, *17,* 47-50.

Richardson, J.T., Stewart, M.W., and Simmonds, R.B. Researching a fundamentalist commune. In J. Needleman and G. Baker (Eds), *Understanding the New Religions.* New York: Seabury Press, 1978.

Robbins, T. Eastern mysticism and the resocialization of drug users. *J. for the Scientific Study of Religion,* 1969, *8,* 300-317.

Robbins, T. Cults and the therapeutic state. *Social Policy,* (May-June) 1979, 42-46.

Robbins, T. and Anthony, D. The limits of "coercive persuasion" as an explanation for conversion to authoritarian sects. Forthcoming, *Political Psychology,* (Fall) 1980 (a).

Robbins, T. and Anthony, D. The medicalization of deviant religion: Preliminary observations and critique. Program for the Study of New Religions, Graduate Theological Union, Berkeley, Calif., 1980 (b).

Robbins, T., Anthony, D., Doucas, M., and Curtis, T. The last civil religion: Reverend Moon and the Unification Church. *Sociological Analysis,* 1976, *37,* 111-125.

Roszak, T. *Where The Wasteland Ends.* New York: Anchor Books, 1973.

Rudin, A.J. and Rudin, M.R. *Prison Or Paradise? The New Religious Cults.* Philadelphia: Fortress Press, 1980.

Sage, W. The war on the cults. *Human Behavior,* 1976, *5,* 40-49.

Schwartz, L.L. Cults and the vulnerability of Jewish youth. *Jewish Education,* 1978 a , *46,* 23-26.

Schwartz, L.L. A note on family rights, cults, and the law. *J. of Jewish Communal Service,* 1978b, *55,* 194-198.

Schwartz, L.L. and Kaslow, F.W. Religious cults, the individual and the family. *J. of Marital and Family Therapy,* 1979, *5,* 15-26.

Schwartz, L.L. and Zemel, J.I. Religious cults: Family concerns and the law. *J. of Marital and Family Therapy,* 1980, *6,* 301-307.

Singer, M.T. Coming out of the cults. *Psychology Today,* 1979, *12,* 72-82.

Snow, D.A., Zurcher, L.A., and Ekland-Olson, S. Social networks and social movements: A microstructural approach. *American Sociological Review,* 1980, *45,* 787-801.

Spero, M.H. Cults: Some theoretical and practical perspectives. *J. of Jewish Communal Service,* 1977, *53,* 330-338.

Staude, J.R. Alienated youth and the cult of the occult. In M.L. Medley and J.E. Conyers (Eds), *Sociology For the Seventies.* New York: Wiley, 1972.

Stone, D. New religious consciousness and personal religious experience. *Sociological Analysis,* 1978, *39,* 123-234.

Straus, R. Religious conversion as a personal and collective accomplishment. *Sociological Analysis,* 1970, *40,* 158-165.

Turner, R.H. The real self: From institution to impulse. *American Journal of Sociology,* 1977, *81,* 989-1016.

U.S. News and World Report 89,(September 1) 1980: 39-40.

Winter, J.A. *Continuities in the Sociology of Religion.* New York: Harper and Row, 1977.

Wood, A.T. *Moonstruck: A Memoir of My Life in a Cult.* New York: Morrow, 1979.

Wuthnow, R. Religion in the world-system. In A.J. Bergesen (Ed), *Studies of the Modern World System.* New York: Academic Press, 1980.

Wuthnow, R. *Experimentation in American Religion: The New Mysticisms and Their Implications.* Berkeley: University of California Press, 1978.

# PERFECT FAMILIES: VISIONS OF THE FUTURE IN A NEW RELIGIOUS MOVEMENT

David G. Bromley
Anson D. Shupe, Jr.
Donna L. Oliver

Early in the 1970s a number of new religious movements appeared in the United States; these groups included the Children of God, Hare Krishna, Divine Light Mission, Scientology, and Unification Church. During that decade several of these movements achieved rapid growth by appealing primarily to young adults (i.e., late teens through mid-twenties). The new religions quickly became embroiled in the most intense religious controversy of the last several decades, a controversy which emanated largely from the struggle between parents of members of these movements and the new religions themselves.

There are two ways in which the family is central to this conflict. First, the most visible of the new religious movements are organized communally, and the communal group serves many of the functions of families. In some cases the familial organization and symbolism is quite explicit, and hence members both join a family-like organization and over time begin to form their own families of procreation within the movement. Second, the opposition to the new religions, which we refer to as the Anti-Cult Movement (Shupe and Bromley, 1980), is composed mainly of parents of individuals who join one of the new religions.

A great deal has been written about the family—new religion conflict by proponents on both sides of the dispute (American Civil Liberties Union, 1977; American Family Foundation, 1979), individual families (Underwood and Underwood, 1979) and social scientists of various persuasions (Bromley and Shupe, 1981; Shupe and Bromley, 1980; Enroth, 1977 and

David G. Bromley is an associate professor and chairman, Department of Sociology, University of Hartford, Anson D. Shupe, Jr. is an associate professor in the department of Sociology, University of Texas at Arlington, and Donna L. Oliver is a doctoral candidate at the University of Massachusetts.

This paper is the product of a combined effort. Authorship is ordered randomly and does not indicate a difference in contribution.

1979), but much less consideration has been given to the organizational logic of the new religions (Bromley and Shupe, 1979a) and aspirations of their members. Therefore, in this paper we shall examine the family structure as it is idealized in the ideology of the Unification Church and as it is envisioned by members of that Church who are moving toward family formation. We have selected the Unification Church as an illustrative case because it has been singled out as the archetypical "cult" by the Anti-Cult Movement and because it has developed and legitimated an alternative family structure most fully.

## Data and Methods

In the fall of 1978, we surveyed 67 members of the Unification Church who were enrolled in the Unification Theological Seminary. The sample constituted approximately two-thirds of the Seminary's student body. Participants were volunteers, and each was assured of personal anonymity. Our access of the study body was gained largely as a result of contacts established in the course of our broader research on the Unification Church (Bromley and Shupe, 1979b). However, other social scientists were also conducting research on church members as at least some church leaders felt that the findings from such research would help to dispel the Church's negative public image. The entire student body, therefore, had been urged to cooperate with the survey. Church officials in no way sought to influence the content of the survey and to the best of our knowledge made no attempt to influence the responses of participants.

The survey focused on Church members' *plans* for marriage and family formation. We stress plans because, like the church membership generally, the vast majority (85 percent) of our sample were unmarried (i.e., never married or divorced); only 15 percent had married since joining the Church.[1] In addition to marital status, our sample is in other respects representative of the movement as a whole. The imbalanced sex ratio (78 percent male and 22 percent female) reflects a continuing problem the Church faces in gaining female members as well as a general predominance of male leadership within the Church. Further, like Church membership as a whole, our respondents were mostly young adults; 15 percent were 25 or younger, 73 percent were 30 or younger and 95 percent were 35 or younger. Finally, racial ethnic and religious backgrounds also are roughly representative. Ninety-one percent of our respondents were caucasian with the rest divided between hispanics and orientals.[2] Religious background was much more diversified. While 37 percent of our respondents were former Catholics, the remainder were scattered among nine different denominational back-grounds.

At the same time our respondents clearly constituted the elite of church membership. Individuals selected to enter the Unification Theological Seminary were more highly educated (99 percent had completed college) than members in general in addition to having demonstrated leadership potential in their church assigned activities. Our respondents had been Church members longer than average; fully 86 percent had joined in 1975 or earlier. It should be added, however, that due to the recent growth of the Church and rapid turnover in membership the majority of respondents (66 percent) had been members for between three and five years. Our respondents, therefore, probably were more articulate and had given more consideration to their futures in the Church than the average member.

### The Family in Unificationist Ideology

Family is one of the most important, if not the central concept, in Unification theology. According to the revelations contained in the *Divine Principle* (HSA-UWC, 1977), God created Adam and Eve who were, according to divine plan, to form a trinity i.e., a family comprised of father, mother and children, based on God. The future was not entirely predetermined, however, as God had ceded to mankind a portion of responsibility for its own destiny in the process of creation. By allowing herself to be sexually seduced, Eve failed to fulfill this responsibility. Rather than forming families centered on God all future generations were centered on Satan and bore the stigma of their satanic lineage. This was the "fall of man."[3] Virtually all of mankind's problems emanated directly or indirectly from this tragic error and his now "fallen nature."

Because mankind had been accorded a portion of responsibility by God and had abdicated that responsibility, the payment of indemnity became necessary for man's restoration to God. God did not interfere with this process, but when sufficient indemnity was paid, opportunities for restoration were proferred. Throughout history a number of "central figures" (including Noah, Abraham and Jesus) appeared at times when sufficient indemnity had been paid to win another opportunity for restoration. In each case, however, these missions had failed. Jesus was the last such central figure, but he too failed to complete the mission of restoration as a result of his crucifixion. He had succeeded in restoring the world *spiritually* but his untimely death prevented *physical* restoration i.e., the formation of a family and the initiation of a God-centered lineage.

It was the failure of Jesus to complete the restoration process that made necessary a new messiah, the Lord of the Second Advent. Now, nearly two thousand years after the mission of Jesus, sufficient indemnity has been paid to earn another opportunity for restoration. In fact, according to Unificationist theology, the new messiah has already been born and begun anew the quest for restoration. Since Moon is widely perceived within the Church to be the new messiah and the new messiah's primary mission is to form families centered on God, the concept of family and the process of family formation are central to Church activity.

Virtually all new Church members spend at least the first years in communally organized groups. Within these groups members participate in a fictive kinship system; Moon and his wife are designated as True Spiritual Parents and other members as "brothers" and "sisters." The goal toward which novitiates are urged to devote their energies is spiritual growth, and in the context of the communal groups this means learning to love others spiritually. Toward this end members face a three year period of celibacy during which they are to suppress all physical concerns and only pursue spiritual goals. It is only after the capacity for true spiritual love has been developed that members can turn their attention to formation of their own families since spiritual love is the premise upon which marriages are to be founded.

Marriage itself is referred to as "blessing" and is endowed within the Church with the status of a sacrament. Moon, as True Spiritual Parent, plays a major role in the blessing process. His approval is necessary for a blessing to occur, and in many cases he matches individuals for marriage based on his spiritual insight. Since marriages are to be spiritually based and Moon's spiritual gifts are superior, many members defer to Moon's judgment although negotiation can and does take place. For most members blessing has taken place in large scale ceremonies over which Moon personally has presided. For example, 36 couples were blessed in 1961, 72 in 1962, 430 in 1969, 790 in 1970 and 1,800 in 1975, all on a single ceremonial occasion.

Because the Church grew rapidly during the mid-1970s and no blessing had taken place since 1975, there was a substantial cohort of technically eligible membership by 1978. In this survey, therefore, we have attempted to ascertain the expectations and aspirations of the still largely unmarried Church membership.[4] Specifically, we have probed four major issues: (1) anticipation of the timing of their blessing and the identity of their mate, (2) the kinds of qualities members preferred in their mates, (3) members' perceptions of the nature of the marital relationship itself, and (4) how members expected to balance their family and church commitments.

## Anticipation of Mate and Marriage

As we have already noted, the vast majority of Unification Church members are unmarried. The lack of marriage and family formation despite the avowed importance of the family as an instrument of change and a building block for the new order is the result of two factors. First, the theologically based expectation of an imminent opportunity for mankind's restoration to God creates pressure and willingness within the Church to forego individual goals and priorities. From the perspective of the Church the future and happiness of the entire human race is at stake. Second, the Church experienced its most rapid growth during the mid-1970s; given the mandatory three year period of celibacy, many individuals have not been members of the Church for a long enough period to be eligible for marriage.

Although Church members are predominantly unmarried, anticipation of mates and marriage is strongly discouraged. The early period of Church membership is to be devoted exclusively to spiritual growth and specifically to the capacity to view and love others spiritually as a precondition to family formation and physical love. Further, of course, the requisites of a communal group in which young men and women have to live in close proximity without sexual competition make such norms highly functional.

Our data indicate that most members anticipate postponing their marriage and family formation beyond the mandatory three year period. Twenty-five percent expect to wait up to a year longer, 23 percent anticipate a wait of up to two years, another 34 percent expect three years to pass prior to marriage, and fully 19 percent anticipate a wait of more than three years. This wait is not always an easy one; only 27 percent of our respondents report no difficulty in avoiding viewing brothers/sisters in a romantic way while 54 percent find it slightly difficult and another 19 percent concede it is moderately or very difficult. At the same time members believe it becomes easier to deal with these problems. Only 19 percent of the individuals we interviewed indicated it became more difficult for them to detach themselves from romanticizing about others in contrast to 81 percent who avowed that it became easier.

Our data also reveal that despite the strong social pressure for total, selfless commitment, members do give some consideration to the timing of their marriage and the identity of their future mates. For example everyone admits to having given some thought to the time of their blessing. Only 18 percent report having given this matter very little thought as opposed to the 46 percent and 36 percent who concede to having given some and a great deal of thought to it. Fewer members indicate having entertained the iden-

tity of their future marriage partners. Sixty-two percent report having given
a great deal or some thought to who their mate might be while 38 percent
assert having given this very little or no thought.

There is a sizeable minority of members who go further and evaluate
others as marriage partners. Although a miniscule two percent of the sample state that they frequently consider other members marriage potential
upon first meeting, 39 percent say they do so sometimes and a like percent-
age 'admit to such preliminary screening on at least a few occasions. Still,
39 percent of those we talked with deny ever doing so. There are, however,
real limits to this screening process. Only three percent of our respondents
report spending time with other Church members on a frequent basis to get
to know them better and 23 percent assert that this occurs rarely. An
overwhelming 74 percent of those interviewed deny ever engaging in such
meetings. It is worth noting that other factors reinforce theological pro-
scriptions and group pressures against the development of deep personal
relationships. The most important of these are the geographic mobility of
members who are assigned to witnessing and fundraising teams, the constant reshuffling of these teams' memberships and the continuous turnover
in Church membership as a whole. Taken together such factors combine to
make future planning difficult at best. Thus whether the result of individual
commitment, group pressure or circumstances beyond individual control,
most members give some thought to the timing of their blessing and to who
their future mate might be. However, relatively few initiatives are taken in
furtherance of such thoughts.

### Marital Preferences

Unificationist theology, at least ideally, provides some basis for individual preferences with respect to the mate selection process as well as the
qualities of a desirable mate. From the point of view of the larger society
certainly the most controversial aspect of the marriage process is the practice of matching ceremonies at which Moon arranges marriages on the
spot, sometimes between virtual strangers. Of course, Moon's status as a
True Spiritual Parent who is undertaking the restoration process by building spiritually perfect families legitimates this practice within the Church.
Nevertheless, arranged marriages clash with the cultural heritage of
American members. What are their expectations for mate selection? Eight
percent of our respondents predict they will either choose or be chosen by
their future mate; 59 percent indicate that they will select a partner from
those suggested by Church leaders; 33 percent expect that Church leaders

will choose their marriage partner for them. Thus, most members seem willing to accept a much greater degree of guidance than most Americans, and a substantial minority expect to leave the matter entirely to the Church.

Not surprisingly, given the emphasis on spiritually based marriage, the vast majority of Church members (75 percent) see themselves as marrying another Church member. The only alternative that draws any measure of support is marriage to an associate member i.e., someone committed to the Church but not involved full time.

Racial preferences for mates are interesting in light of the Church goal of forming a "world family." Sixty percent of our respondents indicate no preference in response to this item, and more express a desire for a partner of a different racial/ethnic group (39 percent) than for a partner of their own background (11 percent). Certainly mixed marriages are much more likely among Church members and reflect their commitment to the goal of world unification. Finally, we asked about premarital sexual activity affecting choice of partner because of the centrality of sexual indiscretion in Unification theology. Twenty-seven percent of our sample report that knowledge of such activity would affect their choice to varying degrees. Surprisingly, perhaps, 73 percent assert that this knowledge would not influence them at all. This latter finding probably reflects the belief within the Church that individuals are spiritually reborn upon assuming membership.

## Nature of the Marital Relationship

In light of the sanctity with which the family is endowed in the Unification Church, one might expect that conservative individuals would be attracted to the Church and that very conservative/traditional values would characterize its' membership. Our data support this expectation. For example, 55 percent of our respondents assert that the husband should have the final say in important family discussions, and 81 percent express a preference for the husband being the primary breadwinner. This is true for both male and female members.

A desire for large families follows from the importance of spiritually based marriages as the building blocks of a new world order. Our respondents anticipate large families indeed. No one indicates an intention to remain childless. Twenty-four percent of the sample states a preferred family size of one to three children, another 44 percent anticipate four to six children, and fully 32 percent express a desire for seven or more children. Such large families certainly are possible in light of members unwillingness to take steps to limit family size. Sixty-three percent of those we interviewed contend that they will not consider any means of limiting their family's size. Of the 37 percent who express a willingness to control family size the largest group (38 percent) state they will simply abstain from sex; the remainder are divided primarily between those who will employ birth control devices (29 percent) and those who will rely on the rhythm method (21 percent).

These generally conservative attitudes extend to contemplation of potential reasons for divorce. Only one individual is willing to list personality or social incompatibility as grounds for divorce while 28 percent assert that marital infidelity would prompt divorce and 71 percent indicate that only a partner's leaving the Church would cause divorce. It is, of course, a difficult matter to assess, but perhaps divorce rates would remain low given the close integration of church and family life. A decision to break either relationship would have profound implications for the other. Indeed, our data indicate that members expect their marriage to be supported within the Church. Virtually all of our respondents indicate that they would turn either to other married couples within the Church or to Church leaders in the event that they experience marital problems. Doubtless there would be substantial pressure on such couples to work out their problems within the bounds of marriage. Taken together, then, these attitudes are predictably conservative and supportive of strong marital and familial relationships.

## Relation of Family and Church

Our final set of questions dealt with the relationship individuals expected between their Church and family responsibilities following marriage. On the one hand, the formation of families is a central objective for both the Church and its individual members. On the other hand, members believe that restoration is at hand if only the opportunity is seized. This conviction leads many to sacrifice their own personal interests for the larger goal of saving mankind. How do our respondents balance these competing demands?

As would be expected from the pattern of responses to preceding questions, virtually all members expect to continue their Church related activity after marriage. Their anticipated degree of involvement varies considerably, however. When we asked about preferred living arrangements following marriage, for example, 16 percent of our sample registers a preference for a separate family dwelling, 28 percent voices a desire to live communally with other blessed couples and 56 percent selects the option of living in communal quarters that include unmarried Church members. Another question reinforces this finding of both deep commitment to the Church and yet substantial variation in anticipated lifestyle. Exactly half of our respondents state they expect to marry and then spend their free time in Church-related work. An additional 31 percent envision working full-time for the Church while their children are in child daycare facilities. Twelve percent of those we surveyed expect extended periods of separation from their children while they pursue Church assigned tasks. Finally, the remaining 7 percent divide equally between those who expect to remain single so as to be free to assume Church responsibilities and those who expect to separate following marriage to pursue Church work. Thus, members differ considerably in the extent to which marriage and family formation would affect their Church commitments. Some clearly hope for something approaching a conventional family life; others obviously intend to continue to give priority to the needs of the Church.

Finally, as an index of responsiveness to family versus Church needs we asked members how much of their family income above living expenses they plan to contribute to the Church. Only 3 percent of our respondents expect to contribute as little as a tithe, another 10 percent anticipate contributions of up to fifty percent of their income, and 87 percent report that they will contribute more than half of their income. Indeed, the most frequent single response (69 percent) is a contribution of all income above living expenses. Once again, then, Church goals seem to supercede individual needs.

## Summary and Conclusions

In this paper we have explored the marital and family futures envisioned by members of a major new religious movement. It is clear that members' visions of the future are strongly influenced by their currently intense commitment to the movement. They clearly expect that commitment to continue, and they project a future in which family and religious life are integrated even more strongly than in fundamentalist denominations. At the same time another intriguing theme emerges, the tension between collective and individual needs. This clash of priorities is not surprising for it has been characteristic of communal groups throughout history. This theme manifests itself in two ways in our data. First, despite the intense commitment necessary to sustain Church membership and the strong social pressure to strive for Church defined ideals, numerous members clearly look longingly for a time when they can address their private, personal needs. This is evident in a desire for a separate residence, work for the Church during *free* time, and living with one's marriage partner. Second, and perhaps more revealing, members' current behavior seems more individualistic than their statements about future intentions. So, for example, members do actively consider who their mate might be and even engage in screening behavior as best they can in the close confines of a communal group. Such activity occurs despite theological and social counterpressure. By contrast, many members anticipate contributing virtually all of their income to the Church—a self-sacrificial decision rather easily made in their present circumstances. This observation in no way demeans the idealism and commitment of Church members. It does, however, underscore the endemic tension of individual and collective needs in communal groups. Self-sacrifice can be sustained only by developing and constantly reinforcing intense personal commitment. The struggle for perfect families like other utopian quests constantly confronts the reality of individual needs. The next decade will reveal how successful the new religions have been in fighting this very old battle.

## REFERENCE NOTES

1. Questions were worded in such a way as to apply to both married and unmarried individuals. Since the number of married respondents was so small, no attempt was made to group these individuals for comparative purposes.
2. Many of the oriental members of the Church were individuals who had been recruited in Japan or Taiwan. Although no black Americans appeared in this sample, the Church did attempt to recruit across racial lines because of its public commitment to creating a "world family."
3. Actually the fall of man was more complex. In addition to the vertical fall precipitated by Eve's physical seduction, there was a horizontal fall when Cain slew Abel. The horizontal fall estranged one human being from another just as the vertical fall had estranged humankind from God.
4. At the time of this writing another large blessing was believed by many American members to be imminent. Several hundred members had already been matched with others in a quasi-engagement ceremony that was designed to permit some mutual assessment of the relationship by the designated partners prior to the final blessing.

## REFERENCES

American Civil Liberties Union. News on conference on religious deprogramming. New York: (January 25) 1977.
American Family Foundation. Transcript of proceedings, Information meeting on the cult phenomenon in the United States. Lexington, MA: American Family Foundation, Inc., 1979.
Bromley, D. G. and Shupe, A. D. Just a few years seem like a lifetime: A role theory approach to participation in religious movements. In Louis Kriesberg (Ed), *Research in Social Movements, Conflict and Change*. Greenwich: JAI Press, 1979a, 159-185.

Bromley, D. G. and Shupe, A. D. *Moonies in America: Cult, Church and Crusade*. Beverly Hills, CA: Sage, 1979b.

Bromley, D. G. and Shupe, A. D. The Unification Church and the American family strain, conflict and control. *New Religious Movements: A Perspective for Understanding Society*. New York: Edwin Mellen Press, 1981.

Enroth, R. *The Lure of the Cults*. Chappaqua, N.Y.: Christian Herald Books, 1979.

Enroth, R. *Youth, Brainwashing and the Extremist Cults*. Kentwood, MI: Zondervan, 1977.

Holy Spirit Association for theUnification of World Christianity (HSA-UWC). *Divine Principle*. Condensed version. Washington, D.C., 1977.

Shupe, A. D. and Bromley, D. G. *The New Vigilantes: Deprogrammers, Anti-cultists and the New Religions.*Beverly Hills, CA: Sage, 1980.

Underwood, B. and Underwood, B. *Hostage to Heaven*. New York: Clarkson N. Potter, 1979.

# OUR INVOLVEMENT WITH A CUL-

Marie Hershell
Ben Hershell

Our daughter, Jean, was 19 when she started as a student at a Western University in January, 1976. She was interested in Wildlife Management, Animal Conservation and related Environmental Sciences. Where to pursue these studies better than the wide open spaces of the great West?

Jean had graduated from high school more than two years before. She had had her so-called fling—traveling, working, and living with a friend away from home and she was ready to go to college. She was idealistic and previously had participated actively in anti-war, anti-nuclear, feminist and new educational movements. Jean was a pacifist, bright, curious and willing to work for her beliefs.

Jean's age group had lived through the Korean and Vietnamese wars; they had lived through three assassinations; they were yet to live through Watergate and Americans being held hostage; they had been a bit disillusioned and wanted to be able to leave their "marks" on the world and make it better.

Jean had been confirmed at our synagogue and had gone on to religious high school training—even so far as to student teach at a center city synagogue.

She had joined us twice (in 1974 and 1975) for two week trips to Cap Haitian, Haiti, when her father, an optometrist, went in charge of a group of interns, giving eye care to the people there. Jean worked the same schedule, along with everyone else involved, in the dispensing area of the makeshift eye clinic at the Justinian Hospital.

In March of 1976, she called to tell us that she was very fortunate to have met a group of young adults that shared her ideals and beliefs. She felt very comfortable with them and they were fast becoming good friends. We learned later that this is part of the technique which the cults employ called "love-bombing." Just before spring break at college, she mentioned that

---

Marie and Ben Hershell are pseudonyms for two parents who write of their daughter's experience in leaving the Unification Church. Ben is a professional and Marie is a homemaker.

*131*

she was going to go on a weekend retreat with her new friends. Shortly afterwards, we received a long letter telling us about her new frineds and their common beliefs and goals. She was going to be a better Jew, a better person and her love for us and everyone else knew no bounds. We were also informed that she had moved out of the freshman dormitory to the Unification Center in order to be with her friends.

Our first impulse was to ignore the letter, but after rereading it, certain things did not ring clear. All freshmen students were required to live in the dorms—how could she have moved out without anyone letting us know? Also, she did not say anything about wanting her dog there, which previously had been an important factor when she would no longer be required to live in the dorms. We thought that her intelligence would help her realize her mistake and she would get over it. But the more we read the letter, the more we became aware of a different flavor from her previous ones, but could not pinpoint the reasons. Too, we had not heard of a Unification Center, and after investigation, realized that it was part of Unification Church, of which we knew nothing.

At that point in time, there was very little information available; most we learned from a recent Reader's Digest article. We went to see our Rabbi. He told us that he did not know much about the Unification "Church" and that it was NOT a religious problem but a psychological one. He said that the cult was "incidious" and "dangerous" and that we must keep communication open with Jean. Fortunately we were able to do that. At our request, Jean called every Sunday and, even though we did not approve of her actions, we listened carefully and gave the impression that we were weighing and questioning, but not condemning.

Our Rabbi had told us about an anti-cult group (which consisted mostly of involved parents) in the area that was going to present a program at the Pennsylvania Institute. For the first time, we heard a parent speak about her son's experience in a cult and his deprogramming, and we heard a young woman who escaped from Unification Church by climbing over a barbed wire fence in the middle of the night. We spoke to them afterward, and the more we heard the more frightened we became.

We called the Dean of Students at the University and even though he was sympathetic when he heard the reasons, he would not divulge whether or not she was attending classes since she was of legal age. He even went so far as to have a psychologist from the University call us. She had had some dealings with the Unification Center but not in several months, so she did not know our daughter. She, too, was concerned, but not helpful.

After much listening to other parents involved with various cults, we analyzed all the information we had gleaned. "Mind control, brainwashing, persuasive coersion, mind manipulation"—these words were all foreign and had no real or practical meaning to our previous realm of experience.

We realized finally that all the cults use variations of the same techniques of mind control, such as: limited sleep, limited nutritional food, fatigue, controlled environment, isolation from others outside the cult, lack of communication, confession, guilt, fear, chanting, constant lectures and reinforcement from other members. They process in a very systematic and controlled manner to gain total control.

We also did a great deal of "soul-searching" at that time. We developed our own "guilt trip." What had we done wrong? Had we been too permissive, too strict? Had we paid too much attention? or too little? What should or could we have done differently? Apparently, most parents go through this same uselessness! We finally realized that it was not what we had or had not done, so we could stop beating on ourselves! It was a combination of many factors: it was the circumstances, it was the timing, it was the approach, it was the deception, the "love-bombing," the interplay. In short, it was the vulnerability of any and all young people. At any given time, any of them could be ripe to be entrapped.

The original approach is so friendly and so casual, seemingly. The cult members are so interested in anything and everything that the new recruits have to offer or say. The members seem to have all the answers to all the questions of life in the world and are so peaceful and calm. Because of the confidence they see, new recruits tend to doubt themselves, and when they voice their uncertainties, they are told to wait until the next lecture or to pray harder or to take another cold shower.

A surgeon in North Jersey whose son had been involved with Unification Church told us, "Your child is no longer the child you think she is." The cults practice and preach "Heavenly Deception." If you are not with them, you are against them, and therefore, a part of Satan. They feel perfectly justified is using any deceptive techniques to win over Satan in the name of God. Many cults have front organizations that sound very idealistic, and even when asked directly, they refute any connection or link with a cult group. C.A.R.P. (Collegiate Association for the Research of Principles), one of the best-known Moonie fronts, is on every major college campus in the country.

Finally, after much information and conversation and deliberation, we arrived at the conclusion that Jean's mind was not controlled by her, that she was in a dangerous situation and that she needed help. We learned that it would be futile to go and try to reason with her, that it would be possible for them even to hide her and send her elsewhere. When we spoke to her on the telephone, we were still being reasonable parents, who accepted but questioned, were interested but concerned.

Eventually, we decided to have her deprogrammed or returned to her original state of mind. Those arrangements were even more difficult to make. Information was almost unavailable. Parents had to check us out before they would tell us anything or give us numbers to call. There were only a few teams doing deprogramming then and two of those were not available. One team was working in Europe (cults are an international menace) and the other was involved in a legal entanglement. We arranged an appointment with Dennis Riley (after he checked on us with other parents) and met with him and his wife, Maureen at the home of Dr. and Mrs. Bucky Smith in Northern New Jersey for about six hours. Our other two daughters went with us—one older and one younger than Jean. Our son, then 14, did not want to have anything to do with the entire situation.

Dennis and Maureen Riley were protecting the Smith family in their own house since their son, Paul, was deprogrammed several months previously. Their house was being watched, their phones tapped, their lives harassed and in possible danger. The Smith family was very supportive of us, and Dennis pointed out the risk of legal involvement and of being sued by our own daughter through the ''church.'' We talked about the possibility of going to a parents' workshop run by the cult. We also talked about the chance that we might have to pick Jean off a street corner in New York City if necessary when she went to the rally there. We also talked about conservatorship, which was just coming into being then (temporary guardianship by parents-awarded by the courts.)

All the ramifications of rescue, deprogramming, rehabilitation, and further services and costs were reviewed. Total family support was necessary and our girls rallied to the occasion. We were frightened, unsure, anxious, and physically and emotionally drained. We had only been going through this for about two months or less at that time—oh! the poor families who have lived with a similar situation for years! We talked and thought about nothing else with each other and were ''paranoid'' about mentioning it to others except those people who helped us. The cult groups have an ''underground'' and they sometimes, somehow know plans that others don't want them to know.

Our sister and brother-in-law were very concerned, supportive and helpful. We talked every day and agonized over decisions. Yet, much of it was not up to us. We were going to put Jean's well-being in the hands of complete strangers who had had experience in deprogramming. We were plotting to capture our own daughter against her will and by force, if necessary. We needed to arrange timing, transportation, and a hiding place for the deprogramming. We talked about barring windows and doors, so that Jean could not use them to escape; we planned to remove objects and medications with which she could harm herself.

Meanwhile, fortunately, Jean was oblivious of our plans. She was playing the game at which the cults are so good, called "Keep the parents guessing." For two weeks she told of arrangements to come east. Occasionally, she even mentioned coming home to our house, but mostly it was to go to New York City. Each time she called it was to tell us of a different method of transportation, with different people, different routes and different times. All the Moonies from various parts of the country were going to congregate in New York City for the "God Bless America Bicentennial Rally" at Yankee Stadium on June 1, 1976. At one point, our older daughter, Ruth, suggested meeting her in New York and they could come home together. But, Jean said they wouldn't find each other (this from a young woman who had gone to England alone just the year before and travelled through England and Scotland with a friend).

Finally, Jean called late one night and said that she and two friends were on their way to our house; they were at the Indiana border and heading here for lunch the next day, so we could meet these wonderful new friends she had been living with. We called Dennis and none of us believed that she would really come home, but we could not take the chance of missing the opportunity. Dennis was committed in Pittsburgh, but the next morning early, Maureen, Paul, and two security people were at our house.

Our brother and sister-in-law came to help. The women stayed at a neighbor's house with the deprogrammers and our house was readied for Jean. We were told that, if Jean started to leave the house in the car with the other Moonies, we were to throw her to the ground or throw ourselves to the ground—anything to keep her there and create a necessary minute's delay. Then the security people would come out and tell the other Moonies to leave without Jean and they probably would. However, they would go to the police station which was two blocks from our home and say that their friend was being held against her will. Then Maureen gave us a map and directions describing where they would take Jean immediately so that when the police would come looking for her at our house, we could honestly say that she wasn't there. Then we could follow where Jean had gone. Just imagine such a scheme! We found all of this frightening. We both are such conservative square people who are careful not to get parking tickets, and here we were part of a plot beyond our kind of imagination.

In the meantime, the men readied the house for the Moonies' arrival.

They nailed the windows shut in the bedroom and bathroom being secured for Jean's stay and the beginning of her deprogramming. The doors leading to a balcony and the bathroom closet door were padlocked and the glass objects, dangerous medicines, and shelves from the medicine cabinet were locked in the bathroom closet. Since Jean and her friends did not arrive at lunch time, we were beginning to panic. When they did arrive four hours later, Jean and a male and a female, we were all in a dither about to have anxiety attacks. We were nervous, sweating and aching. We had been afraid that the powers that be had changed their minds again and the young people were really going right on to New York. However, they had dinner with us—the longest meal of our lives. They each took a shower, changed their clothes and all of them walked the dog around the neighborhood. The Moonies were zombie-like when they talked about the church and because they had been driving for 44 hours. Jean did not drive at that time, so she felt that she had to stay awake when each of the others was driving. We were worried that we would say the wrong thing—we had dreamed up such schemes that we thought we might forget our lies. We need not have worried about that; they paid no attention because they were so concerned with their own problems. They had to be awake another two hours and be presentable to get to New York to the Unification Center on 43rd Street, a building which used to belong to Columbia University. After much ado, the two others left—really leaving Jean at home. We could hardly believe our good fortune as we all stood on the steps waving goodbye. All the cloak and dagger plans proved to be unnecessary.

After a few minutes the deprogrammers rang the doorbell and told Jean that they wanted to talk to her about the church. She was amenable and thought it a challenge to test her faith. After talking for awhile in the dining room, Maureen and Paul took her upstairs to the secured room to speak to her alone while the two security men stayed downstairs and guarded the doors in case she should try to leave. After a couple of hours, Jean came running down the stairs in an hysterical state, crying, "How could you do this to me without listening to what I had to say?" At that point, we were as upset as she. We tried to calm her and tried to make her realize why she should listen—that we were doing it for her—to get her to think for herself again! She did not believe us then, of course.

That night, Jean agreed to go to a place that Dennis Riley had elsewhere and to stop chanting and to try to listen. The next day, the four deprogrammers, Jean, the dog—Baron and I left, so that when her friends looked for her and called when she did not show up in New York three days later, the rest of the family could honestly say she was not at home and they did not know where she was.

That first night at home, Ruth said she would be Jean's friend against the rest of us so they spent some time together. Ruth thought Jean was O.K., that she seemed to be herself when they talked about other things and that she did not need deprogramming. We said that we would have her go through it anyhow, because it would not do any harm. She could not be deprogrammed if she were not programmed.

Jean told us later that she had been allowed and encouraged to come home because she was sure she could convince us to go to the workshop for parents before the rally (that is when Moon bought the old New Yorker Hotel to house the parents). She was also going to persuade her idealistic sisters to join the group with her.

We were one of the lucky families. Jean's deprogramming took a few days until she began to see both sides. She went on "rehabilitation" for a few weeks and helped with other deprogrammings. That reinforced it for her and helped others. They try to have ex-cult members to help because they have the credibility. There were times of danger. She "floated"— thoughts that remind her of the lectures and friends back at the center and perhaps the temptation to go back. There was much self-recrimination about being duped, loss of self-confidence and initiative, severe depressions, etc. The egos have been removed. All decisions were made for them by the cult leaders. Now, even the simplest routines such as when to shower or what to eat became a trying ordeal. At one such point of depression, we obtained the name of Dr. Ralston, a psychiatrist. He was recommended by a psychiatrist in another state who was ably treating ex-cult members. However, when Jean went to see him, he admitted he knew nothing about the cults and even though he was interested, he did not know how to help her.

In the meantime, several cult members were trying to locate Jean. Both the boy and girl called several times within the first ten days of Jean not having appeared in New York at the appointed time. We finally convinced them that she was no longer interested in the church and all their energies went into the rally that was forthcoming. A couple of weeks later, Jean contacted a young student at her University named Beatrice. Beatrice had been one young woman whom Jean had been trying to recruit for Unification Church before she came home. Now she spoke to Beatrice several times on the phone to make her realize that the people at the center were not her friends, but Beatrice was going through some very difficult personal problems. One night when Beatrice was out, there was a message for her from a young man at the Unification Center at the University. Jean was being notified that Beatrice had joined the church, and had been sent to Missouri. Understandably, Jean was very upset, blaming herself for this turn of events. Somehow, just to be sure, she tried to call Beatrice again at her apartment. Imagine her jubilation when Beatrice was there and not in the cult at all! It was just some more of their "heavenly deception" and harassment. In fact, as late as eight months after Jean had come home, a young woman called looking for her, with a story about wanting her to talk at Princeton. This was subsequent to much of Jean's public speaking about the cults. We learned through a newspaper article and a TV program that the young woman was a Moonie at one of the Philadelphia centers and had nothing to do with Princeton.

When Jean's younger sister, Denise, was Confirmed several weeks after the deprogramming, Maureen Riley came with us because she knew that any religious experience would be a torment for her—"floating" again. It was! but it was all right.

After the young people have been deprogrammed from a cult, it's as though the rug has been pulled out from under them. They have to gain confidence, slowly rebuild their egos, and try to socialize again with "real" people doing "real" things in a "real" world. They have to point their lives in a meaningful direction. Through the cults, they had thought they had found a personal purpose in life and now that purpose was obliterated.

Most involved parents we contacted were most sympathetic and helpful. They did not stint at all; they gave freely of their time and of themselves. They held nothing back. They told of the marvels of having their children back as well as the horrors of what they had experienced and their doubts and questions. Then as we heard of another young person being rescued and deprogrammed, we all identified with the family and felt grateful.

Helping young people coming out of cults is frustrating. Their problems do not fit into the ordinary categories. Even when they get depressed, it is different from other depressions—we have to realize what they have been through—where they "are coming from." They have difficulties in areas where they functioned well before the cult experience.

After Jean's deprogramming and rehabilitation, she did a great deal of public speaking in this area for several months—mostly to young people—as much as four and five times a week. When she moved to a new nearby University and enrolled she found it hard to concentrate. It took a long time for her to feel good about herself again. There had been another enormous change in her personality. She WAS and IS a pacifist, and yet, she said she would have gone to South Korea to fight and kill if she had been told to do so. Some young people have told after their deprogramming that they would have killed their parents if they had been told to do so.

Other young people had razor blades in their possession, saying they had been told "it is better to be dead than deprogrammed." They had been told they were going to be tortured and not allowed to eat or sleep, and that the girls were going to be raped. Some groups have suicide pacts.

Young people who are entrapped by a cult generally do not come out by themselves. They need to be deprogrammed. Those who do come out alone usually have lots of questions left unanswered. And all of them coming out need help. They need support from their families. They need to be able to share their thoughts and feelings and to know that their loved ones care. They need caring from professionals and assistance in breaking the mental bonds of the cults. Professional people such as clinical psychologists, clergy men and women, psychiatrists must become familiar with the backgrounds and operations of the cults. They must understand the cults' hold on the young people. These cults represent a whole new host of problems that do not conform to the established routines and standard model approaches. The young men and women coming out of the cults need time and understanding to get themselves back together again.

Jean says she would not have come out on her own, there was too much guilt and fear and confusion and pressure thrown at her. We felt we were walking on eggshells for awhile and it was hard on her sometimes when we hovered over her a bit. However, we felt that nothing could be as bad as the control of her mind that the Unification Cult had. She is back to her own life now. She is still idealistic, still has the courage of her convictions, and still has her causes! Thank God!

Unfortunately, the cults are not dying. They are alive and well and getting stronger because they keep changing their tactics and front organization names and mode of operation to catch young people off guard.

The Hare Krishnas (ISKCON) are now storing arms and ammunition. Several devotees have been involved in drug arrests in recent months.

Scientology has invaded F.B.I. files. Their leaders make a point of harassing people who try to block them with nuisance suits involving millions of dollars.

Unification Church does the same with law suits. There will be another mass wedding ceremony performed by the self-ordained reverend—Moon—supposedly for thousands of members of the group. Many will be between Americans and immigrants from Japan and Korea so that they may stay in the U.S.A.

The Family of Love (formerly Children of God) uses its female members to become prostitutes for God.

The Way, International has as part of its required reading a book stating that the Holocaust of World War II did not really happen. Along with the list of needs for members similar to those of camping is included "bring a rifle—or handgun."

A former top leader of Divine Light Mission says he witnessed physical and sexual torture of members. He denounced Guru Maharaji Ji after seeing similarities of behavior to those of Jim Jones.

Jonestown *can* happen again—here.

# THE CULT PHENOMENON: BEHAVIORAL SCIENCE PERSPECTIVES APPLIED TO THERAPY

Marvin F. Galper

*Cult Movements—Overview and Indoctrination Analysis*

## Introduction

The late 1960s witnessed the proliferation of a substantial number of new religions on the American scene which are directing their proselytization efforts primarily towards the late adolescent and young adult segment of the population. The term "cult" has been applied to many of these new organizations. In this presentation, the latter term will be utilized within the context of a sociological frame of reference. Societal responses to the emergence of these groups has been characterized by an extraordinary degree of public attention and controversy.

Such movements seek to initiate sweeping societal structural change. They pose a challenge to conventional religion and to the biological family. Consequently, they inevitably mobilize conflict with the broader social milieu as a consequence of their (a) ideology, (b) organizational style, (c) economic resources, and (d) recruitment and socialization practices. Allegations of coercive brainwashing have been made by concerned parents whose children have been exposed to cult recruitment. The Unification Church, Scientology, The International Society for Krishna Consciousness, and the Divine Light Mission have received most of the public and professional attention, and consequently serve as a major focus for this paper. Other American cults which have undergone less membership growth and expansion include The Children of God (Wallis, 1976; Davis and Richardson, 1976), The Love Family (Enroth, 1977), The Way (MacCollum, 1978), The Holy Order of Mans, and the Nicheren Shoshu Academy (Dator, 1969).

Marvin F. Galper is a licensed psychologist practicing in San Diego, California.

During the past decade, behavioral science investigations of contemporary cults have begun to emerge in the professional literature. This paper seeks to present and synthesize some of the social science findings which deal with the American religious cult. Studies of totalist organizations emergent in other cultural contexts will also be quoted where relevant. In perusing this survey, the reader's attention is directed to Stone's (1978) cautionary words, addressed to the professional interested in religious phenomena. He points out the inevitability of value orientation influences on the report and interpretation of data, and suggests that both researcher and reader cultivate awareness of ideological and personal biases and their consequent effect on presented information.

## Behavioral Science Investigation of Totalist Phenomena

The literature which deals with the phenomena of "totalism" is of central significance in an overview of the modern religious cult. Although the term was coined by Erikson (1964) without a concise formal definition, the context indicates that he intended to connote organizations and social movements characterized by a polarized world-view and absolutist doctrinal and social boundaries. Lifton (1963, p. 419) defined totalism as "the coming together of immediate ideology with equally immoderate character traits—an extremist meeting ground between people and ideas." He suggested that this is most likely to occur with ideologies which are most sweeping in their content and most ambitious—or messianic—in their claims. He considered the Chinese Communist thought reform movement an example of political totalism, and in a later paper (1976), conveyed the view that marked totalist features are also to be found in the psychosocial world of American religious cultism. This view is consistent with Shupe and Bromley's (1979) description of cults such as the International Society for Krishna Consciousness, The Children of God, and the Unification Church as "world transforming movements" (p. 326) which have sought to initiate sweeping structural change of the society in which they are located.

In his original paper presenting the "identity crisis" concept, Erikson (1964) suggested that radical historical or technological change can increase the potential for precipitation of a tenuous sense of personal identity. During periods of turmoil the person caught in a marginal social position may achieve a synthetic sense of identity through immersion in a totalist sub-culture. Writing from a behavioral science perspective, Eister (1974) expressed the similar view that dislocations in the communicational and orientational institutions of advanced societies open the way for cults to flourish. Evidence in support of this thesis is found in a cross-cultural study by Larsen (1950) which documents the spread of extremist cultism in Germany subsequent to World War I and again in Japan subsequent to World War II. Galper (1977a) pointed out parallels between the latter periods and contemporary American society. He suggested that weakening of traditional American sociocultural institutions has precipitated widespread identity diffusion and concomitant susceptibility to cultism.

Kanter (1972) studied the totalist milieu nineteenth-century American communes and utopias. The extent of thematic parallelism to be found between her report and that of Lifton (1963), though based on the study of social movements which are strikingly different in historical period and cultural context, is of considerable theoretical interest. The combined evidence from both studies points towards the possible universality of the totalist phenomenon as a generic form of social organization. Parallel themes encountered include (a) sharp division of the experiential world into the absolutely good and absolutely evil, (b) control of the individual's inner life and his communication with the outside world, and (c) de-individuating processes which bring about identity change through the community's invasion of phenomenological privacy. These latter processes include confession and mutual criticism which promote symbolic self-surrender and express the merger of self and environment. In my role as a psychotherapist, I have received personal reports from members of each of the four cults herein surveyed with regard to their experiences within the totalist milieu. Their personal experiential reports reveal the presence of the patterns described by Lifton and Kanter, in varying degrees, within the psychosocial world of each cult.

Bourguignon (1974) has stated that many contemporary "marginal" American religious groups and movements tend to foster religious experience of a particular intensity characterized by an altered state of consciousness. Support for Bourguignon's view can be found in a series of psychological studies (Clark, 1977; Galper, 1976; Levine & Salter, 1976; Singer, 1979) of cult members. Reported findings make reference to an altered state of consciousness in this population, variously described as a "trance state" or "disassociative state." Ludwig (1966) has surveyed the broad gamut of scientific studies which deal with the phenomena of altered states. He finds that there are a number of prerequisite psychological conditions which contribute to their emergence. The overall body of research findings in this area indicates that altered states serve as "final common pathways" for many different forms of adaptive and maladaptive human expression.

## Totalism and the Mental Health Professional

Traditional humanistic values of Western society clash profoundly with the totalist value system with regard to the basic issue of the proper relation between man and society. Humanism places priority on the dignity and freedom of the individual as a rational being. This individualistic emphasis is clearly embodied in the personality theory of Western mental health professionals. A classical prototype is Freud's negative view of the "primal horde" and commune. This humanistic perspective is also evident in the emphasis on automomy in contemporary concepts of "positive mental health" (Jahoda, 1958), and is perhaps most explicitly articulated in Maslow's (1948) need hierarchy theory. Maslow states that needs for safety and belonging exist at a lower phylogenetic and ontogentic level than needs for self-actualization.

The totalist perspective reflects a reversal of humanistic value priorities. Successful realization of totalist group aspirations requires ideological homogeneity and unity of collective action. This is accomplished via the molding and submergence of individuality. Consequently, one consistently finds that Western mental health literature consistently views the individual immersed in a totalist organization as experiencing a regressive form of adaptation. Thus Meerloo (1956) views totalitarianism as "man's escape from the fearful realities of life into the womb of the leader" (p. 21). Erikson (1964) sees membership in a totalist movement as "immersion in a synthetic identity" (p. 93), which for Lifton (1963) "poses a profound threat to personal autonomy" (p. 421). In a similar vein, Galper (1976) describes treated cult members as displaying "loss of automomy and delay in personal growth during the period of immersion in the cult sub-culture" (p. 3).

## Treating Cult-Related Problems

I have evolved a modus operandi in dealing with cult-related problems based on my clinical experience. Initial requests for consultation are made either by (a) concerned parents of a young adult who is an active cult member, or (b) a person who has relinquished cult affiliation and seeks assistance in facilitating readjustment to the community mainstream. The majority of cult cases I have treated have been under the former set of circumstance.

Consequently, parent-referred cases will therefore constitute the major focus of the clinical presentation which follows. Parents who arrive in my office for an initial consultation are usually in a state of acute crisis and emotional turmoil. Frequently they perceive their child who is a cult member as an innocent victim of malignant cult leaders who have seductively recruited their child into cult membership for purposes of exploitation. They often are fearful that their child's mental destruction is immanent, unless a rescue can be accomplished. Parents have frequently considered and rejected the option of coercive deprogramming, with two-fold motivation. Firstly, they are concerned about the ethics of arranging for a temporary deprivation of their child's civil liberties. Secondly, they are unwilling to risk permanent alienation from their child which might result from "unsuccessful" deprogramming.

This latter fear has a substantial reality base. It is not uncommon for cult members who have been exposed to "unsuccessful" coercive deprogramming attempts to permanently sever contact with their nuclear family subsequent to their "escape" and return to the cult environment. Crisis-oriented intervention at this stage requires alleviating parental anxieties to a level which permits them to discuss their dilemma and consider realistic options in a relatively composed and rational manner.

The assessment interviews which follow consist of a series of history taking sessions. Diagnostic impressions are formulated with regard to familial interaction patterns and the personality structure of the cult member. Information is gathered regarding the circumstances in which initial cult recruitment took place. Most commonly, the child was experiencing stress and social alienation when initially exposed to prosyletization overtures by cult members. Parental perceptions of attitudinal and behavioral changes which their child has displayed subsequent to cult indoctrination are also elicited. In relatively rare cases, the child had been maintaining a chronic marginal level of adjustment to the community prior to cult indoctrination. For such persons suffering from severe and chronic psychopathology, immersion in the cultic milieu appeared to result in a dramatic improvement in their level of surface adjustment. It seems likely that the highly structured cult environment provided such individuals with a "group ego" which bolstered their fragile and impaired capacities for autonomy and self-direction.

When the initial assessment process leads to a recommendation for family counseling which is accepted by the parents, they are then oriented with regard to the special difficulties in enlisting their child's voluntary participation. Religious cults tend to devalue the potential contributory value of mental health professionals. I have found that cult members will very frequently discourage their peers from participation in counseling. Consequently, I ask parents to extend the invitation for counseling to their child during a private visit off the cult premises.

Advance scheduling arrangements are made so that the cult member can immediately be brought to my office if he or she responds in the affirmative to the parental invitation. During the latter private visit, parents inform their child that his or her involvement in a highly controversial new religion has caused them considerable anxiety and emotional turmoil. They then suggest family rap sessions with a qualified counselor, with the goal of hopefully achieving more family harmony and understanding.

The rationale for couching the latter invitation within a "family problem" context is based on the clinical finding that cult members are frequently highly resistant to accepting the role of identified patient. Most frequently, cult members who agree to participate in family counseling are motivated by a desire to reassure parents that their concerns about his or her cult affiliation are groundless. Post-treatment interviews reveal that on occasion the cult member has an initial "hidden agenda" of hoping to recruit parents and/or the counselor into the cult.

In initial sessions cult members often exhibit a sustained altered state of consciousness. This altered state is a phenomenon of extraordinary clinical and research interest. Intensity of this psychological orientation appears to be correlated with longevity of cult membership. This state is associated with an extreme narrowing and intensification of the phenomenological field of conscious attention. Psychic energies are almost exclusively invested in cult ideology and associated fantasies. Narrowing and blunting in the range of consciously experienced affect is a not infrequent concomitant of the intense altered state of consciousness. Cult members perceive themselves as enjoying an elevated spiritual position which is associated with a sense of distance from the mainstream community. Cult ideology and ingroup jargon are kept secret from non-cult members, which serves to accentuate the sense of special privilege and separation from the "unenlightened" interpersonal world which surrounds them. I have utilized a series of approaches which appear to be of value in alleviating the latter sense of alienation. Firstly, an attempt is made in initial sessions to elicit the child's genuine concerns regarding misunderstandings in his relationship with parents. Whenever possible, clearly delineated and modest short-term family counseling goals are established which seek to resolve relatively superficial parent-child communication problems. Success in achievement of such goals tends to facilitate the cult member's perception of the counselor as one who can to some extent serve as an effective family mediator. Establishment of rapport is further enhanced by informing the cult member of my own philosophical world-view of belief in the existence of a Higher Power. I have also found that openly displaying my knowledge of secret cult ideology and jargon in conversation with the cult member conflicts with his or her initial generalized expectations and tends to promote a heightened sense of intrigue and interest in the counselor. Session "ground rules" are established to facilitate an ongoing flow of family communication. These ground rules prohibit flagrant parental condemnation of cult ideology or socialization practices. Parents are allowed opportunities to openly share their concerns about allegations of deceptive cult recruitment methods and "brainwashing" indoctrination techniques. As one facet of treatment, the counselor provides the cult member with insight regarding features of manipulation and suggestion in the molding of belief systems within his own cult. Concrete descriptions of similar practices in congruent cults permit the cult member to recognize parallels and make relevant comparisons in a setting which minimizes emotional threat and defensiveness.

For persons who reject their cult affiliation as a consequence of the counseling process, one notes a return to the Generalized Reality Orientation (Shor, 1959) characteristic of their pre-cultic existence. In a substantial number of cases, the former cult member's mental state is observed to fluctuate between the Generalized Reality Orientation and the cult-generated altered state of consciousness for a period of time subsequent to exit from the cult. This phenomenon, which has been termed "floating," is of extraordinary clinical and research interest. Former cult members report that they most frequently experience this transient return to the altered state (a) when alone, and (b) in the very early morning or very late evening, before or after their immersion in the round of daily activities. Thus decreased focus of conscious attention on the realities of the immediate environment emerges as a significant factor in this mental fluctuation.

When the individual relinquishes cult involvement, facilitation of his or her readjustment to the community mainstream becomes a major focus of counseling. The establishment of a viable community support system becomes a critical concern at this juncture. As indicated by Schwartz and Kaslow (1979), therapy groups composed of ex-cult members and halfway house arrangements can provide extremely valuable sources of support during this transitional adjustment phase. Persons who emerge from highly structured and authoritarian cults in which they had pursued a dependent and submissive role display varying degrees of impairment in their decision-making capacities. In such cases, professional assistance can facilitate the restoration of decision-making skills and the establishment of long range vocational goals. In the cult milieu these patients had experienced an extraordinary sense of group closeness based on the collective submergence of individuality in the joint pursuit of organizational goals. These persons tend to struggle with an acute sense of confusion regarding the essence of "true" intimacy. Providing orientation to the concept of mature love as involving mutual acknowledgement and accomodation to individual differences is often quite helpful in achieving clarification of their bewilderment. Former cult members often feel intense ambivalence towards their former cult peers whom they have rejected. Some focus on resolution and working through such ambivalence frequently is a significant feature of post-exit counseling sessions. Many young people also struggle with ideological confusion after leaving a cult. Referral to an empathic clergyman with some sophistication in the area of religious cultism may be of help in this regard.

Some of the former cult members seen had been exposed to "successful" coercive deprogramming before arriving at my office. Parental arranging for and participation in their son's or daughter's deprogramming is experienced as a rescue operation which is the culminating event in a major family crisis. This is almost invariably highly traumatic for parents, in large part due to the extraordinary unconventionality of their behavior during the deprogramming process, and the associated intensely conflicted affect. A transient reduction in resistance of the family interactional system to change is seen in most cases during this period. This reduction in resistance is associated with acute conscious awareness of love feelings towards the offspring who had been immersed in the cult environment. Prognosis for effective professional intervention via family psychotherapy appears to be maximal when provided immediately subsequent to "successful" deprogramming. Periodic long-term follow-up sessions may be required to reinforce achieved gains and circumvent the possible reconstitution of chronic family system defenses.

## REFERENCES

Bourguignon, E. Cross-cultural perspectives on the religious uses of altered states of consciousness. In I. I. Zaretsky & M. P. Leone (Eds), *Religious movements in Contemporary America*. Princeton: Princeton University Press, 1974.

Clark, J. G., Jr. The noisy brain in a noisy world. Unpubl. man. New Jersey Psychological Association, 1977.

Dator, J. A. *Soka Gakkai, Builders of the Third Civilization: American and Japanese Members*. Seattle: University of Washington Press, 1969.

Davis, R. and Richardson, J. T. The organization and functioning of the children of God. *Sociological Analysis,* 1976, *37* (4), 321-340.

Eister, A. W. Culture crises and new religious movements: A paradigmatic statement of a theory of cults. In I. I. Zaretsky & M. P. Leone (Eds), *Religious Movements in Contemporary America.* Princeton: Princeton University Press, 1974.

Enroth, R. *Youth, Brainwashing and the Extremist Cults.* Grand Rapids: Zondervan Publishing House, 1977.

Erikson, E. H. *Insight and Responsibility.* New York: W. W. Norton & Co., 1964.

Galper, M. F. The cult indoctrine: a new clinical syndrome. Tampa-St. Petersburg-Clearwater Psychiatric Society, 1976.

Galper, M. F. Indoctrination methods of the Unification Church. Los Angeles: California State Psychological Association, 1977a.

Jahoda, M. *Current Conceptions of Positive Mental Health.* New York: Basic Books, 1958.

Kanter, R. M. *Commitment and Community: Communes and Utopias in Sociological Perspective.* Cambridge: Harvard University Press, 1972.

Larson, E. *Strange Sects and Cults.* New York: Hart Publishing Co., 1950.

Levine, S. V. & Salter, N. E. Youth and contemporary religious movements: Psychosocial findings. *Canadian Psychiatric Association Journal,* 1976, *21,* 411-420.

Lifton, R. J. *Thought Reform and the Psychology of Totalism.* New York: W. W. Norton & Co., 1963.

Ludwig, A. M. Altered states of consciousness. *Archives of General Psychiatry,* 1966, *15,* 225-234.

Maslow, A. Higher and lower needs. *Journal of Psychology,* 1948, *25,* 433-434.

Meerloo, J. A. M. *The Rape of the Mind.* New York: Grosset and Dunlap, 1956.

Schwartz, L. L. & Kaslow, F. W. Religious cults, the individual and the family. *Journal of Marital and Family Therapy,* (April) 1979, 15-26.

Shor, R. E. Hypnosis and the concept of the generalized reality orientation. *American Journal of Psychotherapy,* 1959, *13,* 582-602.

Shupe, A. D. & Bromley, D. G. *Moonies in America: Cult Church, and Crusade.* Beverly Hills, CA: Sage, 1979.

Singer, M. T. Coming out of the cults. *Psychology Today,* 1979, 12, 72-82.

Wallis, R. Observations of the children of God. *The Sociological Review,* 1976, *24* (4), 807-828.

# THERAPEUTIC COMMUNITY AND THE DANGER OF THE CULT PHENOMENON

Donald J. Ottenberg, MD

## Introduction

The burgeoning cult phenomenon witnessed in America during the last twenty years occurred during the same period in which therapeutic communities emerged as a treatment method—probably the most effective available—for narcotic addicts and others with drug abuse problems. Among those attracted to cults are persons who, dependent on drugs and without control or direction in life, readily succumb to a cult as a means of salvation. For these young people the cult is an alternative form of treatment, chosen—or acquiesced to—in preference to conventional therapies, or after these treatments have failed. To this extent, therapeutic communities, like established religions, are in competition with cults for the same members.

Since some elements of organizational structure, methods of operation, and even stated purposes of some cults and some therapeutic communities may appear to be similar, it is important to distinguish between the two and delineate the significant differences that separate them. The therapeutic community has earned trusted status as a legitimate means of help for many persons whose lives are being destroyed by dependence on drugs and alcohol. Only careful differentiation of the therapeutic community from the cult will dispel confusion and protect the therapeutic community from the fearful aversion with which most people view cults.

The need to distinguish the therapeutic community from the cult is made more urgent by the adverse publicity given to the therapeutic community concept as a result of recent events at Synanon. Synanon is the first and most famous drug/alcohol therapeutic community and the prototype from which many other therapeutic community organizations have been derived.

---

Dr. Ottenberg is Executive Director, Eagleville Hospital and Rehabilitation Center, Eagleville, PA 19408.

In this report I will examine similarities and differences of cults* and therapeutic communities and seek to explain how a therapeutic community becomes corrupted into a cult. Safeguards that protect therapeutic communites from this kind of transformation will be identified. Finally, while examining aspects of the therapeutic community that may be considered cult-like, criticisms emanating recently from some European colleages in the drug abuse field will be reviewed. The questioning of some approaches taken in this country interpenetrates the issues to be considered in distinguishing therapeutic communities from cults.

The entire community meets daily, at which time various members speak about their experiences and feelings toward the community. There is a good deal of group singing and group physical activities. Memorable community anniversaries and significant events are noted with special celebrations. There are periodic feasts and festivals.

Members who have been in the community longer have more privileges than more recent arrivals, along with special responsibilities in the orientation and indoctrination of new members. All members must abide by community rules; those who do not are singled out and penalized. Everyone observes the dress code. All members share in necessary labor and participate in various activities to raise funds for the community.

Members are not permitted to leave the community grounds without permission from the authorities. Trips outside the community are

---

*Hundreds, if not thousands, of cults are active in the United States today (Jewish Exponent, Phil. Dec. 5, 1980, Phil. Bulletin, Dec. 26, 1978). In this paper, I am concerned with the quasi-religious type of cult exemplified by (but not limited to) the Unification Church (the "Moonies"), led by Sun Myung Moon; the Divine Light Mission ("Premies"), led by Guru Maharaj Ji; the International Society for Krishna Consciousness (Hare Krishna), led by Swami Prabhupada; the Church of Scientology, led by L. Ron Hubbard; the Children of God, led by David (Moses) Berg; and the Transcendental Meditation movement, with Maharishi Mahesh Yogi as its spiritual leader.

Obviously, not all cults follow exactly the same practices nor adhere to the same beliefs. In comparing cults—as a group—with therapeutic communities—as a group—I have tried to identify features that are typical and essential. A comparison of each cult with each therapeutic community would require an exhaustive treatment, which is neither feasible nor necessary for purposes here.

A number of books, published articles and papers presented at professional meetings have served as a major resource in the effort to define and characterize the cult phenomenon. I wish to acknowledge indebtedness to these authors, whose works are identified by asterisks in the bibliography. Credited in the text are authors whose original work or specific ideas have been used. Some ideas, repeated many times in the literature, have not been specifically credited.

made only in groups; no new member ever goes "out" without "support." As a member of the community one gets to understand that the worthiness and high ethical standards one expects to find in the community are not present in the outside world, which is perceived as dangerous. Prohibitions against communication with outside families and friends is necessary, particularly in the early phase of membership. These restrictions are strictly enforced.

The community creates and uses a private language made up of words with new definitions, phrases, mottos and newly-coined words, all of which have special meaning to members and are not readily intelligible to outsiders. One learns secrets known only to the membership.

One must have faith in the community. Older members are "role models" who help newer members to "trust the leaders" and "trust the process." Sometimes group sessions lasting many hours are used as a means of lowering resistance and penetrating psychological defenses.

As a member, you experience the joy of being part of something greater than yourself. You can't really understand it unless you experience it personally; and to experience it fully you must "let go," "give yourself up," which means abandoning all questions and doubts and immersing yourself without reservation in the community's activities and beliefs. In the early part of membership, before one's faith in the community and its norms is solid, one is expected to "act as if," that is, act as if one were fully convinced, even though one's conviction is still tentative. Do what you are expected to do whether you like it or not, understand it or not, accept it or not, or are motivated or not. Later you can be concerned with the emotional and intellectual considerations. Right now the only consideration is behavioral: Do it!

One's entire life will be different, and better, as a result of membership in the community. One owes full allegiance and loyalty to the community in return.

Do the paragraphs above characterize cults or therapeutic communities? In fact, the description fits many cults and many therapeutic communities equally well. We must inquire more deeply into motives and objectives, carefully examine other practices and observe the limits, location and exercise of power if we are to understand the nature of the communities and their effects on their members. Only then will we be able to distinguish between the two phenomena.

## What Is a Therapeutic Community?

In this discussion, the concern is with the therapeutic community as organized to help drug addicts and substance abusers, and not the type found in psychiatric hospitals. The latter therapeutic community, by virtue of its connection with a larger medical institution, is organized differently. It has a different set of objectives and constraints, and is not subject to the same hazards experienced by the therapeutic community in the drug field. The relationship of one type of therapeutic community to the other, and the degree to which both should be categorized under some overarching principle, is discussed elsewhere (Ottenberg, 1978). Henceforth, the phrase therapeutic community refers to the therapeutic community found in the drug abuse field.

Despite the appearance of hundreds of therapeutic communities in the last twenty years, until very recently no single definition has been widely accepted. Each therapeutic community has its own conceptual and organizational framework, some elements of which may be like other therapeutic communities. "Personality" in therapeutic communities varies as widely as in individuals.

In the last few years therapeutic communities in the United States have been banding together in order to learn from one another and to take united action in matters of common interest. Therapeutic Communities of America (TCA) was organized early in 1975 as a loose federation of therapeutic communities in the United States and Canada. Through TCA collaborative projects have been undertaken aimed at defining and describing the structure and functions of therapeutic communities. In January, 1976, TCA and the National Institute on Drug Abuse (NIDA) co-sponsored a conference on The Therapeutic Community. The fifty participants represented various background and disciplines. The common bond was interest and experience in therapeutic communities. The conference addressed a number of topics, among them "What is a therapeutic community?"

No single definition was derived and several types of definition were elucidated. These indicate the range of goals, methods, values, structures and historical derivation found in therapeutic communities. The following extract is taken from the Proceedings of the Planning Conference published as a Services Research Report by NIDA (The Therapeutic Community, 1976):

—Essential Definitions—These identified the most generic nature and principle of the TC, e.g., the therapeutic community is a group of persons who, by following certain salient interpersonal principles, have largely overcome the pain and pain-reducing maladaptive behavior produced by isolation and who have a high skill and willingness in helping other previously alienated persons achieve a clear sense of community fellowship. It is a community that has people who have been out of the community and know how to help other people get back in.

—Functional or Methodological Definitions—These identify how TC'S characteristically operate to achieve their goals, e.g., the TC provides moral and ethical boundaries and expectations for personal development; it employs potential banishment, positive reinforcement, shame, punishment, guilt, example and role modeling to coerce personal change and development; it says here is a structure and some support, make it work for you.

—Purposive Definitions—This defines the TC by its goals for individual members and for the group, e.g., the therapeutic communtiy aims at the development of a new social self and self-definition; it aims at self-improvement and re-entry from sub-culture to the larger society; it aims at the reconstruction of a lifestyle.

—Normative Definitions—These focus on the norms and values intrinsic to the TC, e.g., trust, concern, responsibility, honesty, optimum self-disclosure, nurturance.

—Historical Definitions—These focus on the derivative, evolutionary forms and processes that have resulted in contemporary TC's.

—Structure Definitions—These definitions focus on both static and dynamic organizational features of the communities, e.g., egalitarian or hierarchical, residential or non-residential, status differentiation, size, membership, open or closed system, upward mobility.

As with definition, no single set of characteristics and program philosophies could encompass all therapeutic communities, but many common elements were identified. These included:

—Trust, the binding element in community;
—Egalitarian structure;

—Family (Note: non-egalitarian) optimism for growth and cohesion;

—A commitment to drama, ritual, myth, folklore, to make a living community;

—Growth concept, feeling of love, dedication;

—Congruence of personal life with ideology of the therapeutic community, investment, idealism, power, movement, a cause;

—Security, freedom;

—Integrated cultural lifestyle, adherence to a set of values;

—Hierarchical communication pattern and upward mobility;

—Invasion of space, approach vs. avoidance, optimum self-disclosure;

—Banishment as a control mechanism, sex as part of the reward system*;

—Re-entry from sub-culture to larger society;

—Punishment and restitution; and

—Optimum size (80 members); 25, minimum effective size; 40, more economically feasible; 80, tends to promote growth outward.

Germane to our purpose is the statement of high priority needs provides insight into the intentions and aspirations of therapeutic communities. TCA was urged to support the following:

—The TC's must put themselves to the task of definition. Before developing specific accountability and evaluation measures, they must develop the classification of components, characteristics, indicators, and processes that identify all TC's and that discriminate good TC's. This will accomplish two purposes: it will assist the communities through this next phase of evolutionary adaptation, and will provide Federal and State agencies with quality control and funding criteria.

—TC's will have to start forging a basic, common stance, and consensus, and a methodology. This agenda is begun in the formation of TCA.

—TC's will have to stop using private language and forego claims to nearly mystical uniqueness. They should aim for clarity, enunciation, and simplicity, and develop a "language of bridging."

—Means must be developed for TCA to police its domain and establish standards of practice. TC's will have to show that some (therapeutic) communities represent distortions of TC principles.

—TC's, having gotten most of these tasks underway, will then need to

---

*This refers to the earned privilege of personal choice regarding responsible sexual involvement, not to sex as a direct reward or promiscuous sex.

undertake a strong, well-designed promotion program demonstrating the need for this small group modality as part of the national health armamentarium.

In April, 1978, the TCA Board of Directors unanimously approved a position paper with the primary goal to foster personal growth by changing one's lifestyle through participation in a community of concerned people where its members work and support one another. Self help and attendant responsible behavior are the major philosophical principles and practices of the therapeutic community.

## Historical Roots

The repeated stress on active participation by all members, along with the obligation to take primary responsibility for one's own progress toward recovery, indicates the self-help nature of the therapeutic community. This, historically, is in direct lineal descent from Alcoholics Anonymous. In 1958, when Charles E. Dederich, III incorporated Synanon as a not-for-profit corporation, The Synanon Foundation, he had been sober for about two years, after 15 years or more of alcoholic drinking (Casmel, 1963, Yablonsky, 1965, Endire, 1966). For about eighteen months Dederich's life had revolved primarily around AA, in which he participated intensively and almost daily.

It was out of the accumulated wisdom and time-tested practices of AA that Dederich and his small band of followers, most alcoholics like himself, at first, but, soon after, with the help of narcotic addicts, evolved the concepts and methods of Synanon. This was a gradual process that moved forward at an uncertain pace, shaping and reshaping itself by trial and error more than design. Although Dederich and his followers soon moved beyond traditional AA concepts, the underlying principles of AA remained at the core: a fellowship brought together by a common problem. Each member was responsible for himself—or herself—yet dependent on the membership for psychological and emotional support. Each person was committed to helping others with the same problem as an integral part of helping himself.

As it developed from its original form, as a club to a shared house where members lived in retreat from the hazards of the world outside, Synanon resembled many small communal groups, that were precursors of the Oxford Groups & the Washingtonians, two movements that strongly influenced the cofounders of AA (Alcoholics Anonymous, 1971). Countless

utopian communities and monastic brotherhoods had appeared and disappeared through the centuries dating back to the apostolic or primitive
Christian movement. The small groups that gathered in the "house
churches" of the early Christian era followed orders and procedures similar
to the rules and practices of therapeutic communities today. The pattern of
life in the Essene sect bears striking resemblance to some aspects of life in
the therapeutic community (Mowrer, 1977). The basic premise of the
Synanon process—full disclosure of self to the membership and the obligation to accept the honest, though frequently harsh, criticisms of the
group—were anticipated in exomologesis. Open confession, absolute and
without deception, was practiced by members of the early Christian church
as a means to achieve personal transparency (*Ibid,* Mowrer). Structures
and practices significant in both therapeutic communities and cults have
common roots in the long tradition of sects, communes and utopian communities that go back to antiquity.

## What Is a Cult?

In a world where few reassuring certainties endure, it is understandable
that many persons, particularly during the turbulence of adolescence, will
seek solutions and solace in cults. The simple surrender of self brings
admission to an enveloping community and its ready-made answers to
perplexing questions. If the answers are cast in the language of idealism
and the ultimate purposes are in line with a person's yearning for significant meaning in life, so much more powerful are the enticements of the
beckoning community. The reasons why cults are attracting Americans in
such large numbers seem obvious and understandable. But what is a cult?
How would one define it?

No national organization of cults exists, comparable to the Therapeutic
Communities of America, from which helpful clues can be derived. Nor do
cults make an effort to explain themselves to the world outside. They
exhibit the opposite tendency, operating in secrecy behind locked gates and
blinded windows. No definition of the cult's character or purpose is offered, beyond the bland superficialities of their corporate charters.

A description of a cult must use a composite of observations and interpretations of those who have experienced cult life and those who have
studied the cult phenomenon over the past several years. These observers
include psychiatrists, psychologists, and others in the health care professions who have treated disturbed persons who are current or past members
of cults.

Members of the clergy have become knowledgeable about cults. Distraught members of their congregations whose children have been alienated from the family by the cult experience have sought help. Some religious leaders have the additional motive of wishing to distinguish between the cult and organized religious institutions.

From these sources; information made public at numerous trials in which cult leaders were defendants or plaintiffs; and from accounts published by persons who have broken away from cult membership, one can piece together consistent patterns of behavior and objectives that can be identified as the cult phenomenon (Conway and Siegelman, 1978; Edward, 1979; Lifton, 1961; Patrick and Dulack, 1976; Patton, 1976; Scott, 1978; Stone and Park, 1977).

Characteristics of cults are found in "The Challenge of the Cults," a report of The Special Committee on Exotic Cults of the Jewish Community Relations Council of Greater Philadelphia (1978). By their definition "a cult is a group that exhibits the following characteristics:

—It is a group of people who follow a living leader, usually a dominant, paternal male figure, or occasionally, a pair or a family of leaders.

—It is a group whose leader makes absolute claims about his character, abilities, and/or knowledge. These claims may include any or all of the following: A claim that he is divine—God incarnate, the messiah, etc. A claim that he is the sole agent of the divine on earth—God's agent or emissary. A claim that he is omniscient and infallible —the possessor of absolute truth and total wisdom.

—It is a group in which membership is contingent on complete and literal acceptance of the leader's claims to divinity, infallibility, etc., and acceptance of his teachings, doctrines and dogma.

—It is a group in which membership is contingent on complete, unquestioning loyalty and allegiance to the leader.

—It is a group in which membership is contingent on a complete and total willingness to obey the cult leader's commands without question.

—It is, then, a group that is by definition undemocratic, absolutist."

Not all groups labeled "cults" show all of these characteristics to the same degree and a group need not be religious in nature to be a cult.

One of the implications of the above defintion is that

it does not assume that any of the more objectionable actions commonly ascribed to cults are necessarily intrinsic to their nature. To put it another way, the fact that a group is a cult does not necessarily mean that it has to raise funds under false pretenses, recruit members through deception, counsel hatred of parents, distort the beliefs of other religions, violate the laws of the state, or forbid its members from receiving medical attention.

On the other hand, there is nothing intrinsic to a cult that would prevent any, or all, of these practices from taking place; in a cult *everything depends on the leader.*

Additional characteristics of cults have been pointed out by still other observers (Clark, 1979; Cath et al., 1980). Singing in unison, dancing and bouncing in a group are common features. So is speaking in whispers. The soft voice may connote the awe with which the spiritual leader is perceived. It may be a mimicking of the leader. The quiet subdued way of talking, the passivity inherent in posture and gait, the vacant staring—all indicate a state of receptivity and non-resistance, and readiness for acceptance of the leader. Meditation and relaxation exercises, important prescribed activities in many cults, also reduce tension, lower defenses and prepare recruits for the unqualified submission required by the leader. Many of these techniques have the quality of hypnotic suggestion, which may help to explain the rapidity with which some people are indoctrinated once they come within the cult's boundary and are enveloped by its teachings.

An element common to many cults is the belief in the apocalypse, the end of the world when true believers will be forgiven and embraced by the deity (*Ibid,* Cath et al., 1980). This is appealing to young people who have had difficulty resolving feelings of guilt and shame and who experience a fragmentation of self, a feeling that everything in life is falling apart. If one can give self over to something larger and more significant than one's being, if one can merge with one's brothers and sisters, and indeed, with all of life—the entire universe—can one fail to have forgiveness? If the world is coming to an end, isn't a saviour needed to protect and prepare us for the end?

In many cults the end of the world fantasy becomes fixed as a rule of mind, a powerful mind-focusing metaphor (*op. cit.* Clark, 1979). This is one way to deal with death and the fear of dying. An obsessional fantasy of death and salvation continues to restrict the focus of the member's mind. It shifts the mind away from the familiar wide-ranging questions and concerns of adolescence to a narrow and intense fixation on a few imperative truths by which one's worthiness and readiness for acceptance in the cult are measured.

While the mind is being conditioned, the body is taxed with physical demands, less sleep, more regulation and disciplined behavior. The demand increases, the penalty of criticism and rejection for failure becomes more painful, and the will to resist, or even question, disappears. The focus becomes so narrow that one is limited to think and act only in the present moment, anything beyond ceases to exist. The usual multiordinal quality of life is lost. Consciousness becomes unilinear in a trance-like state (*op. cit.* Clark, 1980).

This is the time when various "transcendental experiences" occur, and when many persons suffer severe and lasting psychological damage. Hallucinatory and dissociative symptoms are not unusual. With the group providing reassuring support and the leaders saying that God is speaking directly, one is buffered against terrible fear and the psychic decompensation that might otherwise ensue (*op. cit.* Clark, 1980).

After experiences like these many persons are not the same. Changes in personality may be so great that parents have difficulty recognizing their own children. Old interests and values may be replaced totally by concern with the cult. Delusions, hallucinations, and paranoia may persist. All the evidence of mental illness may be present, yet one can remain compensated so long as one lives within the confining demands and allowances of the cult's environment. Eventually one loses "adaptive autonomy" almost completely (*op. cit.* Clark, 1980). One is defined by the cult. One does what the cult demands.

At this point, an attempt to break away, which few have the will to do, will end in failure because of the power of techniques and centering devices currently available. These include preaching, praying, speaking in tongues; ritualized activities of various kinds: sensory deprivation through sleeplessness, exposure to cold, and extreme fatigue (*op. cit.* Clark, 1980). Paradoxically, fear of those in control of the punishing environment competes with fear of being rejected.

Through processes of humiliation and obedience, sensory deprivation and severe discipline, along with various group activities and shared experiences, rules and beliefs are reinforced into ritual. The person is conditioned to accept the leader as the solution to all problems and the sole source of fulfillment. The ability to think independently is lost. Compliance, elevated to worship, earns salvation. In these terms, the incredible phenomenon of mass suicide on command at Jonestown becomes understandable. The control exercised by a cult and the power accorded to its leader is best illustrated in a case study of Synanon.

## The Elevation and Fall of Dederich

### *"Synanon Founder and Two Guards Convicted in Attack with a Snake"*

That bizarre headline from the New York Times of July 16, 1980 announced the sad climax of a court case in which Charles E. Dederich, broken down physically and emotionally, and relapsed to drunkenness, pleaded no contest, along with two members of Synanon's security force, to charges of conspiring to commit murder using a rattlesnake. The rattlesnake attack was on Paul Marantz, a Los Angeles lawyer, who had won a $300,000 lawsuit against Synanon and who also had been successful in having several young persons removed from Synanon by court order. The snake was placed in the lawyer's mailbox. Marantz was bitten but did survive after hospital treatment.

People who had known Mr. Dederich over the years and had been aware of events at Synanon over the last decade really were not surprised. Although the manner and calculated viciousness of the attack were shocking, the fact that hateful violence erupted was seen as an almost inevitable climax to the deterioration of a closed community that allowed its founder-leader to acquire almost unquestioned power. Indeed, some of the community members had come to perceive in Dederich attributes usually reserved for a deity. In its November 27, 1978 issue, New Times wrote of "the thousands of perpetually smiling former misfits who worshipped 'the Founder' as they would a god."

For several years strange reports had been circulating about Synanon (The Philadelphia Evening Bulletin, 1975; Newsweek, 1978). There were stories that Dederich was becoming obsessed with power and control over his followers (New York Times, 1978; Philadelphia Evening Bulletin, 1977; Philadelphia Inquirer, 1978). Except for the departure of a relatively small number of members who refused to obey arbitrary new rules, there appeared to be no person or group at Synanon capable and willing to block Dederich as his edicts became increasingly ominous. Dederich had to stop smoking, for health reasons; it was decreed that everyone at Synanon give up smoking. A few hundred members left, but the great majority remained. In a few days Synanon was converted to a non-smoking community.

Similar decrees were handed down about dieting. At one time all the women in the community shaved their heads. Birth control was enforced. All men in certain age categories were told to have a vasectomy.

In 1977 Dederich's third wife died and he chose a new female companion. It was soon after this, according to an account in the Philadelphia Inquirer (1978), Dederich thought, "wouldn't it be funny to perform some kind of emotional surgery on people who are getting along pretty well." He directed married Synanon members to divorce their mates and pair off in three-year "love matches" with new mates. "Changing partners" was Dederich's label for the new idea (*op. cit.* The Philadelphia Evening Bulletin, 1977).

In the mid-seventies Synanon presented itself as a religious movement. In 1978, a booklet, "The Synanon Religion—The Survival Morality for the 21st Century" was written by Howard M. Garfield, a resident of Synanon since 1971 and, at the time of publication of the booklet by Synanon Foundation, Inc., the head of Synanon's Legal Department and a member of Synanon's Board of Directors.

While these changes were taking place, Synanon was moving farther and farther away from the policy of nonviolence that originally was a cardinal rule of the community (New York Times, 1980; Phil. Evening Bulletin, 1977). Now suspicion and paranoid ideas beset Dederich and the entire community (New York Times, 1978; Phil. Enquirer, 1978). Martial arts and training in defense tactics replaced other everyday activities (*op. cit.* New York Times, 1978). A large cache of weapons was found at Synanon through an investigation by the California Attorney General's office (New York Times, 1980). By the time the attempt on Marantz's life was planned and carried out, Dederich seemed to be in a paranoid state, and his followers joined him in a "folie en masse."

### Why Did Synanon Fail?

Synanon broke all rules that safeguard a therapeutic community against a charismatic leader who—for whatever reason—becomes incapable of continuing as the major source for the moral and ethical standards of the community. Allowing one person to become dominant beyond challenge, Synanon put the entire community at the will of the leader. No mechanism remained by which the leader's judgment could be questioned. Even the Synanon game, in which for years Dederich could be challenged and criticized, ceased to provide a corrective to his irrationality.

Synanon as a self-contained community associated with the outside world only on Synanon's terms. Not requiring, or respecting, the give and take that occurs naturally where there are competing interests, and seeing no need to abide by the larger community's values and norms, Synanon ventured outside the walls of its "cities" only to conduct necessary business, to "hustle" needed goods, services and money, or to recruit new members. Synanon desired no more from the outside world than to be let alone, provided it could continue to enter that larger world at will for its own purposes.

As Synanon became a world within itself, soon it was a law unto itself. No one knew what was good, or right, for Synanon better than Synanon; and Synanon, with gates closed, saw no obligation to abide by rules other than its own.

Synanon as a community lacked the corrective effect of honest intercourse with peers. Some visits to Synanon took place, but outsiders always were guests privileged to observe Synanon's way, never colleagues and equals with whom Synanon would engage in mutually instructive discourse. Dederich rarely participated in conventions or meetings with leaders of other programs. On the few occasions when he was willing to attend he invariably cast himself in the role of teacher and others in the role of student.

Synanon missed the leavening effect a program can have if its population is made up in part by its own graduates and in part by professionals who come to provide services, but not to be inducted themselves into the mythic system. Synanon's source of strength—its homogeneous tribe of true believers—was also its greatest vulnerability. In order to be at Synanon, one had to join up, not as a professional, but as a lifetime adherent to a philosophy and a religion. The subjugation of individual judgement and conscience to the group's will was the price of admission.

Synanon prided itself on its ability to remain self-supporting without governmental or foundation help (Endore, 1968). By denying itself funds from these sources Synanon avoided any obligation to abide by regulations that monitor and constrain the use of tax-based dollars and provide protection from illegal or unethical activity.

Synanon refused to join organizations of therapeutic communities, both national and international, thereby missing the opportunity to hear questions and criticism from knowledgeable peers who take divergent views. Synanon's insulation against a world it perceived as hostile and evil was also a barrier separating it from friends and colleagues who had many common interests and concerns. Synanon lost touch with the subtle but significant shifts of attitude and public policy shaping the environment to which therapeutic community approaches, as a movement with common interests and methods, must accommodate. Synanon never saw itself as part of a larger movement. It was *the* way, a movement in and of itself. There were no shared goals. The only way to cooperate with Synanon was to join it.

Synanon was willing to accept new members—on its terms—but had no wish or need to join forces with any other body. This gave Synanon a monolithic character not seen in other large and successful therapeutic communities that participate in a free exchange of ideas and share tasks toward common objectives.

Operating beyond the scrutiny of other therapeutic communities, Synanon did not participate in the creation of standards considered necessary and appropriate. These standards, addressing ethical issues in the organization and operation of a therapeutic community, were created to protect the basic rights of individuals and the integrity of the therapeutic community as an organization.

An example of the standards promulgated by Therapeutic Communities of America is a Clients' Rights Statement ratified recently by the TCA Board of Directors.* This statement aims to assure fair, considerate and ethical treatment to every individual who enters a therapeutic community and speaks specifically to basic rights of individuals which must not be denied. TCA also has adopted a Staff Code of Ethics for its members. This code, reproduced on the application form for membership, is concerned with behavior towards members, staff interactions, responsibility to the employing agency, behavior towards other agencies, personal responsibility and to the larger community.

### Important Differences Between Cults and Therapeutic Communities

#### Power

In the cult power ultimately rests with one person, the leader or guru, whose word is law and whose person in many cults is considered to embody the deity. Power in the therapeutic community rests with the whole community, within which a hierarchical staff structure is answerable, ultimately, to a board of directors. No single person in the therapeutic community is law.

#### Focus of Interest

In the cult concern is with the apocalypse, the universe, eternity, or life after death. The therapeutic community focuses persistently on the here and now and on the elements that determine an individual's problem and the means to relieve it.

---

*Copy available on request from Therapeutic communities of America % Samaritan Halfway House, 118-21 Queens Blvd., Forest Hills, NY 11375.

The therapeutic community values self-searching, self-awareness and self-acceptance. It fosters appreciation and expression of one's unique identity. The cult stresses selflessness, loss of individual identity, merging with the group and with the universe. The ego the therapeutic community strengthens, the cult suppresses.

## Goals

The goal of the therapeutic community is to help the individual member achieve self-awareness, self-control, responsibility for self, and the ability to function autonomously outside the therapeutic community. The cult goal is to incorporate the individual into the cult—permanently—in order to strengthen the cult in its efforts toward its political, economic and religious objectives.

The therapeutic community, despite great potency derived from a highly organized, cohesive community, remains a member-centered community. This idea is expressed in O. Hobart Mowrer's aphorism: "Only you can do it, but you can not do it alone." The cult is centered on the word and person of the leader. He—or she—not the individual member and not the community as a whole, is the pivot around which the life of the cult revolves.

## The Right to Challenge

The therapeutic community provides opportunities for any member to challenge any other member of the community, regardless of relative positions or levels of authority.

The cult requires obedience and acceptance of the cult's beliefs as revealed by the leader. Any real challenge is met by a variety of measures: punishment, isolation, preaching and teaching, induced fatigue from hard labor, exercise and minimal sleep, fear, "love bombing," absorption into the group by means of shared activities, such as chanting, hopping, jumping, dancing in unison. The use of physical restraint—unheard of in a therapeutic community—is not unusual in the cult.

## Accountability

Responsibility for the therapeutic community is invested ultimately in its board of trustees and they, in turn, are answerable to the community from which tax funds and tax exempt status are derived. Numerous local, state and federal bureaucratic agencies keep the therapeutic community accountable to their regulatory and supervisory function.

Most cults define themselves as religious organizations and use constitutional protections to avoid accountability to outside agencies. They are not subject to licensing and accrediting requirements comparable to those with which therapeutic communities must comply.

*Openness to the Outside Community*

Therapeutic communities restrict communication between the individual resident and persons outside only during the earliest phase of membership. This "blackout" period usually lasts from two weeks to a month. The limitation is imposed to permit orientation of the member to the program and entry into the community without countertherapeutic influences from family members and friends outside. Most therapeutic communities attempt to involve the family in the resident's program beginning in an early phase of treatment.

Therapeutic communities are open to visitors, both lay and professional. Tours, open house events, educational and training programs for outsiders are frequent.

Many cults permit visits to take place at their residences, but accounts from many former cult members indicate that visitors are carefully guided through the facility and visits are arranged so that guests see only selected parts of the environment and interact only with carefully chosen members (Edwards, 1979; Patrick and Dulack, 1976; Stoner and Parks, 1977).

*Pre-Entry Information*

Therapeutic communites provide accurate and complete information regarding their programs, indicating objectives, policies, procedures and expected duration of stay. Most therapeutic communities distribute a resident's handbook that spells out this kind of information. Cults rarely inform the prospective member about the cult's practices or goals. Numerous accounts from persons enrolled in various cults indicate that deceit, subterfuge and a carefully orchestrated process of manipulation are used. Thought control is designed to draw the individual deeper and deeper into a situation, the nature and implications of which he or she does not comprehend (*op. cit.* Edwards, 1979; Patrick and Dulack, 1976).

*Aftercare*

Basic capabilities and skills needed to support oneself in a stable and autonomous life are a major target in therapeutic communities. Remedial education, vocational counseling and training, and the teaching of life skills are incorporated into the therapeutic community program.

The cult does not release the individual from the cult and its influence, so the concept of aftercare is meaningless.

## Change of Personality

The therapeutic community provides an environment in which growth and maturation can occur. Those who successfully complete the therapeutic community program realize major gains toward self-realization, knowledge of personal assets and limitations, and the ability to mobilize personal resources toward meaningful goals. Remarkable changes occur in the countenance and behavior of some individuals. But the person remains the same person, who simply has used the opportunity to express him or herself in a different way. This shift in personality occurs gradually and the progress of the individual is evident to those around him. This differs from the rapid personality change observed in many cult members.

In the cult the shift away from the established personality is accompanied by the loss of ability to maintain continuity between the former and the new personalities. Something sudden, severe, unintentional and, usually, irreversible has taken place. The exact nature of this change is not established. Whatever the nature of the change and its underlying mechanisms, the sudden shift of personality resulting from the cult experience appears to change the way in which the brain functions. The person is altered. From the perspective of qualified observers, this is not growth, but induced pathologic change (Conway and Siegelman, 1978; Lifton, 1961; Scott, 1978; Ungerleider and Wellisch, 1979).

## International Concerns

How authority and power are distributed in the governance of therapeutic community programs emerged as a controversial question in recent meetings of The World Conference of Therapeutic Communities, a section of the International Council on Alcoholism and Addiction. Disagreement became evident in the first meeting, which took place in Norrkoping, Sweden in 1976, and has reappeared at the four annual conferences that have followed (*op. cit.* Ottenberg, 1978). The issue has been joined in the texts of prepared presentations, but to a greater extent has been in the discussions which followed and in the informal give and take that occurred outside meeting rooms.

Some of the European participants took strong anti-authoritarian positions, in conflict with the views—and practices—of American therapeutic communities in the lineage of Synanon, Daytop, and Phoenix House (Casriel and Amern, 1971; Sugarman, 1939; De Lem, 1974).

Approaches described by some American programs made some European colleagues uneasily mindful of organizational style and practices remembered from youth movements under totalitarian governments. They expressed their deep conviction that the danger of misusing the power of the community under a charismatic leader might outweigh any positive results expected of the program. They questioned the extent therapeutic effectivness depends on authoritarian and charismatic leadership in a therapeutic community, and how safeguards against misuse of power can be built into the system (Fifth World Conference of Therapeutic Community; Grimberg, Kalibaba, and Pomella; Kerr; Ladisich-Raine; Palmgren; Jones; Schaap; Setiabudhi, 1980).

This issue—and others that emerged at the Conference—probe once again the ethical position of those who use powerful methods to bring about change in others. In another form, this is the same question Robert Jay Lifton referred to in 1961 in his book on brainwashing, *Thought Reform and the Psychology of Totalism*. He alludes to the "...responsible—even tortured—self-examination which leads professional people to ask whether they in their own activities might not be guilty of 'brainwashing'...." The question is perhaps even more pertinent today. Since the time when Lifton did his studies, methods of controlling behavior and engendering change in the therapeutic context are more sophisticated and more predictably "effective." Now more than ever we need to explore the grounds on which we justify the methods we use, even as we must carefully define the circumstances and limits within which we use those methods. Simply going ahead because "it works," or because people in trouble "need our help," is not sufficient, any more than uncourageous retreat in the face of these challenging questions is acceptable.

### Summary: What Lesson for the Therapeutic Community?

A comparison of cults and therapeutic communities of the type organized to help persons with drug and alcohol problems leads to the following conclusions:

1. The differences that distinguish these two types of program from one another are striking and far more substantial than superficial similarities that identify one with the other.

2. The prime purpose of the therapeutic community is to provide assis-

tance toward a fresh start in life, outside the therapeutic community, to persons caught in the trap of addiction or drug abuse. The prime purpose of the cult is to attract, indoctrinate and hold members in the cult community of believers. Ultimate dissociation of the member from the cult and its practices is not intended. Joining a cult is a lifelong commitment, although many initiates are not aware of this at the time of entering. Admittance to a therapeutic community is a temporary involvement, comparable to a stay in a hospital, convalescent home, rehabilitation center, or a live-in school.

3. Therapeutic communities take pains to insure that a prospective resident understands the purpose of the therapeutic community and the way it operates. This understanding is essential in gauging motivation of the intended new member and in deciding whether this modality of treatment, or some other, is appropriate. The new member entering a cult has only a vague idea of the cult's purposes and usually no true concept of what will be experienced as a result of joining.

4. The most important fact about cults is that each is dominated by a single person whose status is elevated above all others, usually to the extreme of taking on god-like qualities. Therapeutic communities are organized in pyramidal structures and usually have an individual in the position of director, or executive director. The leader in the therapeutic community may be charismatic but, unless the therapeutic community has shifted from its original mold into the form and practices of a cult, the leader is not considered omnipotent, omniscient or unchallengable, nor is he or she considered to be pre-ordained for the role.

5. Cults live by rules and standards they create for themselves. By virtue of their status as quasi-religious, self-financed, private organizations, cults avoid close scrutiny and bureaucratic regulation by governmental bodies. Therapeutic communities, with a few notable exceptions, receive public funds as part of the network of community health care service providers. They are accountable to various official agencies. Therapeutic communities are generally open to the public and have many interactions with outside persons and groups. Cults characteristically remain aloof from the world, have very limited intercourse with outsiders, and keep their operations hidden from view. A high priority objective of therapeutic communities which are members of Therapeutic Communities of America (TCA) is to forego private language and claims to mystical uniqueness, which cults depend on.

6. A large body of evidence indicates that the cult experience is damaging to many individuals. Profound changes in personality and intellect occur. Many instances of psychosis directly precipitated by involvement

with a cult have been documented. Changes of this kind are rarely observed in persons who have participated in a therapeutic community.

7. Therapeutic communities, as powerful, self-contained, social organizations, are susceptible to corruption if a single individual is permitted to assume a dictatorial role and the community becomes fixed on a messianic mission and an absolutist creed.

8. The therapeutic community method is protected against the danger of transformation into a cult when it remains open to the outside world. It is required to live by ethical standards that provide boundaries for the authority and activities of leaders and assure practices that guard the safety and basic rights of individuals. At meetings of national and international organizations of therapeutic communities these concerns are shared by persons representing a wide variety of viewpoints and approaches, including persons who are not themselves members of therapeutic communities. This open diversity challenges attitudes and beliefs that otherwise might tend to become entrenched and unassailable.

Forums provide the free exchange of ideas out of which standards of good practice and ethical guidelines emerge. By operating within these acceptable boundaries therapeutic communities preserve their integrity while continuing to develop as a powerful and legitimate therapeutic method.

A few European colleagues have criticized some American therapeutic communities for their authoritarian structure, aggressive behavior modeling techniques, and the "fusional relationship" that encompasses everyone in the community. These critics deny that the therapeutic community deserves to be called a therapeutic method, even though it "works" for some.

That these questions are raised and discussed in open international forums can only be seen as healthy. An important underlying issue is the extent to which powerful methods employed in therapeutic work mimic techniques some think of as "mind control," or "brainwashing." This question has relevance far beyond therapeutic communities. Methods should not be used without considering whether they violate ethical principles that must be upheld; but neither should a method of proved efficacy— like the therapeutic community—be renounced simply because challenging questions about it are raised.

## BIBLIOGRAPHY

*Alcoholics Anonymous Comes of Age,* New York: AA World Services, Inc., 1971, pp. 39, 58ff, 64-68, 74ff, 77, 124ff, 160ff, 262.

Authors alarmed by fanaticism, Jewish Exponent, Phila., Dec. 5, 1980.

Casriel, D. *So Fair A House: The Story of Synanon,* Prentice-Hall, Inc., Englewood Cliffs, N.J., 1963.

Casriel, D. & Amern, G. *Daytop: Three Addicts and Their Cures.* New York: Hill and Wang, 1971.

*Cath, S. H.; Clark, J. G.; Marks, E. S.; Etemad, B.; at Cults: Clinical Significance, 17th Annual A.P. Noyes Memorial Conference, Norristown, PA: October, 1980.

*Clark, J. G. Cults. *JAMA,* July 20, 1979, Vol. 242, No. 3, pp. 279-281.

*Conway, F. & Siegelman, J. *Snapping.* Philadelphia: J. B. Lippincott, 1978.

DeLeon, G. *Phoenix House: Studies in a Therapeutic Community (1968-1973).* New York: MSS Information Corp., 1974.

*Edwards, C. *Crazy for God.* Englewood Cliffs, N.J.: Prentice-Hall, Inc., 1979.

Endore, G. *Synanon.* Garden City, N.Y.: Doubleday & Co., Inc., 1968, 291-296.

Expert says cults create zombies, The Bulletin, Philadelphia, November 26, 1978.

Grimberg, M.; Kalibaba, N.; Pomella, J. D. The French Social Workers Question The T.C. Model, pp 37ff, The Fifth World Conference of Therapeutic Communities, ICAA, The Hague-Netherlands: August 31-Sept. 5, 1980.

Jones, M. Therapeutic Communities in Perspective, pp. 135ff. The Fifth World Conference of Therapeutic Communities, ICAA, The Hague-Netherlands: August 31-Sept. 5, 1980.

Kerr, D. H. Some responses to the paper entitled "French Social Workers Question the T.C. Model," p. 4ff, The Fifth World Conference of Therapeutic Communities, ICAA, The Hague-Netherlands: Aug. 31-Sept. 5, 1980.

Ladisich-Raine, A. Towards a Democratic, creative therapeutic Community, p 53ff. The Fifth World Conference of Therapeutic Communities, ICAA, The Hague-Netherlands: Aug. 31-Sept. 5, 1980.

*Lifton, R. J. *Thought Reform and the Psychology of Totalism,* New York: Norton and Co., Inc., 1961.

Mowrer, O. H. Therapeutic Groups and Communities in Retrospect and Prospect, *The Proceedings of the First World Conference on Therapeutic Communities,* Montreal: The Portage Press, 1977.

Ottenberg, D. J. Therapeutic Community—Bastard Child of Public Health, *The Addiction Therapist,* Special Issue, Part II, Vol. 2, Nos. 3 & 4, Montreal, Canada: 1978, pp 2-7.

Palmgren, L. Abstract, pp. 59ff. The Fifth World Conference of Therapeutic Communities, ICAA, The Hague-Netherlands: Aug. 31-Sept. 5, 1980.

*Patrick, T. & Dulack, T. *Let Our Children Go.* New York: Random House, Inc., 1976.

*Patton, J. E. *The Case Against TM in the Schools,* Grand Rapids, Michigan: Baker Book House, 1976.

Schaap, G. E. Democratic and Concept-Based Therapeutic Communities, pp. 155ff. The Fifth World Conference of Therapeutic Communities, ICAA, The Hague-Netherlands: August 31-September 5, 1980.

*Scott, R. D. *Transcendental Misconceptions.* San Diego, CA: Beta Book, 1978.

Setiabudhi, T. The possibility for setting up a therapeutic community in the developing countries, pp 203ff. The Fifth World Conference of Therapeutic Communities, ICAA, The Hague-Netherlands: Aug. 31-Sept. 5, 1980.

*Stoner, C. & Park, J. A. *All Gods Children.* Radnor, PA: Chilton Book Company, 1977.

Sugarman, B. *Daytop Village: A Therapeutic Community.* New York: Holt, Rinehart & Winston, Inc., 1939.

Synanon's Dad: The parallels to Jones are eerie, Philadelphia Inquirer, Dec. 5, 1978.

Synanon Game: 'Change Partners', The Evening Bulletin, Dec. 17, 1977.

Synanon Chief Arraigned by an Alleged Murder Plot, New York Times, Dec. 3, 1978.

Synanon Recordings Seized in Snake-in-Mailbox Case, New York Times, Nov. 23, 1978.

Synanon Friends and Two Guards Convicted in Attack with a Snake, New York Times, July 16, 1980.

*The Challenge of the Cults,* Jewish Community Relations Council of Greater Philadelphia, Philadelphia, PA: January, 1978.

*The Therapeutic Community.* Proceedings of Therapeutic Communities of America Planning Conference, Services Research Report, NIDA, U. S. Dept. of HEW: January 29-30, 1976, pp. 32 & 33.

The Synanon Horrors, New Times, November 27, 1978.

The Trouble at Synanon, Newsweek, June 26, 1978.

Ungerleider, J. T. & Wellisch, D. K. Coercive Persuasion (Brainwashing), Religious Cults, and Deprogramming, *Am. J. Psychiatry 136* (3), March, 1979.

Women Shave Heads for Freedom, The Evening Bulletin, Philadelphia, Feb. 28, 1975, p. 52.

# INFORMATION SEARCH STRATEGIES: CULTS AND THE FAMILY

Jonathan B. Jeffery
Patricia W. Jeffery

A knowledge of reference sources and services available in libraries today will assist the social scientist and interested layperson in collecting information on cults or any other phenomenon relating to marriage and the family. Keeping in mind the interdisciplinary and dynamic nature of the family, primary reference sources for retrospective and current literature will be given.

## Abstracts and Indexes

Since scholarly journals provide the major vehicle for reporting research, it is advantageous to emphasize the abstracts and indexes that organize the literature. Two sources whose contents are devoted to marriage and the family are *Sage Family Studies Abstracts,* 1979-, and the *Inventory of Marriage and Family Literature.* The latter publication is as good a place as any to begin a retrosepctive review of a marriage and family topic. In the *Inventory,* an effort was made to cover the literature from 1900 to 1964 in Volume 1, with additional volumes continuing coverage up to 1979. Besides the standard subject and author indexes, there is a Keyword-in-Context (KWIC) index that allows the searcher to locate references by all of the key words in the article titles. To supplement and update this source, the searcher could next turn to the *Sage Family Studies Abstracts.* As in the *Inventory* reference volumes, this abstracting service covers books, articles, pamphlets, and other fugitive material. In addition to its currency, another advantage of this Sage publication over the *Inventory* is its provision of summaries or abstracts of each publication listed.

---

Jonathan B. Jeffery is acting head, Documents and Maps Department, Morris Library, University of Delaware. Patricia W. Jeffery is a lecturer for the Writing Center at the University of Delaware.

*175*

The Institute for Scientific Information emphasizes in its reference publications currency, thoroughness, and interdisciplinary coverage of scholarly periodicals. Marriage and family articles may be retrieved in the *Social Science Citation Index,* 1969-, by author, corporate source, or paired key words. The Permuterm Index is like the KWIC index in that the searcher may look for key words in the titles. It differs in that each key word is paired with every other word in the article title. Here, any prominent term that describes the research topic may be searched through thousands of journals. The topic of "cults" may be sought directly here, which is often not the case in other indexes. For instance, in the 1979 Permuterm Index, People's Temple, Scientology, Divine-Light, Hare Krishna, and Moonies were all listed. *Current Contents: Social and Behavioral Sciences,* another ISI publication, is a weekly which reviews journals up to a recent date. Here the researcher would look up the marriage and family journal by name in the index and scan the table of contents of one of its recent issues. Also, a brief subject index is provided where articles may be located under the subject "family."

Numerous references to journals and books on marriage, the family, and cults will be found in *Sociological Abstracts,* 1953-, and *Social Sciences Index,* 1907-. *Sociological Abstracts* is arranged by a classification scheme, so the classification number 1900 for "family and socialization," and 1941 for "sociology of the family" will remain the same from index to index, allowing the searcher to quickly identify the location for these topics in each index. For completeness, the subject indexes also should be checked under various family headings. Suggested headings for cults are: sect(s), cult(s), convert(s, -ed, -ing, -sion), religion(s, -ous), irrational (ism, -ity), mystic(ism, -al), youth(s, -ful). What is not covered in *Sociological Abstracts* probably can be found in the *International Bibliography of Sociology.* It also has a scheme with a subdivision for family (i.e., Population. Family. Ethnic Group.). The alphabetical author-subject index of the *Social Sciences Index* delineates the field into many headings which will be noted as "see" references under "family." Another Wilson publication, the *Education Index,* 1929-, is an author-subject index to educational periodicals, proceedings, and yearbooks. The topic "cults" is located here under the term "sects."

As psychology plays an integral role in many family studies, *Psychological Abstracts,* 1927-, and *Child Development Abstracts and Bibliography,* 1927- would be two necessary candidates for any source list on the subject. The type of literature to be found in *Psychological Abstracts* is revealed by a sample of the subject index words and phrases:

cultism, family relations, family crises, family counseling, and family members. *Child Development Abstracts* often repeat *Psychological Abstracts*, but are more extensive in pediatrics and physical medicine. *Women Studies Abstracts*, 1972- was introduced into the communication network to assist in the retrieval of the burgeoning literature on women's studies. Other articles on women, including such topics as dual careers and personal finances, are indexed in *Human Resources Abstracts*, 1966-.

Four indexes were particularly helpful in the search for articles on cults. The greatest single index to popular news magazines is probably the *Readers' Guide to Periodical Literature*, 1890-. Possible subject headings for this index are : "cults," "religious conferences," "religion and law," "conversion," "youth-religious life," and individual cult names. *Religion Index One: Periodicals*, 1949- (formerly *Index to Religious Periodical Literature*) has articles indexed under "sects," "conversion," "mysticism," and under "family." *ABC Pol Sci, A Bibliography of Contents: Political Science and Government* will provide articles under "deprogramming," "Jonestown," and "cults." One line of investigation on cults and kidnapping may lead to the *Index to Legal Periodicals* for additional information.

## Books

Keeping tabs on book publication in the field of marriage and family can be accomplished by examining a variety of catalogs, review journals, and bibliographies. Theodore Besterman's *A World Bibliography of Bibliographies* is one source that lives up to its name. The author of this monumental work compiled a list of bibliographies from the earliest printed books up to 1963. There is a subject heading for family in this volume that covers books, pamphlets, periodicals, and other print materials. Current bibliographies on the family and on cults may be found in the *Bibliographic Index: A Cumulative Bibliography of Bibliographies*, 1937-. The two editions of Roberta Scull's *A Bibliography of United States Government Bibliographies* extend the search for bibliographies to government documents. Books published in the United States are noted in *Subject Guide to Books in Print* and *Subject Guide to Forthcoming Books*. In these two works, cults are each given a separate heading. Reviews of new books may be found in *Sociology: Review of New Books*, 1973-. For cults, look under "religion," and for family reviews, look under "marriage and family." Using a similar heading, "marriage and the family," the latest reference books can be found in *American Reference Books Annual*, 1970. If one's goal is to build a personal reference collection on marriage and the family, this work would do so with its listing of books, government publications, audiovisual materials, pamphlets, and bibliographies.

In any field of study, handbooks are a useful means of determing the status of research. Also, those less familiar with the field can see at a glance how specialists organize material for the purposes of study. The various editions of Marvin Sussman's *Sourcebook in Marriage and the Family* answer this need for a handbook for family studies. Another reference source that can be a vital link in the communication network of scholars is the review journal. One example of its usefulness is the 1963–64 review article on the impact of urbanization and industrialization on the family written for *Current Sociology*. A review journal of particular interest to researchers on the topic of cults is the *Annual Review of Sociology*. In the 1979 issue, a review article entitled "The Sociology of Contemporary Religious Movements" cites a great deal of the cult literature from the last decade.

## Government Publications

Since national social programs address the family as well as the individual, sources on families can be acquired through government publications. The *Monthly Catalog of United States Government Publications,* 1895- is considered to be the premier index to government documents. Publications on the White House Conference on Families will be indexed here under "family-United States" or the "White House Conference on Families." Because of the large volume of government publications, a separate index, the *Index to United States Government Publications,* 1970-, is needed to index periodicals produced by over one hundred agencies. Government statistics from such major statistical agencies as the Bureau of Census, the Bureau of Labor Statistics, and the National Center for Health Statistics, are indexed in the *American Statistics Index,* 1974-. To pinpoint hearings, committee reports, and committee prints of the federal government, referral to the *Congressional Information Service,* 1970- is recommended.

## Fugitive Materials

Sources that are dedicated more exclusively to fugitive materials are: the *Alternative Press Index,* 1969-, and the *Vertical File Index,* 1932-. In the *Alternative Press Index,* articles on cults and families can be found under such headings as "International Society for Krishna Consciousness,"

"Family," "Black Family," "Divorce," "Marriage," and "Parents." "Family" as a subject heading in the *Vertical File Index* will cover much of the pamphlet material available.

## Audiovisuals

The major educational media of audiovisuals should not be overlooked as a potential source of information. Hal Rifken's book, *The Selective Guide to Publications for Mental Health and Family Life Education*, is an aid with an AV section on adults and family life for mental health program planners. For one of the most complete listings of AV materials, one should consult the *National Information Center for Educational Media* (NICEM) catalogs. Access to 16mm and 35mm educational films, 8mm motion cartridges, educational records, audiotapes and other AV materials are possible with NICEM catalogs. In most of the directories, there is a separate heading for marriage and the family under "Sociology."

## Computer Searching

The on-line computerized literature searching is yet another means of locating sources of information in libraries. Computer technology has taken hold in libraries in the past few years enabling librarians or the end user to search well over a hundred indexes and abstracts through on-line bibliographic data bases. Two advantages to searching bibliographic data bases are the time savings and the potential for greater variety of search term combinations when retrieving articles. As a result of this precision, it is possible to search by the name of the cult, the name of the cult leader, or specifications of any social, cultural, or psychological condition which in combination with cults defines the topic sought. Relevant Lockheed data bases for searches on family and the cults are: the Educational Resources Information Center (ERIC), Social Sciences Index, Psychological Abstracts, Comprehensive Dissertaion Abstracts, Sociological Abstracts, Magazine Index, Public Affairs Information Service, Philosophers Index, Smithsonian Scientific Information Exchange (SSIE), and the National Newspaper Index. The choice of data base and subject words depends on the breadth and depth of the topic sought. Search words that may retrieve information from some or all of these data bases are: brainwashing, mind control, alienation, snapping, deprogramming, coercive persuasion, chant, dianetics, and prophetic leader. If cult names appear in the titles or abstracts, then the searcher may use headings such as: Hare Krishna, Children of God, Church of Scientology, Divine Light Mission, People's

Temple, Unification Church, etc. These cult names may be combined with thesaurus terms. For instance, *Sociological Abstracts* will index articles under "family," "brainwashing," "religious cults," "coercive deprogramming," and "youth cults."

The current years (past two decades) of ERIC, Psychological Abstracts, Social Science Index, Sociological Abstracts, CIS Index, and ASI Index are all available for computerized bibliographic searching. There is usually an accompanying fee charged by the library that provides this service. However, this service allows the searcher to search by all key words in titles, subject fileds, and abstracts (if available). A good approach to searching the bases is to explore the on-line dictionaries for your key words. This is done by expanding, on-line, any words such as marriage or family to set aside all related terms for easy manipulation. Once a search logic has been established, it may be stored by the computer for periodic automatic searches. This service, the Selective Dissemination of Information (SDI), if requested by the user will allow the search to be automatically run each time the file is updated.

Our coverage of reference sources on the family, in general, and the cults, in particular, has ranged over many years of the literature in a variety of its reference forms. To keep abreast of research, the knowledge of reference services and sources is invaluable.

# ANALYTIC ESSAY
# CULTS

Kris Jeter, PhD

In this analytic review, I will discuss four of the more recent, diverse, and significant books on social movements, which may or may not have been through a cult stage. Each book describes a different movement—ancient Gnosticism, The Church of Scientology, the Process, and *est*. My intention is to express the author's purpose, procedures, and barriers in obtaining the material for the book; to present a brief history of each social movement; and to indicate how families are viewed and treated by those who represent the leadership of the social movement. The full citation for each book follows:

—Pagels, Elaine. *The Gnostic Gospels*. New York: Random House, 1979.
  Wallis, Roy. *The Road to Total Freedom*. New York: Columbia University Press, 1977.
—Bainbridge, William Sims. *Satan's Power: A Deviant Psychotherapy Cult*. Berkeley, California: University of California Press, 1978.
—Bartley, William Warren, III. *Werner Erhard: The Transformation of a Man: The Founding of est*. New York: Clarkson N. Potter, 1978.

## *The Ancient Gnostic Christians*

I begin with Elaine Pagel's work because of its historical origin in relation to the newer social movements and cults and for the possible application of the Gnostic Christian experience to the interpretation of later day movements and cults. Pagel's purpose in writing *The Gnostic Gospels* was to examine the Nag Hammadi texts and traditional ancient sources to "see how politics and religion coincide in the development of Chris-

Kris Jeter is a trainer, human development specialist and associate with Beacon Research Associates, Ltd., Inc.

tianity." Because "it is the winners who write history—their way" ecclesiastical Christians called themselves "orthodox" and their opponents "heretics." I will examine what forces allowed the orthodox to grow and survive through today and what forces dictated the Gnostics to be considered a cult and to eventually disappear as a group.

The barriers to this study are enveloped in intrigue and mystery. These conditions by themselves can introduce and sustain the lay reader's interest in the subject. In December, 1945, an Arab peasant went with his brothers to Jabal al-Tarif, a mountain in Upper Egypt perforated with over 150 caves. While digging soil to use as fertilizer, he hit a red earthenware jar. He wondered if it might hold a spirit. Then, thinking that it could hold gold, he broke it and found thirteen leather bound papyrus books. These were taken home and piled on the ground next to the oven. Much of the papyrus was burned to kindle the fires. Several weeks later the brothers sought revenge for their father's death by killing a man. Afterwards, they asked a priest to keep the books so that the police investigating the murder would not find them. A local history teacher saw one book and had a friend go to Cairo to ascertain their value. The books were soon sold to Cairo antiquities dealers on the black market. What follows is a twenty year story involving the smuggling of some books out of Egypt; government nationalization of the collection; confiscations; and court injunctions. Fifty-two texts of the early Christian era were salvaged.

Scholars competed to view the books. Most were prevented so that fame would not come to just one researcher. In 1961, a group of international archeological and Biblical scholars urged UNESCO to photograph and publish the manuscripts and to make these available to all serious scholars. Ten volumes were published between 1972 and 1977. Pagels, who studied Coptic as a graduate student, was able to work with mimeographed transcriptions the international team commissioned by UNESCO had privately circulated to scholars.

The history of the Gnostics and Christians indicates that politics alone separated the cult from the religion. Following the death of Jesus, numerous gospels were written and circulated and many Christian cults holding radically differing beliefs and practices developed. Then, Bishop Irenaeus in the second century maintained that there should be only one church—orthodox ("straight-thinking") and catholic ("universal")—and all cults were procalimed "heretic." With the conversion of Emperor Constantine in the Fourth Century, the Catholic Church was the only approved religion and military support was effectively used to punish cults. Possession of books was a criminal offense and books were burned and destroyed. It is believed that in Egypt a monk from a nearby monastery of St. Pachomius hid the Nag Hammadi texts.

We shall now explore the beliefs of the Gnostics and compare them to the Orthodox. The Gnostics claimed insight, intuition, and knowledge of self and of God. Jesus was a guide to spiritual understanding. Gnostics individually evaluated each candidate for membership on the basis of spiritual maturity. The Orthodox Christians, however, in their effort to be the only religion did not want to limit membership and did not want to establish a complex administration for membership evaluation and so established objective criteria for church membership—baptism, verbalization of the creed, obedience to the clergy, and participation in formal worship.

Gnostic Christians interpreted the resurrection as occurring in a dream, a trance, or a vision. In contrast, Orthodox Christians adopted the doctrine of physical resurrection as a political issue—to legitimize the authority of apostolic succession of bishops as successors to the apostle Peter. The three rank hierarchy of bishops, priests, and deacons was a symbol of the present experience of Jesus.

Gnostics believed in the spiritual body, rather than the physical, sexual body. Sexual equality was practiced. At each meeting all Gnostics would cast lots to determine who would take the roles of priest, bishop, and prophet. Gnostic Christians regarded the diety to be androgynous, a Mother/Father God. Orthodox Christians were and to this day are sexist. It is hypothesized that sexism originated from two sources. The first source was the influence of the Hellenized Jews. The second source was the shift from favoring recruits from the lower class who needed and prized the labor of both sexes to enlisting members of the middle class who valued only the labor of men.

The Orthodox considered Christ's death as a model for martyrdom. Martyrs were used by the Orthodox to warn Christians of danger; encourage Christians to be brave and victorious martyrs; and strengthen the organization. Gnostics regarded physical experience and martyrdom as a diversion to the spiritual life.

Thus, Gnostics disagreed with the Orthodox on such issues as membership, authority, the form of God, participation of women, and martyrdom. These differences were threatening to the universality and acceptance of the Orthodox church. The political and military organization of the Orthodox church destroyed the Gnostic Christian movement and other Christian cults. Some beliefs, ideologies, and practices persisted, however, and are the tenets of todays new religious movements and cults. I will come back to this later.

## The Church of Scientology, Ne' Dianetics

The next movement discussed learned from Orthodox Christianity to adopt both defensive and offensive approaches to survive. Dianetics, and later Scientology, has a history in English speaking countries of over 20 years.

Sociologist, Roy Wallis, began his research into Scientology in 1971 as a graduate student. He selected Scientology as his thesis topic because: 1) he wondered how people could adopt and commit themselves to "a system of beliefs and practices which at that time seemed altogether bizarre;" 2) there was controversy and conflict with government agencies and mass media in the United States, England, and Austrialia; and 3) there existed an "apparent authoritarianism and even occasional totalitarianism of this movement." *The Road to Total Freedom* draws on influential Scientology texts and data from 83 interviews, 46 questionnaires, and a two day participant observation of a group session conducted by the Church. The participant observation lasted only two days because personal participation was necessary rather than mere presence and Wallis experienced inner conflict about what he should communicate. Preceding the publication of the book Wallis published several research papers. In an earlier article Wallis used Scientology to illustrate his theory on the concept of sects. The consequence was that Wallis experienced "a campaign of harassment"— undercover investigation and forged letters describing Wallis as a homosexual and a drug agent. Wallis, to avoid a libel suit from the Church of Scientology whose "record of litigation must surely be without parallel in the modern world"—made the manuscript available to the Church. He amended and incorporated over 100 negotiated statements and included an appendix written by a sociologist member of the Church. Wallis warns researchers of powerful groups with strong self concepts to be aware of possible aggression and censorship. Sociologists and other researchers of human behavior have a heritage of honoring the interests of powerless groups. Now censorship threatens the relatively powerless researcher.[1]

The history of scientology revolves around the life and practices of L. Ron Hubbard, born in mid-America in 1911. After numerous jobs, he practiced hypnosis and, in 1948, Hubbard wrote his views of psychotherapy into an article which was rejected by the *Journal of the American Medical Association* and the *Journal of Psychiatry*. Not to be excluded from influencing people, he rewrote his thoughts for lay readers. In essence, he wrote that the mind is a calculator which works best when it is "cleared" and such lucidness is best accomplished after training in scientology.

Hubbard's book, *Dianetics: the Modern Science of Mental Health,* was first published in 1950. That same year, the Hubbard Dianetic Research Foundation was incorporated in New Jersey with branches in five cities across the United States. Spontaneous grass-root groups emerged. As a movement, Dianetics bordered on healing, popular psychology, science-fiction, and self-improvement. Accusations against Hubbard, bankruptcy action, Hubbard's divorce from his second wife, poor administration, restraining orders, and warrants followed the early enthusiasm about dianetics. Hubbard moved to Cuba and later to Phoenix, Arizona, where Scientology was born.

Hubbard learned from the demise of Dianetics and organized the Church of Scientology with an elaborate bureaucracy. Friends could no longer informally "clear" each other. Rather, people were to take courses for $500 and up. A centralized, formal bureaucracy controlled the certification of practitioners, communication, copyrights, and franchises and demanded strict discipline.

As a charismatic movement, Scientology is dependent on Hubbard's character and his ability to change the belief system and doctrine without internal opposition. In 1959, Hubbard's eldest son, L. Ron Hubbard, Jr., and other executives defected the Church. A Guardian's Office was created as an internal disciplinary system and charged to be vigilant for heretics, notable defectors, and schismatics.

The economy of the movement depended on recruitment. Members were enlisted by advertising a personal counseling service; contacting next of kin during periods of grief; corresponding with persons whose names appeared on mailing lists, purchasers of reading materials and self study guides on health and mysticism; and individuals being solicited as subjects for research projects on particular diseases.

Church members were obligated to accomplish a "Dessemination Drill"—meet á possible contact, defuse hostility, identify a personal problem, and sell Scientology as the solution to the problems. Recruits initially tended to be orientated toward desiring a career in psychology, pursuing truth, or resolving problems.

A movement's identity can be discovered by portraying its antagonists. Those who defected expressed dissatisfaction with the organization's authoritarianism, financial expense, and social control and with their career growth and status within the Church. Defectors desired wider philosophical study, had disassociated themselves from partners who were committed Church members, and questioned whether they were "clear." The enemies of Scientology include clergy, ex-scientologists, FBI, FDA, neighbors and relatives of scientologists, physicians, politicians, the Press, and psychiatrists whose rationale for the dislike centers around the unorthodox training and therapeutic claims. Alleged reaction to enemies by Scientology indicated by various observers includes character assassination and forged documents to discredit the "evidence" of the detractor.

Proaction by Scientology involves professional public relations designed to attract new members, arouse sympathy and support for the movement, and incite antagonism towards Scientology opponents. Social reform activities sponsored by Scientology are in areas in which they feel misjudged. For instance, in 1968, the Citizen's Commission on Human Rights was formed to combat prejudice; and Narconon, created in 1966, supports research on drug addiction and related problems.

## The Church of the Final Judgement, Ne' The Process Ne' Compulsions Analysis

The two movements just discussed survived. Interest in the Gnostics has reearthed after almost 2000 years and Scientology has a modern history of approximately 30 years. William Sims Bainbridge's work is discussed because The Church of Final Judgement, despite its birth in Scientology and metamorphosis like Scientology into church status, is now extinct.

Bainbridge, a sociologist, writes "an analytic ethnography, a psychohistory" entitled *Satan's Power: A Deviant Psychotherapy Cult.* To protect his sources, the names of people and in fact the names of the groups are changed. In this discussion we shall use his names for the group, The Power and The Establishment, although the real identity has been deduced by readers to be The Process and The Church of the Final Judgement. The purposes of his research are: 1) "to discover the way a new culture is socially produced" and 2) to study the only polytheistic group readily available to him.

Bainbridge approached this research using Malinowski's classical anthropological method. He was initiated into the Power in 1970 and acted as a "friendly associate" and an "interviewer of native informants." He collected their artifacts and publications, recorded the observations in a lengthy field diary, and photographed and tape recorded their rituals and other occasions. Bainbridge's photography impressed the members and actually served as a medium for reciprocity—research data for photographs.

The cult started in Great Britain in 1963 as a personal relationship between Kitty McDougal (actually Mary Ann de Grimston), a counselor with Techniacity (Scientology), and Edward de Forest Jones (Robert de

Grimston), her client. Independently, they had studied Alfred Adler's theory of human goals and together they developed a psychotherapy movement called Compulsions Analysis in which clients could discover and share their compulsive goals. Clients developed an intense intimate relationship, a feeling of family.

From 1965 to 1967, Compulsions Analysis developed into a religious sect because the goals expressed by clients became more mystical and spiritual and united the group in a social implosion. They decided to build a self-supporting community abroad. In June, 1966, thirty Powerites and six German shepherd dogs left by ship to Nassau and then to Xtul on the Yucatan coast.

In September, a British Consul visited the commune to warn members of Hurricane Inez and invite them to shelter. They voted to stay and for two days experienced the personal psychological commotion and natural meterological disorganization of the hurricane—a mixture of God and Demon powers. While 298 Mexicans died, the commune members survived unharmed and even spiritually enlightened. Thus was laid the foundation for a religion with four Gods—Christ, Jehova, Lucifer, and Satan with some emblems and many rituals to formalize it. By the end of the year, most of the Powerites had left Xtul; some were minors and accompanied away by an attorney; some wanted to be home for Christmas. Within a year, all had returned to Great Britain.

The church authorized begging. Its legal incorporation freed the group of tax payments, and it began a program to change public attitudes. The Power from 1967 to 1972 recruited its young people largely from middle and upper class families and divorced families. All recruits were seeking intimacy. In fact, persons were actively recruited who were uncommitted to any cause and without any strong social ties. The tenth Chapter of Matthew was used as the rationale to send recruits in pairs without money or belongings to European and American cities to beg. These adventures served as initiation rites where members learned to deal with strangers and to maintain themselves in strange environments.

In August, 1969, Charles Manson and his followers murdered Sharon Tate and six others. With Manson's capture several months later, rumors spread and a chapter in a book and magazine articles published that the influencing factor in the killings was the Power. Powerites had not met Manson and sued for libel. In the United States, an agreement was reached and a retraction was printed.

Headquarters were established in Boston in 1970 complete with the popular attraction of the times, a coffee house called the Cavern, used primarily for enlisting new members. From this time on, recruits tended to have limited creativity and talent and a strong dependence on parental figures.

With the Manson experience and the first American headquarters in the United States, a change of image was in order. Uniforms changed in color from black to gray and then to medium blue. A popular radio show featuring interviews with rock stars was aired on WBZ, the NBC affiliate in Boston, and syndicated to over 20 other stations. The Power entered social service work, giving free food and clothing with the view that such community spirited activity would effect more public tolerance to their recruitment efforts.

Begging was the major money making activity because the Powerites felt unable to compete with credentialed therapists. Therapy ceased as a major activity by the end of 1973. In 1972, the Power was influenced by Kathryn Kuhlman, an American faith healer, and healing was incorporated into their practices.

In 1974, "The Great Separation" occurred. There were many reasons with the most evident being Edward's desertion of Kitty and travel with Lilith on cult funds to Mexico and New Orleans. A divorce followed. The organization, however, had been dying for some time. First, the Church had no congregation; at best, the clergy/laity ratio was 1 to 1. The clergy were ordered in a very elaborate organizational hierarchy. Edward and Kitty had been living in luxury in a secret mansion and taking expensive world trips. Meanwhile, the original followers entered different developmental stages—working in normal jobs, being married, having children, and attaining community status. There were 20 children born from 1967 to 1970 to Power members. Some of these members quit the Church and moved into conventional lifestyles. Other members felt non-acceptance from the public, lost their sense of purpose, and were burned out from constant giving and in turn, receiving little money from their begging.

With the Great Separation, Kitty and some supporters tried to replace the charismatic leader Edward had represented but were unsuccessful. All of Edward's publications were withdrawn from circulation. Rituals lost their mysticism and became performances with entertainers and collection plates. Lectures on varied psychic and therapeutic theories were sponsored and admission charged.

Meanwhile Edward attempted to form a group in Boston, the Waltham Power; however, the people he recruited had little in common and no bonding occurred. For the first time in the history of the cult, he participated in the rituals, which caused some unrest. In 1975, Edward went to

Boston and addressed a group of former Powerites and said that religion, not the Church, developed self awareness and ended with these words: "To put it bluntly, you're on your own."

## est (Erhard Seminars Training)

The fourth book concerns a modern worldwide movement, *est*. Like Edward of the Power, its founder deserted his wife. Unlike the Power, he returned twelve years later to his parents and first wife and succeeded at reinstating a positive feeling among all of the people he deserted—an enviable feat.

Philosopher William Warren Bartley III wrote *Werner Erhard: The Transformation of Man: The Founding of est*. His writing has three purposes: 1) to tell the story of Werner Erhard's education, transformation, and completion of his relationship with his family; 2) to give an account of the disciplines Werner encountered in developing *est;* and 3) to present *est* theory and practice. He interviews Werner, family, and associates and reads writings which influenced Werner. Bartley was referred to *est* in 1972 by a physician to deal with a 9 year case of insomnia. The insomnia was cured. Bartley's curiosity was aroused and he began to ask questions about Werner and *est*—especially how philosophy and free enterprise could be combined. Bartley's work was supported by free access to available information. The book has been well received by Werner, *est* graduates, and critics. The account is personal, and throughout, Bartley writes of "Werner," as we shall.

Werner was born in 1935 as Jack Rosenberg, the first child to Joe, son of an immigrant Russian tailor, and Dorothy Clauson, American Revolution stock. Joe converted from Judaism to being a conservative Baptist; Werner was reared Episcopalian. Werner had a series of violent accidents he feels now were his way to attract attention, punish himself, and fulfill the Oedipus complex.

He experienced a close bond with his mother. At 12 he broke his nose and his pregnant mother said, "you know where the doctor is. Why don't you go to the doctor yourself?" This marked the end of the special mother-son relationship.

Werner became lonely and detached and as a teenager read all night, especially the plays of Tennessee Williams. This made morning wake up difficult. One morning, after the usual requests, his father woke him with a punch and a black eye. About nine months later, Werner became a father after marrying Pat Campbell. He was successful at selling cars, however, both Werner and Pat felt cheated at having their life plans interrupted. In 1959, he met June Bryde and after leading a doublelife for a year, flew with her to St. Louis. They changed their names to Werner and Ellen Erhard and invented new life histories. These biographies proved unnecessary because Werner's car selling ability got him employed, not his record.

In St. Louis, he began to use hypnosis and to read success books. From reading Napoleon Hill's *Think and Grow Rich,* he learned that ideas form reality. Maxwell Maltz through his book *Psycho-Cybernetics* indicated to Werner that a change in self image changes behavior.

Werner and Ellen than moved to the West Coast. Werner worked over the years in several posts as administrator of sales for Encyclopedia Britannica's Great Books Program, Parent's Magazine Cultural Institute, and the Grolier Society.

Meanwhile, he studied various systems which are discussed chronologically. The writings of Abraham Maslow and Carl R. Rogers on determinism, group growth, optimism, and truth telling were important. He became a neighbor of Alan Watts and was most influenced by Zen and the difference between self and mind. In 1967, he took the Dale Carnegie Course which is about "being yourself" and contains "sophisticated principles." He spent a year with Subuh meditation. Werner received 70 hours of Scientology auditing which he described as the "fastest and deepest way to handle situations that I had yet encountered." Bartley writes: "Werner Erhard is virtually the only consciousness leader, and the only person of distinction in American society to have stepped outside this childish quarrel between Scientology and society and to have acknowledged both his indebtedness to Hubbard and his emphatic differences with him." Werner then took and later taught Mind Dynamics, a mind expansion program with more activity than theory.

In March 1971, a transformation occurred when Werner was driving on the freeway. "I realized that I knew nothing—I realized that I knew everything." He created three goals from this experience: to share his self, to take responsibility for his ego, and to correct the lies in his life. These are the fundamental principles of *est.* These are abstracted in *The Book of est,* authored by Luke Rheinhart. He stopped drinking alcohol and coffee, eating sugar, and smoking without withdrawal symptoms. He lost twenty pounds in two weeks, his posture changed, and within a few months, his face looked young. He mellowed and began to communicate more intimately.

Throughout the job shifts and the experiencing of disciplines and techniques, he was developing a loyal cadre of employees who enjoyed participating in his sales trainings and working with him. For instance, he said that parents were to be sold educational products on the individual basis and counseled about preschool children, not pressured with hard sales techniques. Werner found his teaching of Mind Dynamics was deviating more and more from the prescribed curriculum. Werner asked his staff if they should remain with Grolier Society and Mind Dynamics or set up another organization.

The staff voted for the latter. With the services of the controversial tax attorney, Harry Margolis, *est* was incorporated as a profit-making educational corporation. A small fee—initially $150—would be charged and the training would be aimed at the maximum number of people.

In 1972, Werner went back to Philadelphia and reopened the relationship with his family. He was honest and "let them discharge all the things that hadn't been said over the past thirteen years." His family was pleased. Every family member took the *est* training between 1973 and 1975 and many now work with or for *est.*

Thanksgiving Day, 1974, the entire family—parents, wives, children and in-laws—celebrated. "Problems occur in families because the people in them are in mystery about one another. When you are really clear about me, you don't have a problem—whatever way it is." The reunited family is a testimony that Werner "practices what he preaches."

The company, "*est,* an educational corporation" was formed to be a facilitator for people who would actualize a transformed view of life into constructive action. Since 1971, over 1000 individuals complete the basic four day training each week. In other words, approximately 300,000 people from over 100 nations are now *est* graduates.

On May 31, 1981, "*est,* an educational corporation" was renamed the Centers Network with 30 Area Centers in Canada, England, India, Israel, and the United States. Projects which had been developed originally by *est* graduates and friends such as the Breakthrough Foundation, the Holiday Project, and the Hunger Project are now under the name of Werner Erhard and Associates. This unincorporated entity acts as an information and referral service for an informal, worldwide network of individuals and groups working toward personal and social transformation.[2]

## Conclusions

Three major areas emerge for concluding discussions: 1) the influence of ancient Gnosticism on the three discussed modern day movements; 2) the factors dictating survival of a movement; and 3) the research of movements.

The beliefs, ideologies, and practices of ancient religions do recycle in movements throughout the ages. The Gnostic philosophy of spiritual maturity seems to have been adopted in essence by Scientology and *est.* The spiritual body, rather than the physical body, was stressed in Gnosticism and with members of the Process, although not their leaders. Movements of today such as *est* have no place for martyrdom valued by the Orthodox Christians. Some might wonder if Scientology's incidents with society might be a form of martyrdom.

Bainbridge wrote that he was interested in "the complex interplay between deviance and conventionality in the formation and persistence of a cult. . . . Cult is a culture writ in small." For a movement to survive the interweaving of a sophisticated accounting, bureaucracy, economy, and philosophy plus the provision of a feeling of family is necessary. Surviving movements work in the system. For instance, imagine if the Gnostics had attorney Harry Margolis as their counselor and a public relations firm to combat the traditional Christians and Roman Army.

Members of a movement are often active only during a particular stage of growth and development when a feeling of specialness, uniqueness and inclusion are needed. Many modern movements lose members through conventional marriage and childbirth stages when other needs surface. To maintain members, movements, like *est,* have activities for all members of the family—children, adolescents, and adults as well as the total family.

Wise researchers know and teach that one should be in love with their research topic. This love was highly evident in the works of Pagels, Bainbridge, and Bartley. Some readers might feel after reading Wallis' book with stoic language and almost as much space devoted to footnotes as the text, that his love of the subject might be of a different kind, perhaps "love in spite of harassment." With the lessened incidence of ancient tribes to study, researchers are turning to modern day movements. The spears and arrows of the "uncivilized" can be just as sharp as harassment and libel suits of some popular movements. Cautious pre-analysis of the movement's true use of establishment safeguards before "absorbing the culture" is prescribed.

## NOTES

1. Wallis, Roy. "The Moral Career of a Research Project." *Doing Sociological Research,* edited by Collin Bell and Howard Newby. New York, New York: The Free Press, 1977.
2. *The Graduate Review.* San Francisco, California: Werner Erhard and Associates, July/August 1981.